# Praise for
## *The New Bottom Line*

"This anthology effectively captures a spiritual renaissance taking place in the business world today. Without question, it is only by aligning ourselves with a moral compass based on universal principles that we can continue to progress in a direction that will take us into the next century."
—Stephen R. Covey
author, *The 7 Habits of Highly Effective People*

"Mother Theresa and other thoughtful social observers have often commented on the spiritual hunger and poverty that are rampant in America today. Perhaps the workplace, where most of us spend a large chunk of our lives, is the perfect place for people to find spiritual sustenance, personal significance, uplifting community, and answers to the really *important* questions about the meaning of life. *The New Bottom Line* is food for the mind, heart, spirit and soul—a *feast* for hungry seekers."
—Barbara "BJ" Hateley, co-author, *A Peacock in the Land of Penguins: A Tale of Diversity and Discovery*

"For the business executive that is looking for a thoughtful examination of today's workplace, *The New Bottom Line* goes far beyond simple solutions. A thoroughly holistic approach to business success."
—David Jamison
Jamison Cawdrey Benjamin Advertising

"It's past time to separate fact from fancy. Business is not driven by profits, by return on investment, or by enhanced shareholder value. Business is driven by something much less definable but very real nonetheless. Call it spirituality, call it community, call it family, call it teamwork, call it heart and soul. Whatever we call it, we can no longer fail to recognize that people drive business—people working together, people committed to what they have chosen to do together. People, not systems. Cooperation, not competition. Any leader who is able to face this truth and who would understand how to work and manage in this environment should buy and read *The New Bottom Line*. I predict this will be among the year's, perhaps the decade's, most useful and rewarding leadership books."
—James A. Autry, author, *Love and Profit,* and his new memoirs, *Confessions of an Accidental Businessman*

"It's an exciting moment in our thinking about organizations; we are willing to contemplate the fact that people have spiritual desires that they want and need to bring to work. This book adds depth to our contemplations by bringing together so many different thinkers. These authors provoked my thinking, and inspired my sense of hopefulness for our future."
> —Margaret Wheatley, author, *Leadership and the New Science* and (with Myron Kellner-Rogers) *A Simpler Way*

"This book is for everyone who grew up in an autocratic work environment, where you were hired only for your hands—and maybe, at times, your mind. We need to be constantly reminded that there is so much more we have to offer—from our hearts and from our souls. This book is a cornucopia of treasured stories that will transform your thinking. Remember, if you touch the heart and soul of another human being, you change them forever!"
> —Rick Gutherie, Supervisor Ford (MP&L) Team Learning and Creativity Center

"This book eloquently proposes fact, not fiction, reality, not opinions on what most certainly will be the essence and acceptable ingredients of successful business leaders in the 21st Century. It is a well constructed book or should I say journey into the changing world of business that is happening now."
> —Ben Mancini, CEO and President Institute of Transpersonal Psychology

"With today's cynicism, fragmentation, and shifting relationships has come a yearning for a greater purpose in our lives. While the world erupts with the quakes of change, we seek to calm our fears by searching our souls and reaching out to our companions. This brilliant collection of essays teases the brain and touches the heart. It, paradoxically, challenges convention and reinforces long-held traditions. It makes you joyful and also makes you want to scream. Sometimes you think the authors have landed from some distant planet, and then you think they have their feet planted firmly on the ground. Soul, spirit, love, healing, consciousness are not yet concepts in good currency in business, but they will be soon. I guarantee it. *The New Bottom Line* is an essential and invaluable guide to every explorer on a search for meaning at work."
> —Jim Kouzes, Chairman and CEO, The Tom Peters Group Learning Systems, co-author, *The Leadership Challenge* and *Credibility*

"This book is an eye-opener, more precisely a heart-opener. It deals with issues rarely encountered in management writings; spirituality, love, and community. Without understanding those ideas, managers deal with, at most, the half-life of work."

> —Warren Bennis, author, *On Becoming a Leader*,
> and the forthcoming *Creative Collaboration:*
> *Leading Groups to Greatness*

"In the best companies, a new spirited-ness is emerging as people work at levels of higher creativity and teamwork synergy. The perspectives found in *The New Bottom Line* have helped me understand and welcome this new energy, and foster its vitalizing effect on my company's financial *and* human fulfillment bottom lines."

> —Mary E. Anderson, President
> Index Sensors & Controls, Inc.

"The purpose of any business organization is to create value for all of its constituencies, which is also the source of its success. The same is true for humans. Both require accessing mind, body, and spirit. Artificial attempts to separate the spiritual nature of people from organizations, or vice versa, are doomed to fail. *The New Bottom Line* points out this inevitability and leads us up the path of human and organizational spiritual integration."

> —W. Mathew Juechter, Chief Executive Officer
> ARC International Ltd.

"Renesch and DeFoore's *The New Bottom Line: Bringing Heart and Soul to Business* defines spiritual leadership and clearly assesses its force as a new approach to leadership, one focusing and integrating values-based leadership, visioning, empowerment, and trust. I recommend it to anyone who is seeking coherence in the muddle of leadership studies today."

> —Gil Fairholm, Virginia Commonwealth University
> author, *Capturing the Heart of Leadership:*
> *Spirituality in the Workplace* (forthcoming)

"*The New Bottom Line* is a magnificent collection—it should be required reading for everyone considering working for a living. It's so timely and to the point. I love this book!"

> —Lorna Catford, Stanford Graduate School of
> Business and California State University, Sonoma,
> author (with Michael Ray), *The Path of the*
> *Everyday Hero*

"*The New Bottom Line* is an indispensable guide for those who are suspicious about New Age "spirituality" in the workplace. Wherever one is on the believer/skeptic continuum, readers will find this anthology to be unusually thought provoking."
> —James O'Toole
> author, *Leading Change*

"If we are to truly regenerate our communities and our society, we must also regenerate ourselves and our human enterprises. *The New Bottom Line* shows the way, making a powerful argument for an undeniable new business logic that acknowledges the inextricable links between personal growth and economic growth, between soul and success."
> —Joel Makower, Editor,
> *The Green Business Letter,*
> author, *Beyond the Bottom Line*

"*The New Bottom Line* is a ground-breaking contribution to defining what spirituality in business life is, how it shows up in the workplace, and the impact it has on organizations and people's lives."
> —Richard Barrett, Founder, World Bank Spiritual Unfoldment Society,
> author, *A Guide to Liberating Your Soul*

"*The New Bottom Line* is a fascinating collection of insights, essays, and powerful new models about what is possible in an "enlightened" business organization. What all of the book's contributors have in common is a clear commitment to and compassion for those of us who spend our lives working in corporate environments. Hopefully, this work will make it a little easier and a lot more fun as we purse the often difficult work of reinventing our companies...and ourselves."
> —Jim Selman, Principal
> ParaComm Partners International

"*The New Bottom Line* is a work which touches and explores every aspect of our working selves. This is a 'must read' for anyone who is in business."
> —Laurie Beth Jones, author
> *Jesus, CEO* and *The Path*

"This book is a gold mine for any business person looking for ways and means of making a transformation from traditional to 'new' business."
>—Rolf Österberg
author, *Corporate Renaissance*
co-author, *The Search for Meaning in the Workplace*

"Renesch and DeFoore have produced an anthology that takes us a giant step closer to addressing the human spirit in the mainstream of business. In the pursuit of reduced cycle time and shareholder equity, spirit is still ignored or denied access to the corporation. The papers in this collection argue persuasively for bringing the full human experience to work."
>—John Adams, Director
Sun Microsystems,
Editor, *Transforming Work*

"What a challenging and inspiring marathon of testimonies all expressing the urgent need and the diversity of ways to foster and release the flowering of the human spirit in business. Hopefully, business enterprise will at last see that its fundamental propose is to nurture human creativity and bring beauty into our daily lives and harmony into the world! Reading this anthology should fire us all to work so that love itself becomes the 'new bottom line.'"
>—Godric E.S. Bader, Life President
Scott Bader Commonwealth, U.K.

"In a world where business leaders are measured and rewarded by the size of their layoffs, this is a refreshing look at the deeper meaning of work."
>—Joyce Wycoff, Director
Innovative Thinking Network

"*The New Bottom Line* compellingly highlights how consciousness, caring, and doing good can enhance, rather than impede, real profitability. This timely and invigorating book inspires us to become co-creators of a dynamic new world of commerce guided by an ethos of partnership rather than domination."
>—Riane Eisler
author, *The Chalice and the Blade*,
*Sacred Pleasure*,
and (with David Loye) *The Partnership Way*

# THE NEW BOTTOM LINE

## Bringing Heart & Soul to Business

# THE NEW BOTTOM LINE

## Featuring writings by:

Tom Peters • William George • Ian Mitroff • Gil Fairholm
Allen  Cymrot • Thomas Moore• Angeles Arrien
John Renesch  • Kymn Harvin Rutigliano
Jacqueline Haessly • Michael Scott Rankin
Perry Pascarella • Joel Levey • Rae Thompson
David A. Schwerin • Margaret Molinari
Sajeela Moskowitz Ramsey • Barbara and Randy Powers
Barry Heermann • Evangeline Caridas
Karen Lundquist • Steve Jacobsen • Kay Gilley
Dave Potter • Laura Hauser • Bill DeFoore
Gerard J. O'Neill • Margery Miller
Ken Blanchard • Anita Roddick

Editors: John Renesch and Bill DeFoore

**NewLeadersPress**

STERLING &
STONE, INC.

San Francisco

New Leaders Press/Sterling & Stone, Inc.
1668 Lombard St.
San Francisco, CA 94123
Tel: 415.928.1473; Fax: 415.928-3346; email: staff@newleadearsnet.org

To purchase additional copies or inquire about bulk discounts for multiple orders, contact the publisher at 1.800.928.LEAD.

Bookstores and wholesalers, please contact National Book Network, 4720 Boston Way, Lanham, MD 20706; Tel: 301.731.9515, 1-800.462-6420; Fax: 301.459.2118.

### Permissions and Credits

The editors and publisher wish to acknowledge the following sources:
The Tom Peters Group and TPG Communications who allowed us to reprint Tom Peters syndicated column:
©1993 TPG Communications. All rights reserved. Reprinted with permission.
and his newsletter, *Tom Peters On Achieving Excellence*
©1994 TPG Communications. All rights reserved. Reprinted with permission.

Blanchard Training & Development, Inc. who allowed us to reprint "The Spiritual Workplace" by Ken Blanchard. ©1996 by Blanchard Management Report. Reprinted with permission.

William George, who granted us permission to publish his open letter to Tom Peters.

Photo Credits: Photo of Bill DeFoore (p xii and p. 284) by Thomas Judd Photography; Kymn Harvin Rutigliano (p. 50) by Deboarah G. Alicen, PhD; Michael Scott Rankin (p. 82) by D. Brant Studio; Rae Thompson (p. 120) by Robin Reid Photography; Margaret Molinari (p. 148) by S. Kay Young; Evangeline Caridas (p. 202) by Gittings; and Anita Roddick (p. 320) by Michael Zinn.

 Printed in the United States of America on recycled paper.

Library of Congress Catalog Card Number: 96-69103


*The New Bottom Line.*  Edited by John Renesch and Bill DeFoore.

ISBN 0-9630390-9-1
First Edition

# Contents

# Foreword

One morning in the Spring of 1993, I opened the business section of our local newspaper, the *Minneapolis Star-Tribune,* to find a startling headline, "Spiritual Talk Has No Place In Secular Corporation." The opinion piece, authored by Tom Peters, argued that spiritual business leaders like Max DePree of Herman Miller and the late Robert Greenleaf of AT&T were out of place in a secular corporation.

I got to know Tom Peters back in 1983 when he ran an off-site seminar for my sector at Honeywell shortly after his now-famous book, *In Search of Excellence,* was published. However, I had no idea of the fervor with which Tom objects to the existence of a sense of spirituality in the workplace.

Concerned that Peters' viewpoint misjudged the motivations of employees in the corporate setting, I decided to write him an "open letter" which was published in the *Star-Tribune,* not only reflecting my own views on spirituality in the workplace but also sharing the experience of Medtronic and the spiritual influence of our founder, Earl Bakken.

A few weeks later, John Renesch, publisher of *The New Leaders,* called and asked permission to reprint my article in his publication. John later got Peters to write a rebuttal to my letter, which he published in his own house organ.

This exchange only served to confirm for me the gulf in understanding which exists between business writers and academics on the one hand and those of us in corporate leadership roles on the other. I have often wondered why the subjects of ethics, values, and spirituality remain so untouchable by these same writers when, in my view at least, they are such a powerful motivating force for employees and corporate leaders. As in the case of Peters' views, discussions of ethics and values lead directly to the source of those values, spirituality. Too often these writers confuse spirituality and religion, and therefore demur in fear of imposing a certain set of religious beliefs. But to write about "organization culture" without fully understanding the power of these motivating forces often leads writers like Peters to mistake symbols for substance.

We are all spiritual beings, composed of minds, bodies, and a spiritual side, whether we acknowledge this portion of ourselves or not. In his article, Peters cites Frederick Taylor, one of the founders of the science of industrial engineering, for bringing "human freedom" to the workplace. In fact, Taylor's efforts did more to dehumanize the workplace by utilizing workers' physical skills but not their minds. He quite correctly acknowledges the later work of Douglas McGregor in tapping into the mental capacities of workers.

To ask employees only to utilize their minds and bodies, while not acknowledging the power of the spirit which resides in every person not only diminishes their individual gifts and contributions but it limits their ability to contribute fully to their work and their organization.

Why should we ask employees to "check their values and their spiritual selves at the door" when they come to work? They lose, the organization loses, and ultimately the customer or beneficiary of the company's work loses! No wonder so many organizations ultimately "lose their souls."

To unleash the whole capability of the individual—mind, body, *and* spirit—gives enormous power to the organization. It truly empowers members of the organization to devote their entire beings to the ultimate purpose for which the organization exists, which is to serve others. That's what I believe is "spirituality in the workplace," to unlock the real sense of significance of the organization's purpose.

Contrary to Peters' views on spirituality, this has nothing whatsoever to do with religion. People of many faiths, or no faith at all for that matter, can join together in a common cause of service to others through their work. To confuse spirituality with religion only diminishes the capacity of the organization to tap into the spiritual reservoir which resides in each of us.

At Medtronic we have seen the power of that spirit and what it means to the patients and physicians whom we serve. I generally begin presentations to our major shareholders as well as employee groups by telling them that Medtronic is not in the business of "maximizing shareholder value," but, rather, our purpose is to "maximize patient value." We like to say that "the real bottom line" for Medtronic is the 1,300,000 patients who were restored to full life and health last year by Medtronic products.

Unfortunately for many organizations, these topics—values, spirituality, and unlocking the full potential of the individual—generally go unaddressed in business books and in many corporations.

Now, thanks for the yeoman-like efforts of editors John Renesch and Bill DeFoore, we have a broadly based anthology of essays and articles on the subject of spirituality and work. In this complete edition, entitled *The New Bottom Line: Bringing Heart and Soul to Business,* Renesch and DeFoore have sought out the leading thinkers in this field, ranging from Ken Blanchard to Anita Roddick, to compile a rich and deep collection of philosophies on this vital subject. In many ways this anthology is a sequel to their earlier work, *Rediscovering the Soul of Business,* which included essays by Thomas Moore and Matthew Fox. Whereas other authors have written on the subject of *individual* spirituality, Renesch and DeFoore have focused primarily on the *environment* for spirituality in the business organization.

The complete reading of this series, I believe, gives the individual refreshing new insights on what constitutes a spiritual workplace and what it can mean both for individuals and corporations in terms of fulfillment and accomplishment. This book takes the dialogue to a new level and will stimulate its readers to think more deeply about their own values and worklife, as well as that of their organizations.

We owe John Renesch and Bill DeFoore and their contributors a deep debt of gratitude for advancing the dialogue on these vital subjects. It is my hope this work will stimulate both new leadership on the part of corporate managers, and result in new depths of intellectual exploration and dialogue on the part of business observers and writers on the meaning of spirituality in the workplace.

William W. George, CEO
Medtronic, Inc.
Minneapolis, MN
June, 1996

"We need an intellectual breakthrough into a new direction. And that means that the state of the human spirit assumes paramount importance."
— Mikhail Gorbachev
*The New Leaders*, Sept./Oct. 1995

# Preface

The challenge addressed by this book is the blending of two worlds—communities that usually never integrate: the world of commerce and the world of spiritual values (not to be confused with religion). By attempting to merge these two domains, this book has accepted an historic challenge.

The world of business has been the exclusive domain of the rational and pragmatic thinker who has been rewarded for consistent "reasonable" behavior. The world of the philosopher, the cosmologist, has been the domain of the irrational conceptual dreamer—not at all considered practical or pragmatic.

Is there a new field coming into being? Could be! The field of cosmology, representing the study of larger philosophic issues involving the universe, human destiny, and creative futures, has been encroaching on the business community for the past several years. It started with the advance stages of Taylorism, where scientific management theory became the rage beginning after World War II.

Organizational development theory and all its related disciplines, growing into a myriad of conceptual models and theories, have been steadily making inroads into traditional business circles. The mix of cosmologists and Taylorists became widely apparent in the early 1990s. The *Fortune* magazine article, "The New Age of Business?" was a start, followed by many articles in mainstream business media, including *The Wall Street Journal, Harvard Business Review,* and The American Management Association's *Organizational Dynamics* journal. This "movement" has also resulted in the beginning of several "new business" periodicals including *Business Ethics* magazine, *Fast Company* magazine, the *At Work* and *The Systems Thinker* newsletters, *World Business Academy Perspectives* quarterly journal and *The New Leaders* newsletter.

*The New Leaders* has a mission statement consistent with this phenomenon. It reads: "The mission of *The New Leaders* is to encourage and support the full expression of the human spirit and the evolution of consciousness in the business community."

Part of this new "business cosmology" is a return to basic values—values once held as sacred in the days of Adam Smith, the father of modern capitalism. Smith's philosophy was based on an 18th Century morality that is no longer apparent in our modern society.

This collection of essays integrates much of this new thinking into today's values. The title of this book reflects this new integration, recognizing that new values are needed to drive enterprise—more than simple economic "bottom lines" that have become so influential over the past century.

The reader of *The New Bottom Line* will need to develop a level of comfort in the paradox—living in the tension between traditional Taylorism and the esoteric, between the different experiences of "reality," holding the conflict as a texture or a climate in which to learn, not as a problem to be solved.

This ability—to live in the tension of paradox—is a skill that will be much in demand for tomorrow's leaders. In this book, the reader will have an opportunity to practice and observe the habitual routine of trying to ease the tension, solve the problem, and reconcile the contradiction.

Part of these new, or renewed, values is gratitude—acknowledging those whom we wish to thank, for whom we are grateful. Everyone associated with this book, consistent with this philosophy, wishes to thank those who were inspirations, supportive, and meaningful in their own endeavors.

# Acknowledgments

To begin, our contributing authors wish to thank those who were significant in their own lives—personally and professionally.

Michael Scott Rankin wishes to thank the most influential three women in his life and three writers—Mom, Margaret Pinder, E.S., William James, Soren Kierkegaard and Meister Eckhart—for their sustained spiritual nurturing.

First and foremost, Joel Levey would like to acknowledge his wife, Michelle Levey, for so skillfully co-crafting his essay with him. Heartfelt thanks also go to their "all star" teams who have demonstrated the profound synergy of innerwork and ordinary work at Hewlett-Packard, Weyerhaeuser, The Travelers, Group Health Cooperative, AT&T, SRI, MIT, PetroCanada, Imperial Oil, Shell, Gulf, TransAlta Utilities, and NASA. For their inspiration and living examples, he thanks his dear colleagues Bill Veltrop, Jon Dunnington, Shirley Swink, George "Duri" Pór, Peter & Trudy Johnsen-Lenz, Loren Blackman, Eric Vogt, Bill Maynard, Chris Thorsen, Ruth Thorsen, Richard Moon, Geoff Hulen, Darla Chadima, Jim Channon, Joan Steffy, John Renesch, Herman Maynard, Willis Harman, Tom Hurley, Jeffrey Mishlove, Alex Pattakos, Joe Jaworski, Peter Senge, Jim Ullery, Don Krebbs, Jim Seferis, Gary Jusella, Blake Emergy, Suzanne Mamet, Mario Narduzzi, Gary Hockman, Andre Leite Alckmin, Leo Puga, Rich Raimondi, Forrest Whitt, Chuck Walter, Janet Buschert, Von Hansen, Ormond Rankin, Bruce Schrepple, Lynda Davis, Vivian Wright, Sylvia Dolena, Diane Robbins, Chris Rahn, Terrell Poeton, Ruth Shuck, Anne Murray Allen, and all the inspired leaders and warriors of the heart who are actively keeping the spirit alive in the world of commerce and consciousness.

Kymn Harvin Rutigliano wishes to acknowledge her husband Vince, her family and friends who generously supported her during her doctoral program, and AT&T Senior Vice-President Ken Bertaccini who listened intently ten years ago to a young woman's dream of making a difference at AT&T and helped bring that dream into reality.

Jacqueline Haessly wants to acknowledge several who gave shape to her own thinking about spirituality and transformation. These include Eleanor Roosevelt, Dorothy Day, Coretta Scott King, Patricia and Gerald Mische, Diane Eck, Sylvia Ashton Warner, Pam McAllister, Gita Zen, Dorothy Odell, Marjorie Tuite, and the women of Church Women United. Dr. Angelyn Dries introduced her to the writings of visionary women from other cultures. Bill DeFoore's excitement about this portion of an earlier essay gave her the courage to explore it further in this book. John Renesch, who took a chance—sight unseen—on her first essay for Sterling & Stone five years ago, continues to offer support, encouragement and friendship in this unique partnership. Lastly, she wants to acknowledge her life partner, Dan Di Domizio and their five children and two grandchildren, who give new meaning to the call to care for the seventh generation, and who make the business of peacemaking such fun.

Rae Thompson gratefully acknowledges the love and support of each person who contributed to the personal insights and growth that made her writing possible. She is especially thankful to Robert Stevens for helping her find her own bottom line; to Carol Heckman for providing stimulating and passionate review of her drafts; to Sanda Jasper for her continued inspiration and friendship; and to her father, James Thompson, who, in his last moments with her, communicated volumes without ever saying a word.

David Schwerin wishes to acknowledge, first and foremost, his wife and partner Joan who not only edited his essay but who has supported him in all his endeavors throughout their 30 plus years together. Pat Fenske, PhD has been a wonderful mentor both in the development of his dissertation and his spiritual understandings. Barbara Good, PhD has been a generous and welcome source of wisdom and support for more than a decade. Bob Bobrow and Arnold Shapiro have provided valuable counsel throughout his business career. Finally, he is most grateful to his son, Eric, whose warm heart and wise soul enliven his spirit whenever he erroneously thinks that things are not going the way he believes they should.

Margaret Molinari honors the many allies that have accompanied her on her own heroine's journey. Beth and Jonah Duckles have consistently supported her emotionally and technically.

Mary Powell and Ann Greene bolstered her bottom line when it was flagging. Jean Houston and Peggy Rubin's ever-growing insight and originality inspired and deepened her. And she is grateful to all of the executives with whom she has worked and shared a passion for change, including (and certainly not limited to) Barbara Glazer, Alan Smith, Marina Whitman, Bob Hendry, John Rock, and Howard Carlson, Helen Moye and Marty Laurent.

Sajeela Moskowitz Ramsey wishes to thank the Paul Reps Estate for granting the use of the illustrations from Paul Reps' book. And she wishes to ackowledge Bob Marshack for his generosity in helping her shape her ideas, inspired by his thinking on similar subjects.

Barry Heermann dedicates his chapter to twenty Union Institute learners doing PhD work in organization behavior and development who participated in a seminar that he convened in Tiburon, California in 1992. This seminar was a transformational experience for Barry and his learners, one of whom is a contributor to this volume, Jacqueline Haessly. This seminar served as the catalyst for Barry's explorations into spirit in organization, leading ultimately to the formulation of the team development process called Team Spirit. Barry especially acknowledges Alexandra Kovats, seminar co-convenor and a Union Institute learner for whom he serves as a core faculty member.

Evangeline Caridas would like to express her warmth and gratitude to her mentors and people in organizations who were open and candid in sharing their experiences with her. She would like to extend her sincere appreciation to her colleague and friend Frank Heckman, whose innovation was to combine Flow, Active Job and the Emery Participative Processes to create a healthy and productive work environment. People who deserve special acknowledgment are Merrelyn and Fred Emery, Nancy Sammis, Mihaly Csikszentmihaly, Shelly Winthrow, Garey Stark, Nancy Cebula, Mike Noon, Debi Kalinin, and her grandmother Evangeline Ivannidis.

Karen Lundquist thanks her business partners, Magaly d. Rodriguez and Carol Ann Cappuzzo, for their practical insight, principled faith and, most of all, their loving friendship. They opened up new worlds of opportunity that are a continuous source of joy and meaning in her life. To her colleagues with whom she worked at the Midwestern plant, Lundquist sends thanks and admiration for their incredible business courage, leadership and spirit: "May you always be so open to the gifts of discovery and learning." Finally, she thanks the staff at Creative Breakthroughs, Inc. whose incredible talent, commitment and determination cannot be matched anywhere. She says, "We are a family—growing, learning together and empowering one another to realize our dreams."

Steve Jacobsen is indebted to the 31 people who participated in his research project; his dissertation advisor, John Gardiner; dissertation committee members Carol Weaver and Phil Burroughs; Steve Hinkle; co-workers Jeannie, Michelle and Peter; and Ann, Autumn, Allegra, and Aria.

Kay Gilley humbly thanks Jim Hargreaves for his loving support and encouragement during her midlife graduate education and business start-up, and especially on her own spiritual journey. She also thanks the many others who helped in that growth process, but especially Kay Porter and long-time friend and partner in growth, Mary Jeanne Jacobsen. Special recognition goes to Paul Frishkoff, Maggie Moore, Meg Wheatley, Peter Senge, and Scott Peck, who each in their own way contributed to the evolution of her thinking about developing more conscious leaders.

Dave Potter thanks his wife, Lauren, for her help in deepening, clarifying, and sharpening his thoughts during the writing of his chapter for this book. Also, no one familiar with the community-building model of M. Scott Peck or the models used by the modern-day practitioners of dialogue, such as Bill Isaacs, could miss their influence on the model presented in his essay. Students of Scott Peck will recognize the "Chaos" and "Emptiness" elements and dialogue practitioners will recognize "Creative Emergence" as "Creativity in the Field." Peck's and Isaac's work have provided great inspiration, both in the writing of the essay and in the author's own work with other companies. Finally, a special thanks to John Renesch for his enthusiastic encouragement and for providing the opportunity to contribute to this anthology.

Laura Hauser wishes to express her deep appreciation to the many people who were inspiring and helpful in the creation of her essay. To her husband, Dave, for his unwavering love and support, and for promoting her work. To her Pepperdine sisters, Sally and Deborah, for nurturing her spiritual warrior. To her son, Chris, for illuminating the lessons of understanding, compassion, and forgiveness. To Gail Fox for enthusiastically and exquisitely coaching her through the writing process. To Michael

Esnard, Karen Hanen, Ann Kruse, and Randy Brooks, for honestly critiquing her essay. To her many teachers, such as Bob Tannenbaum and her mother, for sharing their wisdom and love. To her family, friends, and clients for being a source of inspiration and learning. And to John Renesch for inviting her into this momentous project.

Margery Miller wishes to acknowledge her incredible team of co-workers in Miller & Associates, without whom she would not have all the free time and energy to write, speak, consult, and teach about humanity in business. She is also deeply grateful to Susan, Rody, Vicki, Mona, Lana, and Belinda, with whom she meets monthly, for pushing her to face herself and grow into the woman she truly wants to be. And further, she expresses thanks to all the clients and associates who have taught her how to put her ideas into practice and have been willing to take the risk of challenging themselves to build businesses with a new bottom line.

Co-editor John Renesch wishes to acknowledge his partner in this book—Bill DeFoore—for his trust, respect, and caring. "It has been a pleasure and a privilege to work with him on this, the second book we've co-edited together."

He also acknowledges all the authors—for their soulful contributions to this collection, their wisdom and creativity, their vulnerability and inspiration. In particular he wishes to thank Tom Peters and William George for being so openly engaged in a discussion about spirit and work. "Their willingness to do so publicly is of an enormous benefit to many," he concludes.

Co-editor Bill DeFoore wants to thank John Renesch for including him in this project as well as their earlier book, *Rediscovering the Soul of Business.* This has opened new doors and provided new opportunities that would have been virtually impossible, otherwise. He would also like to thank Tom Peters for "stirring the pot" and bringing up such a wonderful mix of feelings, thoughts, and perspectives, as reflected in this book's first chapter.

New Leaders Press, the book's publisher, thanks everyone connected with the design and production of this book. This includes the composition team of Carolynn Crandall and Chuck Karp, New Leaders Press staff members Michael Mulcahy, John Renesch, Amy Kahn, Claudette Allison, and Tatiana Roegiers. For her creative cover design, we thank Sue Malikowski of Autographix.

As the final stage of the book's production, our printer deserves special thanks: Lyle Mumford and his colleagues at Publishers Press have been terrific allies over the last several years and we are grateful for their support. Special thanks are also sent to Michael Lash for his very special support for this project.

The publisher also wishes to thank William George for offering to expand his endorsement for this book into a foreword. Being the CEO of a much-admired publicly-held company like Medtronic adds further to the legitimacy for the ideas in this book. Thanks also to Jack Lowe, CEO of TDIndustries, who offered some valuable input before going to press.

The advisory board of New Leaders Press/Sterling & Stone, Inc. has been invaluable as a continuing resource and we wish to acknowledge each of them: Pat Barrentine, David Berenson, William Halal, Willis Harman, Paul Hwoschinsky, William Miller, Shirley Nelson, Christine Oster, Steven Piersanti, Catherine Pyke, James O'Toole, Michael Ray, Stephen Roulac, Jeremy Tarcher, Peggy Umanzio, and Dennis White.

For those generous people who agreed to preview the collection in advance of its publication, the editors and authors are profoundly grateful. These people are John Adams, Mary E. Anderson, James A. Autry, Godric E.S. Bader, Richard Barrett, Warren Bennis, Lorna Catford, Jim Channon, Stephen R. Covey, Riane Eisler, Gil Fairholm, Michael J.E. Frye, Rick Gutherie, William E. Halal, Barbara "BJ" Hately, David Jamison, Laurie Beth Jones, W. Mathew Juechter, Jim Kouzes, Joel Makower, Ben Mancini, James O'Toole, Rolf Österberg, Martin Rutte, Margaret Wheatley, Joyce Wycoff, and Jim Selman.

This collection has been a true collaboration—a partnership in a very real sense among the authors, editors, and publisher who worked together in creating this unique offering. We thank you one and all for a job well done!

**John Renesch** (left) is editor and publisher of *The New Leaders*, an international business newsletter on transformative leadership, and managing director of Sterling & Stone, Inc. He has edited or co-edited a number of published collections including *New Traditions in Business*, *The New Entrepreneurs*, *Leadership in a New Era*, and *Learning Organizations*. Renesch speaks publicly on transformative leadership in business and has addressed audiences in Seoul, Tokyo, Brussells, and various U.S. venues.

**Bill DeFoore,** PhD (right), is an author, psychotherapist, consultant, and president of the Institute for Personal & Professional Development. He was the organizer and convenor of the September 1993 conference "Searching for the Soul in Business." He speaks and conducts workshops internationally on emotional intelligence and emotional health in personal and professional relationships.

Introduction

# Restoring Consciousness To Business

## John Renesch and Bill DeFoore

Do people live in order to serve and maintain companies? Or, do companies exist to serve people? Most of us would agree that the second premise is the "correct" one—the way we'd like to think our modern lives are structured. However, to larger and larger degrees the first premise is one gaining momentum—not out of conscious intention but from unconscious "system creep."

Over the past two hundred and fifty years, materialism-based capitalism has become the dominant force in society—at least in the industrialized world. In Adam Smith's day, in the mid-1700s, society was presumed to be a moral, compassionate and relatively frugal marketplace, dependent on much less efficient means of production than the present day. Business was presumed to have a conscience and, even if it didn't, there was limited negative effect it could have on the rest of society. Travel and communications took months, even years. Manufacturing was a craftsman's art.

Gradually, over the past couple of centuries, the Industrial Age has created a huge production-consumption machine—a system that is so complex, so vast, that it finds itself pulling all of the industrialized world along in its tracks. And the rest of the world is lining up to board the train too!

This system of production-consumption is insatiable. It has become an engine—a machine—that has only one goal:    to produce the most profit for the owners of the enterprises of commerce.  That is what it does best.

Roger Terry, editor of the award-winning alumni magazine of the Marriott School of Management at Brigham Young University, writes:

> Capitalism, no matter whose model you like, requires a constantly expanding market, requires that luxuries become necessities, that we constantly improve and replace products in an endless upward spiral, that we extract an increasing amount of profit, and that we infuse new money regularly into the economic flow. Everyone agrees on this.  These are the assumptions behind everyone's solutions.  No one questions the insanity of the system at its most fundamental levels.
>
> —Roger Terry, *Economic Insanity*

This fixation on the "bottom line"—fueled by the insatiable appetites of the investment community who demand increased profits on a quarter-by-quarter basis—has compromised the system's sense of right and wrong.  Terry quotes World War II hero General Omar Bradley who quipped decades ago: "The world has achieved brilliance without wisdom, power without conscience. Ours is a world of nuclear giants and ethical infants."

America has led the parade in this fixation — leading the world through most of the industrialization of business. With our revolutionary roots and our pioneer spirit, we have developed what David Korten calls "cowboy economics" in a spaceship world —a powerful combination of metaphors contained in his book *When Corporations Rule the World.*

The preoccupation with the bottom line drives business and industry to ever more productive methodologies, to produce more and more goods with less and less workers.  A by-product of this preoccupation is that the industrialized human has balked at the price of this incessant growth.  Running parallel with the honeymoon ending with the Industrial Age has been a growing interest in understanding human consciousness.  As the industrialization of humanity has grown, requiring people to think and act more machine-like, the human spirit has been fighting for its life as it stands on the precipice of extinction.

Some have referred to this phenomenon as "spiritual bankruptcy." It is the result of a loss of meaning in our lives and in our work. Meaningful work is the birthright of the soul.

More and more people, in more and more regions of the world, are waking up to find themselves riding a runaway train—a constant push for improved bottom line—and asking deep questions about the system's viability. These people are also at the forefront of an evolutionary shift for humans—a shift to an "Age of Consciousness," as futurist Peter Russell has called it in his book *The Global Brain Awakens.*

In this new awareness more people may come to a similar conclusion as those who advocate a new worldview. This new perspective believes that consciousness is causal. As has been stated by many visionaries over the past several years, we can evolve from a scientific worldview of "I'll believe it when I see it" to a causal perspective of "I'll see it when I believe it."

As these two worlds overlap—consciousness and commerce—a new bottom line is being born. This new bottom line puts people and nature ahead of profits. It is not anti-business, nor against profit-making. However, some may see this kind of a shift in priorities as a threat—a threat to the system that has become so powerful that nothing has been able to slow it down so far.

We know from general systems theory, that all systems resist change and that big systems can be brutally resistant. They can kill (in both real and metaphoric terms) anyone or anything that is seen as a threat to their survival. In the case of this economically-driven system, its survival is based on the need to continuously increase production and consumption.

The new bottom liners, therefore, will meet some serious opposition. However, the human spirit is superior to any mechanisms, especially those that are operating on automatic pilot—those systems that evolved unconsciously out of our obsession with production, materialism, science, and consumption.

As we recognize the growing disparity between the "haves" and the "have nots" in the U.S. and the rest of the world, the human spirit reminds our consciences of our humanness—of our rootedness as spiritual beings. The new bottom line values meaning, diversity, integrity, caring, service, community, connectedness, creativity, intuition, balance, and grace. It challenges the excessive focus on the old bottom line values of toughness, wealth-amassing for its own sake, stress, domination, control, and individual heroics.

Springfield Re-Manufacturing CEO Jack Stack revealed his own prescription for narrowing the gap between the "haves" and the "have-nots" in an interview with *The New Leaders* newsletter. He feels everyone in the company should know business. All the employees learn how to evaluate financial statements and other intricacies of the enterprise. And it works! The success of the company has been so outstanding, the story has been told on network television news and in national newspapers over the past several years.

Part One of this book contains the keystone of the entire collection, a summary of a dialogue that began when a syndicated column by management guru Tom Peters appeared in newspapers across the U.S. Questioning the idea of integrating spiritual values into the workplace, Peters' column generated responses from a range of individuals including CEOs, academics, and authors. In addition to Peters' writings, this part contains views from bestselling author Thomas Moore (*Care of the Soul*), USC's Ian Mitroff, real estate expert Allen Cymrot, Virginia Commonwealth University's Gil Fairholm, and Medtronic CEO William George.

Part Two examines work from the perspective of spiritual values. It contains essays by *One-Minute Manager* co-author Ken Blanchard, Michael Scott Rankin, *Industry Week*'s Perry Pascarella, and Joel Levey. Part Three focuses on the heart of business—with being human, first and foremost. It contains essays by Angeles Arrien, author of *The Four Fold Way*, AT&T's Kymn Harvin-Rutigliano, and Jacqueline Haessly.

Part Four probes the personal journey of inquiry and self-discovery. Essays in this portion include ones by Rae Thompson, financial advisor David Schwerin, Margaret Molinari, and Sajeela Moskowitz Ramsey. Part Five looks at participation and teamwork in the context of merging consciousness and commerce. It contains the writings of Barry Heermann, Evangeline Caridas, and Karen Lundquist.

Part Six examines leadership in this context and includes essays by Steve Jacobsen, Kay Gilley, Dave Potter, and Laura Hauser. Part Seven is the final group of essays, examining the more pragmatic or practical side of these writings.  It contains essays by coeditor Bill DeFoore, Ireland's Gerard O'Neill, Margery Miller, and The Body Shop founder Anita Roddick.

Information on how to contact all the authors is contained in the back of this book, along with lists of books, periodicals, and organizations that may be a resource for the reader in continuing an inquiry into this field of study.

We encourage you to read and enjoy this compilation of original writings by incredible harbingers of a global movement toward a new bottom line. Enjoy!

Part One

# SPIRIT AND WORK

Chapter 1
## Spirit And Work: Can Business And Consciousness Co-Exist?
John Renesch

Featuring contributions by:

Tom Peters
author, consultant, speaker

Allen Cymrot
president, Cymrot Realty Advisors, Inc.

Gil Fairholm
professor, Virginia Commonwealth University

William George
CEO, Medtronic, Inc.

Michael Munn
consultant, Lockheed Missiles & Space Co., Inc.

Thomas Moore
author, *Care of the Soul*

**John Renesch** is editor and publisher of *The New Leaders*, an international business newsletter on transformative leadership, and managing director of Sterling & Stone, Inc. He has edited or co-edited a number of published collections including *New Traditions in Business*, *The New Entrepreneurs*, *Leadership in a New Era*, *Learning Organizations*, and *Rediscovering the Soul of Business*.

Renesch speaks publicly on transformative leadership in business and has addressed audiences in Seoul, Tokyo, Brussells, and various U.S. venues.

His career includes a wide variety of business experiences: real estate, financial services, event promotion, public relations, and publishing. He served as managing director for a real estate investment firm and was the founding CEO for a secondary market real estate securities brokerage firm in the mid 1980s.

# Spirit & Work: Can Business And Consciousness Co-Exist?

## John Renesch

Is there a role for spiritual values in the modern workplace? Can our experience at work be enhanced by bringing the softer human qualities into our business relationships? Will this ultimately be a lasting benefit to our corporate communities or is this talk of "soul" and spirit at work a mere distraction or passing fad?

Based on my experience as a career businessman with over forty years of self-employment and more than twenty years of personal development and study, I am convinced that the "search for meaning" from our toil is not a fashionable trend. This growing desire for wholeness and meaningfulness is fueled by a sense of purposelessness or "spiritual bankruptcy" experienced by many workforces around the world, a by-product of an Industrial Age mindset gone to extremes.

Recently, the subject of spiritual values at work has become the focus of a debate in the U.S.—a debate that could be one of the most significant business issues for this decade. Before I examine this debate, let me provide a brief overview of how we've arrived at this crossroads of thinking.

In the mid-1980s, following on the heels of the human potential movement, an informal grassroots network began to focus on "organizational potential," largely motivated by the frustrations of bureaucracy, ineffectiveness, and mediocrity of corporate and institutional life. This movement was given even greater energy as the excesses of the "decade of greed" became more and more unconscionable.

In the late 1980s and early 1990s more and more people began to talk and write about a nonreligious spirituality—a sense of interconnectedness that encompassed systems thinking, respect of indigenous cultures, civility, mythology, and social responsibility. In the U.S., these elements gained much attention from the likes of Joseph Campbell, Peter Senge, M. Scott Peck, the Native American traditions, Twelve Step programs, and the environmental movement. The continued influence of the women's movement, joined by the subsequent men's movement in more recent years, has provided another dimension to this social trend toward a more inclusive, holistic approach to life.

Much of this phenomenon can be attributed to a reaction to the overbearing influence of the Industrial Age, which resulted in the mechanistic, reductionistic thinking that has dominated the West (and parts of the East) for more than a century. We have come to think that the whole is the sum of the parts, that value exists in what is external to us, that rationality and the mind are the ultimate "justifiers of our actions."

This kind of thinking has been valuable for technological advances and creating much wealth for a relatively few people, but it has not done much for maintaining a sense of community with each other, for developing sustainable lifestyles that allow our environment to continue supporting us, or for enriching our inner lives, our intrinsic sense of self identification.

As peoples' minds and bodies go to work each day, the tension grows as they fail to feed their hearts and souls—those parts of themselves that the Industrial Age demands that they leave at the factory or office door. This growing tension motivates people to search for connection with a force beyond personalities. Since tension tends to relieve itself, people deal with it in one of two ways: they explore their inner selves in a quest for intrinsic values or they "numb the pain" that results from this discrepancy through addictive distractions that include consumption, overwork, gossip, alcohol, television, overeating, drugs, or other compulsions created by a negative ego.

It is no surprise, therefore, that the works of spiritual scholars and philosophers have begun to cross over from philosophy to the world of business, labor, and organizational life. In the U.S., we have seen increasing numbers of "spiritual business books" appearing on the shelves of our libraries and bookstores. In 1990, *Fortune* magazine published a feature entitled, "The New Age for Business?" which examined the progression of "enlightened" business practices over the previous generation. A 1992 issue of *The Wall Street Journal* pointed to the growing popularity of spiritual business books. Today the number of these books continues to grow exponentially.

Richard Barrett was working at the World Bank when he was inspired to start a support system for employees who saw a place for spiritual values in the Bank. The result was the establishment of the World Bank Spiritual Unfoldment Society. In an article for *The New Leaders* business newsletter he writes:

> For anyone who is experiencing a similar situation let me encourage you to go ahead. There is a great need to bring spiritual values into the corporate setting. Persuading your organization to shift from a paradigm of competition, exploitation and self-interest, to cooperation, empowerment and the common good is one of the greatest gifts you can give to society.

U.S. management guru Tom Peters, who wrote a syndicated newspaper column in the U.S., decided to focus on this topic in April 1993. In his column, he expressed concern over this growing phenomenon and wrote:

> In his own fashion, time-and-motion man Frederick Taylor increased human freedom. His schemes for objectively determining "best practices" for every imaginable job helped free front-line workers from the capricious discipline of unscientific, turn-of-the-century foremen.
>
> A half-century later, MIT's Doug McGregor gave us Theory Y, based on the then contrarian idea that "the capacity to exercise imagination, ingenuity and creativity in the solution of organizational problems is widely, not narrowly, distributed in the population." About the same time, Peter Drucker marveled at the potential power of employee suggestions at GM—long before Toyota, acting on its employees' suggestions, embarrassed GM in the marketplace.

Taylor, McGregor, Drucker et al. have done us an enormous favor. In an age of brainwork, chaos, globalism, and shifting alliances, we must empower fast, or else. There's no room for the oppressive managerial practices of the past.

I'm a long-time champion of employee involvement, even the frivolous parts—T-shirts, caps, buttons, badges and "one-minute praisings." Cynics take special glee at ripping the latter (from "One-Minute Manager" Ken Blanchard), but the world would be a better place if we thanked employees more often for jobs well done.

Still, I have a nagging concern something has gone a little haywire. Call it the advent of the spiritual leader.

Years ago, Robert Greenleaf, a retired AT&T exec, wrote *Servant Leadership.* Its simple premise was right as can be. The leader, from shop supervisor to Bill Clinton and Boris Yeltsin, should serve his or her constituents.

Greenleaf's slight but powerful treatise has a spiritual feel, as does, more openly, Herman Miller chairman Max DePree's 1989 *Leadership is an Art.* In fact, a recent business book publisher's catalog seemed to feature borderline mystical books; the importance of a leader's spirituality popped, unabashedly, from at least half the texts.

Part of me sees no problem with that. I've long argued that effective individual and organizational perfor-mance is largely a by-product of ethical, committed, spirited, joyous labor. "Put love where your labor is," the very secular The Body Shop founder Anita Roddick urges in her book *Body and Soul.*

Yet another part of me is antsy. The late Bill McGowan, MCI's legendary chief, thought corporate paternalism was bunk. McGowan was one of the toughest and most inspiring guys I've met. And I fell in love with MCI almost as much as with him: It was/is a madhouse. Action-oriented. Antibureaucratic (to the extent that any $10 billion-plus firm can be). Disrespectful of job boundaries.

Empowerment is MCI's hallmark. "We don't shoot people who make mistakes, we shoot people who don't take risks," Dick Liebhaber, MCI's head of strategy and technology, says with a smile.

CNN rings the same bells. "'Doing it' means figuring out how to do it yourself," said former CNN President Burt Reinhartdt. "If your way works most of the time you'll get promoted." I like that! CNN is action-oriented, empowered, spirited. But hardly spiritual.

Respect for the individual at MCI and CNN puts traditional corporations to shame. But both firms are performance fanatics, and they "don't coddle" (per MCI's Liebhaber). Truth is, if I were young and starting out, CNN and MCI would top my list of résumé recipients.

So what's my beef? I'm not sure. It's just that several recent business tracts seem to cross a line, to blur the borders between church and corporation.

I relish telling managers that they're first-class jerks if they don't listen to employees, then act on what they hear. Hey, I've repeatedly said we should *eliminate* 90 percent of our managers, because the troops don't need them!

But when the talk turns to the spiritual side of leadership, I mostly want to run. It should be enough if I work like hell, respect my peers, customers and suppliers, and perform with verve, imagination, efficiency and good humor. Please don't ask me to join the Gregorian Chant Club, too.

GE boss Jack Welch, one tough cookie, uses the word "liberation" more often than I. And he tells his managers, in no uncertain terms, to tap the brains and zest of *all* employees—or catch the next train out of town.

Welch may be deeply spiritual. Or not. I don't know. And couldn't care less. His liberation plea, I do know, is aimed at enhanced competitiveness—which is the point, as I see it, of our secular corporations.

If Welch sneaks off to spend summers working with Mother Teresa, I'd respect him all the more, personally. But as a GE shareholder—or employee—I just don't give a hoot.

By all means let's empower, then empower some more. Those who fail to tap the imagination and curiosity of workers will fail in the viciously competitive '90s. Good riddance. But in tapping the needed imagination and curiosity, let's leave the Bible, the Koran and facile talk of spiritual leaders at home.

Within a few days of its publication, an open letter to Peters was published by the *Minneapolis Star Tribune*. Written by William George, CEO of publicly-held Medtronic, Inc., the response directly addressed Peters' discomfort. As George wrote:

Dear Tom:

You've got it all wrong! After 10 years of inspiring us with anecdotal tales of corporate excellence and employee empowerment, your column "Spiritual talk has no place in secular corporation," which appeared in the April 6 edition of the *Star Tribune*, shows a lack of understanding about what really motivates employees, and people in general.

My business experience suggests the vast majority of employees of corporations are motivated not by "balloons in the atrium," as you often suggest, but rather by making meaningful contribution to others through their work.

Appealing to these deeper motivations is indeed the spiritual side of leadership that Max DePree and Bob Greenleaf have both practiced and written about so meaningfully, yet which you say makes you "want to run."

The dictionary defines "spiritual" as (1) "the animating or life-giving principle within a human being," (2) "the part of a human being associated with the mind or feelings as distinguished from the physical body" and (3) "the real sense of significance of something."

This "significance" is precisely what DePree and Greenleaf are appealing to. After all, we spend more time at work than in any other part of our lives. Shouldn't we find significance in our work and the opportunity to use our mind and feeling while appealing to "the animating or life-giving principles" within us? This isn't practicing religion per se but rather devoting our whole being toward a higher purpose in our work.

You accuse people like DePree of "crossing a line, to blur the borders between church and corporation." But "spiritual leadership" in the workplace has nothing to do with church or with religion.

Medtronic was founded more than 40 years ago by a spiritual leader named Earl Bakken. Sure Earl is a great inventor who created the first battery-operated wearable pacemaker. He also is a great visionary who in 1960, when the company was near bankruptcy, wrote a mission statement that laid out Medtronic's future for the next 100 years. But even more important than that, Earl is still the spiritual leader, or "soul," of Medtronic, despite that he has been retired for four years.

The mission he wrote more than 30 years ago, not one word of which has been changed, calls for Medtronic to restore people to the fullness of life and health. Our 9,000 employees are totally dedicated to that mission, regardless of whether they work in the R&D lab, the factory, the accounting department, or in the hospital.

Earl still meets with every new employee of Medtronic, all around the world. In these three-hour sessions with 15 to 20 employees, he describes the founding and mission of the company, answers questions and then awards each employee a medallion symbolic of his or her work with Medtronic. I have been with Earl in Minneapolis, Tokyo, and in the Netherlands as he does these inspiring sessions. Last June he even traveled to former East Germany to meet with 29 employees of a small pacemaker company Medtronic had acquired the previous year.

Earl also carries his spirituality into the marketplace. You will find him at every major medical meeting around the world at the Medtronic exhibit from 8 am until 6 pm talking to doctors, young and old alike, about the importance of their work in saving lives with Medtronic products.

The most meaningful event of the year for Medtronic employees is the annual holiday party, held each year in late December. There nearly 2,000 employees (and several thousand more by videotape) gather at Medtronic to hear the personal stories of the patients whose lives have been saved and restored by Medtronic products. Last year's program included an 18-year-old immigrant from Czechoslovakia who had been in a near-fatal automobile crash and quite literally had his life saved through the use of an experimental emergency bypass system. Many of us, quite unashamedly, had tears in our eyes as he and his mother told their story.

The latest focus in our organization is to stress "leading by values," rather than "management by objectives." We believe that if all of us, employees and managers alike, agree on the values that guide our work, employees can be fully empowered to realize them. This emphasis is especially important to the many self-directed work teams that are becoming the backbone of our organizational structure.

What are those values? They are, first of all, restoring people to full health; next, serving our customers with products and services of unsurpassed quality; recognizing the personal worth of employees; making a fair profit and return for our shareholders; and maintaining good citizenship as a company. Not surprisingly, these values are taken directly from the Medtronic system which is well understood by all Medtronic employees.

Tom, you may be surprised to see that "maximized shareholder value" is not our first objective as it is for many companies. At Medtronic we believe that if we first serve our customers well, provide products and services of unsurpassed quality and empower our employees to fulfill themselves and the company's mission, we will indeed provide an outstanding return for our shareholders. And, the results of the past 30 years, or the past eight years, seem to validate that approach; $1,000 invested in 1960 in Medtronic stock would be worth $1.65 million today, or $1,000 invested in 1985 would be worth $9,000 today.

At Medtronic we don't mix religion and business, but we certainly do not shy away from the spiritual side of our work and the deeper meaning of our mission to save lives. If all this makes you want to run, so be it. For all of us, it is the real reason we go to work every day.

Concurrent with George's articulate response, my newsletter, *The New Leaders,* published a short commentary, inserted just as we were going to press. I wrote the commentary which follows:

The outspoken Tom Peters has done it again. True to his reputation as a "roughrider" management guru, Peters criticizes talk of any spiritual side to business leadership. In his column in the *San Jose Mercury News* on April 5 [1993], Peters seems to confuse the application of spiritual values such as inner-directedness, authentic power, and intuitive management with joining the Gregorian Chant Club.

Perhaps he doesn't understand what most credible writers, academics, and leaders mean when they use the term "spiritual." He seems to believe it is synonymous with corporate paternalism, working with Mother Teresa, or singing in a choir.

Most advocates of spiritual principles for the workplace clearly distinguish between religion and spiritual, something Peters doesn't seem able to grasp.

To use his own words, he writes that "something has gone a little haywire. Call it the advent of the spiritual leader."

Even the title of his article, "Top Execs Need to be Spiritual Leaders, Not Spiritual Gurus," suggests that he doesn't understand that the new breed of leader in business is not a "religious" guru but an individual who assumes responsibility for an outcome, who is self-empowered, and can work in harmony with his or her environment.

Michael Munn, at the time senior quality consultant for Lockheed Missiles & Space Co., Inc., sent us his response to the Peters column. Here is an excerpt of his letter:

Three words run around in my head. They bounce back and forth until I begin to feel dizzy. They won't stop. I can't turn off the screen of my mind. I see wild horses stampeding across a plain as the word "spirited" flashes briefly before me. A near relative follows it, but the picture changes in a split second. I see myself, eyes closed, and hands clasped in a peaceful posture as the word "spiritual" flickers momentarily. A question forms with the third word. I see myself old and gray. I am on my deathbed. I wonder why I've been here. "Did my life have *meaning?*"

I wonder if everyone thinks of these words in the same way? When I use them, do others see the same pictures? How different are those pictures? I've done many workshops in which people compared their interpretation of words. Even simple words like "communicate" take on as many meanings as people. The differences are huge. How can people ever make sense to each other?

What does Tom Peters think when he hears these words? I've read his articles. I can't tell for sure. I know meaning is important. I know spirited leaders are good for Tom. I know spiritual leaders in business are not as good. The way I see these words, I've been a spirited and spiritual leader as I tried to bring meaning into my work life. My coworkers and employees seem to have appreciated both. We've all grown together.

In early 1994, I wrote Peters to see if he would respond to the reactions to his syndicated column. I included William

George's open letter, which had been reprinted in *The New Leaders* earlier in the year. Peters replied, to me as well as to George, in a two-and-a-half page article in his own newsletter, *Tom Peters On Achieving Excellence.* He wrote:

> John, let me be clear. I find the idea of "spirituality in the workplace" appalling. Before flipping the dial, at least give me a chance to explain. I am a First Amendment freak, a free-speech anarchist. I consider the American experiment, little more than 200 years old, to be (warts and all) a raging success; and I consider the 45-word First Amendment, guaranteeing freedom of speech (and religion) the cornerstone of that success. We're a nation that talks back to authority, that savors contention, that doesn't cower before petty tyrants (political or corporate). In addition to spawning unparalleled personal liberty, it's the engine of our matchless entrepreneurial spunk.

> On a similar plane, I salute Justice Louis Brandeis' contention that the right to be let alone (privacy) is the most important and fundamental of human rights. Institutions are institutions. They're all too damned intrusive, from the DMV and the IRS to my own company, The Tom Peters Group.

> Now that we've got that out of the way, let's move forward. I guess I know a sacred (spiritual?) cow when I see one. I find it amusing—instructive—that the two columns of mine (out of 490 in the past nine-plus years) that have drawn the most flak are the one on spirituality and one that derided, during the 1992 presidential campaign, Ross Perot as a potential tyrant-in-waiting (whose protectionist ideas are wrong-headed—but none of my attackers worried about economics, that's for sure. They were on my case for not seeing a savior when I looked Perot in the eye.) Hmmm.

> In his original, 15-paragraph letter, Mr. George gave a dictionary definition of spirituality (that's *always* a show stopper. Who'd dare disagree with a dic-tion-ar-y?). He wrote: "The dictionary defines 'spiritual' as (1) 'the animating or life-giving principle within a human

being,' (2) 'the part of the human being associated with the mind or feelings as distinguished from the physical body' and (3) 'the real sense of significance of something.'"

Sadly, Mr. George didn't identify his dictionary. Hence, I went to my own trusty jillion-pound *Oxford English Dictionary*, which traces the origin of "spiritual" to AD 1377. Here are the *OED*'s first two definitions of the word (or should I say Word):

"1. Of or pertaining to, affecting or concerning, the spirit or higher moral qualities, esp. as regarded in a religious aspect. 2. Of, belonging or relating to, concerned with sacred or ecclesiastical things or matters, as distinguished from secular affairs; pertaining to the church or clergy."

Rings a tad religious to me.

But look, I'm not going to hang my case on an un-American (British) dictionary. My hackles were raised by George's resorting to the cheapest debater's trick in town (one I often use): the *straw man*. My beef with spirituality is that church and corporation don't mix, as I see it. Yet George says, "My business experience suggests that the vast majority of employees of corporations are motivated not by 'balloons in the atriums,' as you often suggest, but rather my making meaningful contributions to others through their work."

Then (also in the original) he laid out Medtronic's virtuous corporate values (No. 1, "Restoring people to health"—surprise? They make pacemakers, for heaven's sake) and concludes, "Tom, you may be surprised to see that 'maximized shareholder value' is not our first objective, as it is for many companies."

Jeez, I reread my original column and glanced through all five books I've written, and I've never said a damned thing about balloons in the atrium being the primary human motivator, or about increasing shareholder value as the No. 1 corporate animating idea (though I have no moral objection whatsoever to either balloons or making money for shareholders).

Okay, let's get off this "he said, she said" seesaw. What *does* gore my ox, unequivocally, is this: "Shouldn't we find significance in our work...? This isn't practicing religion per se but rather devoting our whole being toward a higher purpose in our work."

Look, Mr. George, I am terribly sorry, but I really don't wish—even in my own company—to "devote [my] whole being toward a higher purpose in [my] work."

Don't get me wrong. I get a kick out of what I do. And folks tell me, from time to time, that it's useful. And, I'm glad. But I sure as hell never, ever think of it in terms of devoting my whole being to a higher purpose. (If my "employees" do, fine; but if they don't, fine, too—at least the "don'ts" have company—the boss and principal shareholder, namely me.) To be more self-disclosing than perhaps I ought to be, as a matter of personal (rather than professional) opinion, I find it insufferable to be around people who take themselves too seriously, on the golf course (I don't play golf) or at the annual strategy retreat (I try not to go to those, either).

I like to raise hell. Cause a fuss. Be part of the fray of the times. Get under folks' skin. I'm always tempted to write in the space calling for "occupation" on customs forms when I enter a country, "curmudgeon," "pain in the ass," "hellraiser." I must admit I was positively thrilled when *Business Week* called me business' "best friend and worst nightmare."

Look, I've got to come clean: My little company (publisher of this newsletter [*Tom Peters On Achieving Excellence*], among other things) doesn't have a *vision statement* (our balance sheet is not such that we can afford the plasticized cards—only kidding). But your letter got me thinking about what "my" corporate value statement is, or might be. Here's a draft document.

1. Do fabulous work, and be known around the world for our innovativeness.

2. Attract exciting people—more than a few of whom are a little offbeat.

3. Raise hell, question "the way things are done around here," and never, ever rest on our laurels. (Today's laurels are tomorrow's compost.)

4. Have those who leave us voluntarily or involuntarily testify as to having learned a lot, had a special experience and made fast friends while they were here. (Ye shall be known by your alumni!)

5. Have a collegial, supportive, yeasty, zany, laughter-filled environment, where folks support one another, and "politics" is as absent as it can be in a human (i.e., imperfect) enterprise.

6. Have no question or innuendo ever surface about our ethics.

7. Dot the *i*s, cross the *t*s, answer the phones promptly, send out errorless invoices, and in general never forget the devil *is* in the details.

8. Work with exciting customers (and other partners) who turn us on, who stretch us, from whom we can learn, and who we enjoy being around (and who pay their bills on time, too).

9. Take in substantially more money than we spend (where spending includes above-average compensation and a very high level of investment in the future).

10. Grow via quality services and customers, not via growth for growth's sake.

Does that show abiding respect for the individual? Our customers? Our suppliers? Our community? I hope so. I think so. Is it spiritual? I think not. I *hope* not.

I am asking folks to work their buns off, have a good time, fawn over customers, constantly learn new stuff, screw around in pursuit of innovation—and take in more bread at the end of the day than we expend baking it (at least over the long haul—we've frequently run in the red, short-term, in pursuit of long-term advantage and doing things the way we think they ought to be/must be done).

John, I'll tell you *exactly* who I want to employ. Actually, I'll let *Inc.* tell you. In its July 1993 issue, the editors presented this fictitious memo:

To: *Inc.* magazine

From: Determinedly seeking the Perfect Job

I don't want to screw around any more in a place that's badly managed, poorly run, and so stupid I'm just wasting my time. Or a place where you have to be a vice-president to get a window. I want to take my dogs to work, at least on Saturdays, and if I break into a chorus of "Oklahoma" at 4 p.m. I want two people to harmonize with me—not look at me sideways....

I like that. I love it. Is she available? I'll hire her. Now. For her spunk. For her spirit. For her irreverence. For her dogs. For her *voice*. But not for her spirituality.

Let me offer one last example of "higher order" stuff, if that's what it is. David Sheff's *Game Over* traces the meteoric rise of Japan's unconventional Nintendo. The essence of Nintendo is aptly captured by a simple exchange. A game designer, Gunpei Hokoi, asks his boss, "What should I make?" Nintendo President Hiroshi Yamauchi replies, "Something great."

What should I make? Something great. Wow! What a turn-on! I hope my tiny company is in a place where folks feel encouraged to "make something great," a wee bit guilty if they fall short of that. What does that have to do with spirituality? Frankly, I have no idea.

I responded to Peters, thanking him for providing greater venue for this discussion and volunteering to represent the concerns of many leaders in business. Here are excerpts from my letter:

Dear Tom:

I am absolutely delighted that we have engaged on this issue of spirituality and work....I feel that a lively debate has begun and am looking forward to what we all can learn from it.

...Your column has sparked an exhilarating discussion on what I have called "business cosmology." By serving as a catalyst, you have brought significant profile to the discussion whereby good-hearted people can disagree on certain principles. This debate feels very "clean" to me, with opposing viewpoints clearly defined and willingly engaged. I am excited about the engagement *and* the inquiry. Once again, I applaud your outspokenness and your passion about the subject.

I presume you have read some of the books written by authors we have included in our anthologies—writers who have clearly defined their values as based on spiritual principles, not religious dogma. These people include James Autry, Warren Bennis, Max DePree, Charles Handy, Michael Ray, Anita Roddick, Peter Senge, and Margaret Wheatley. Of course, there are also the works of Tom Chappell, Steve Covey, and Paul Hawken who have been quite popular authors of values-driven business books.

None of these writers have condoned the imposition of religious practices or beliefs on co-workers or employees. None of them would suggest that workers be asked to engage in any "practice" or to conform to any specific dogmatic tenet. All of them would agree, I believe, that values-driven, spiritually-based principles...have a role to play in the social changes going on in the world.

Business is the dominant player in [society] these days, providing it with the greatest opportunity to affect our evolution positively or negatively. Many of us in this field of inquiry believe that it is business' responsibility to be a leader in this evolution. As a result, there are many advocates for business being more socially responsible, more humanistic and holistic in its approach to the marketplace.

At the risk of coming across as one of those too seri-ous for your tastes, I see this perspective as one of necessity for long-range sustainability, not a form of missionary work to convert workers to the "gospel of whomever." I see the need for new fundamental val-ues in how we lead, manage, and work in the future if we are to continue evolving in a post-modern world.

For example, one of the primary principles that most of these authors would support is that of the value of diversity. Many of us envision significant possibility of synergistic power and creativity in diverse workforces, wishing to truly embrace ethnic and gender mixes, not just paying them lip service. Diversity cannot flourish when any one culture—be it religious, racist, elitist, or sexist—dominates the others.

It is clear from your recent article in the *Total Quality* newsletter that you are occasionally touched emotion-ally—moved to cheer the socially responsible heroics of our current crop of principled entrepreneurs (e.g., Ben Cohen of Ben & Jerry's). I commend your com-mitment to "do something about" the social condition and suggest that you are as moved to be individually responsible as some of those who may be in the camp of the "spiritual pioneers" in business.

By taking the stand you have, are you disagreeing with these scholars of business cosmology? Are you saying there is no place for philosophy and commerce to overlap, for that is what is clearly occurring these days? Or, are you opposing the imposition of religious dogma and practices on workers who feel the need to comply to protect their jobs? If this latter is your contention, I argue that this is not what these people are advocating and that you are confusing spiritual values with religious structures.

USC School of Business professor Ian Mitroff sent us his thoughts about the Peters' stance. He writes:

It is amazing the lengths to which we humans will go

in order to deny and avoid the topic of spirituality. For Tom Peters, spirituality is equivalent to religion, and the mix of religion and business is strictly forbidden under the First Amendment. Thus, religion/spirituality ought not to intrude in the workplace. Second, spirituality is not necessary in order for organizations to function at a high level. To demonstrate this, Peters lists ten principles that represent his "corporate values" and presumably, if followed, would allow organizations to perform effectively. Spirituality is thereby unnecessary.

Wouldn't it be peachy if Peters', or any limited number of principles, allowed organizations to function effectively? You bet it would! The trouble with all such lists is that they assume away the very problems they are supposed to address! The lists already presuppose that an organization is functioning well in order for them to work.

I take a darker view of both human nature and organizations. This is not the same as saying that I am thereby utterly without hope for individuals, organizations, or humankind in general.

I believe that most organizations, like most families, are deeply dysfunctional. As one of my friends puts it, when you mention the words "families" and "organizations," you don't need to mention "dysfunctional." It's automatically included.

I know of one highly intrusive program composed of twelve extremely unorthodox "management principles" that is highly successful in treating severe dysfunctions. This is the Twelve Step program of AA. Surprisingly, the same debate rages here as well, i.e., whether spirituality is necessary to cure alcoholism. As a result, some have even formulated twelve step programs that do not mention spirituality at all.

I believe that spirituality is a vital element of all humans and human institutions. I know of nothing great or small that can be accomplished without *enthusiasm.*

My Oxford dictionary defines enthusiasm as the conjunction of two words, "ens" and "spiritus." Thus enthusiasm literally means to listen or follow the God or spirit within. This definition makes spirituality much broader than religion. This definition has nothing per se to do with religion, although it can. Religion is only one of a number of institutions that have tried, often unsuccessfully, to make spirituality their central concern and mission.

I do not see how organizations can function at a high level and truly meet the "ethical needs and wants" of all their stakeholders unless they learn to grapple seriously with spirituality. All of the fundamental issues we are confronting today with regard to organizations are due in large part to their spiritual emptiness, or the blockages that they place in the path of spirituality.

Virginia Commonwealth University professor Gil Fairholm, author of *Leadership and the Culture of Trust*, wrote us with his reaction to Peters' stance as well as George's reaction. Fairholm writes:

Tom Peters is wrong! There is a clear difference between spirituality in religion, founded on sacred writ, and the spirit or soul of man, defined as body *and* spirit.

People are much more than just a bundle of skills and knowledge, as some managers think. As Mr. George's dictionary says, people also come to work armed with a spirit, a life-giving principle that is concerned also with (Mr. Peters' dictionary definition) higher moral qualities. Defined this way, people engage in work with their whole soul, whether or not management theory, or some managers—or management pundits—take note of it.

People want more from work than just excitement, a good job, and a chance to innovate. The new work force is more intelligent and informed than those of a previous generation and, importantly, they are more "wanting." Today's workers are generally better educated and aware of what is possible of the good life. And, many come to work wanting to take responsibility, accept challenging work, and make a contribution to organizational success from the foundation of their whole self, not just the few skills, knowledge, and abilities defined in a position description.

Peters knows—his books trumpet it—that success in today's global market demands innovation, creativity, commitment, and vision from all of us. These capacities are not easily reduced to writing in a position description. Nor can they be measured on standard measures. Yet they are essential to the kind of employee Peters himself advocates in his own newsletter: "People who do fabulous work, are innovative, exciting, questioning, highly ethical, constantly learning, a joy to be with, seek growth, and make money."

Workers may, on occasion, "talk back to authority,"... "savor contention," refuse to "cower before petty tyrants (political or corporate)." But they want passionately to be engaged in work that makes a difference.

Of course, church and corporate life differ, but the committed religionist, like the committed corporate executive (or minion) brings their passion with them 24 hours a day. Today's leaders recognize this and are creating corporate cultures that foster this whole-soul—spiritual, if you will—commitment.

I would agree with Peters that there should be built into any organizational culture a distinction between corporate rights and personal rights to the private enjoyment of religious convictions. But there should also be mechanisms present to allow workers to see the larger societal purposes and results of their work, and to make personal, individual contributions to those higher-order goals along with the routine of day-to-day task-accomplishment.

I think Tom Peters is wrong also in his statement that he doesn't "...wish to devote [his] whole being toward a higher purpose in my work, as Mr. George advocates." His books, his taped seminars, the ideas he is so passionate about say as much about this personal (dare I say, whole-souled) commitment as they do about his caring for his subject matter. If he could get past his confusion of doctrinaire religion and the personal spiritual (whole-soul) needs we all have to become our best selves, I think he would make a most articulate advocate of corporate spirit in today's work world. Because the spiritually-tuned worker wants to "make something great" and does, indeed, "feel a wee bit guilty if they fall short of that."

In a November 1994 issue of *Industry Week* magazine, editor-in-chief Charles R. Day, Jr. applauds the idea that personal faith, virtue, and values are all welcome in the current business climate. He mentions the "private searches for meaningful lives" and introspections of "inner feelings" that are now commonly discussed in executive circles. He writes, "If all this qualifies as a *trend*—and I'd like to think it does—more power to it."

Recently, a survey of twenty-two U.S. leaders was conducted by a doctoral candidate from Southern California, in which the link between spirituality and leadership was examined. Notre Dame president emeritus Theodore Hesburgh, former New York state governor Mario Cuomo, and U.S. senator Claiborne Pell were among the industry and organizational leaders who participated. In his survey, Steve Jacobsen discovered that 77 percent of the respondents reported that spiritual/central values play a "strong and vital relationship" influencing their leadership. Surprisingly, the work environment was the most often cited place where these leaders found "support, renewal, and insight," suggesting a market for community building efforts in our modern workplaces.

Since part of this debate pivots around how spirituality is defined, it might be worthwhile to examine the distinctions between spiritual and religious ideals. One modern U.S. business consultant and author, Jack Hawley, compares these two in his book *Reawakening the Spirit in Work.* He describes spirituality as the "goal" and religion as the "path." His comparison identifies spirituality as a personal, private journey, containing elements of all religions, and focused on oneself and personal inquiry. He identifies religion as group-oriented, with a set of specific beliefs and rituals, with a more institutional focus.

In an interview published in the March 6, 1995 issue of *Industry Week* magazine (now called *IW*), Editor-at-Large

Thomas Brown met with consultant Laurie Beth Jones whose book *Jesus, CEO* had just been published.

Brown asked Jones if it was wrong to keep religion out of the workplace, as most managers (even those who are religious) agree. Jones responded:

> Religion is a system developed to grow and disseminate a set of particular beliefs. When I hear the word "religion," I think of something that is necessarily man-made and therefore highly fallible.
>
> So I personally agree that religion should be kept out of the workplace. Whose religion would be imposed? And at what price? While not everyone is religious, everyone is spiritual, because we are composed of mind, body, and spirit. Therefore, our spirit is already in the workplace, because our minds and bodies are. *Spiritual* principles are universal; they can and should be applied everywhere. Treating people the way you want to be treated is a simple yet profound spiritual principle, one which led to the abolition of one of the worst labor practices in history—slavery.

The interview covered comparisons of Jesus' leadership style to the challenge of modern day managers and concluded with Brown asking: "How will you answer those who feel there should be a separation of religion from business?" Jones responded:

> Yes, keep religion out of business. But recognize that spirituality is already in business, because people are the basis of any organization. And people are *spiritual* beings. To recognize and harness spiritual principles is to purposefully and actively engage the forces that are already hovering in and around every business, the spiritual dimension of workers...leaders and managers can unleash what I call the "S," or Spirit, factor—the most powerful element which exists inside people. To let this factor go untapped is to underutilize at least 30 percent of each employee. Engage it, and productivity and morale will soar!

Management consultant Nancy Austin addressed the growing interest in spirituality and business in an article in *Working Woman* magazine (March 1995), entitled "Does Spirituality at

Work Work?" She writes:

> Call it what you will—spirituality, yin and yang,
> dharmic management, following your bliss—the
> unspoken, untested assumption is that merging your
> whole being with your work in order to serve a Higher
> Purpose is a worthy, even essential business practice
> in turbulent times. That idea goes a long way beyond
> the merely unorthodox. It is just plain nuts.

> Unfazed soulmeisters insist they have solid business
> reasons for their philosophies. An expanding American
> economy and robust job market simply covered up our
> real problems, they say, but now, following years of
> economic upheaval, we see them all too clearly: self-
> doubt, greed, cynicism, arrogance and moral decline.
> None can be vanquished by fancy technology or clever
> marketing; these are problems of faith. Tapping that
> wellspring requires a personal journey, a spiritual quest
> that will enrich your organization as well as your soul—
> if you can muster the courage to attempt it.

> Plenty of people are adopting this stance—the busi-
> ness world's embrace of New Age tactics simply ech-
> oes the search for spirituality that is sweeping the
> nation. How else to explain the mainstream appeal of
> *The Celestine Prophecy* (over two million copies, 20
> languages), about a regular guy who treks to Peru in
> search of a mysterious ancient manuscript whose
> nine secret Insights are transforming life on earth?

> People are frantically searching for something to help
> them make sense of the world today. But that an
> individual manager (my boss? yours?) might hole up
> in his or her office and devise company strategy or—
> yikes!—review an employee's performance guided by
> strange Celestine bromides, the I Ching or the funny
> way you dot your i's scares the hell out of me.

> Asking an employee to devote her whole being to some
> higher spiritual purpose is wrong, even dangerous. For
> one thing, it makes mincemeat of the First Amendment.
> For another, it obscures and demeans the real, tough

work and artistry of management. It's not hard to
image the so-so manager who blames a bad quarter
on a shortage of spirituality while turning her back on
the pressing issues: global competition, union unrest,
flagging sales.

I don't want any corporation messing with my soul. I
will, however, gladly contribute my best talents,
efforts and productivity in the interest of superb
service to customers. I won't shy away from the new
or difficult. I'll work my rear end off. Just keep your
mitts off my spirit.

Matthew Fox, the ostracized Catholic priest who is the
author of *The Reinvention of Work*, proposes work as a sacra-
ment—a "holy endeavor in the spirit of service"—as opposed to
the machine that it has become over the past couple of centuries.
He warns us that outlawing Spirit from our culture "is inviting
addictions—addictions that hide the cosmic loneliness people
feel, addictions that derive from immature efforts to find Spirit on
one's own or with one's peers." Fox also addresses the tension I
mentioned earlier: "Dualistic work—that separates our lives
from our livelihood, our personal values from our work values,
and human work from the universe's work—is passé. This very
dualism constitutes the heart of the problem of our Earth
crises and youth crises and poverty crises the world over."

This tension between our personal and our work values has
finally gained some factual recognition. In a survey co-sponsored
by my company, Sterling & Stone, Inc., over 1,200 people were
asked to compare their personal values with their organization's
values. This survey was surprising in many ways. There certainly
is a gap—what we've nicknamed the "pain index"—between the
company and the individual's values, according to the respondents who were grouped into four main geographic areas—Pacific
Rim, U.S., India, and Europe. The different cultures were quite
similar in some areas and very distinct in others.

In addition to a values gap that suggests an area in need
of attention by corporate management around the world, ninety-
four percent of the respondents acknowledged that they used
intuition or a "natural knowing" in their jobs, either sometimes
or frequently. Only six percent claimed they never use it.

National real estate expert Allen Cymrot of Cymrot Realty

Advisors, Inc. wrote a response to my invitation to offer his thoughts on this debate. Cymrot and I were both active in the real estate boom of the 1980s, when he was CEO of McNeil Corporation and chairman of the National Multi-Housing Council. He writes:

> Like one large symphony orchestra, the success or failure of a company will be determined by its coordination and execution of these activities. The responsibility for orchestrating this coordination and execution belongs to the management of the company. What is management's role in these activities? Although many definitions and descriptions exist, I believe one *real world* universal application is, "To identify all existing and/or possible sources of energy within a company, and then to direct those energies into productive efforts for achieving the company's goals."
>
> What is energy within a business organization? Webster says it is a source of power. In business, energy is created from many different sources. Some are ambition, the many forms of security, recognition, self-satisfaction, and competition.
>
> A lesser understood source which creates energy is spirituality. For management to disregard it, or treat it as a throw-away would be irresponsible. In a world where success does not come easy, and increasingly has to be earned, every qualified tool at management's disposal should be identified and applied. There are only three qualifications for determining management's decision to use or not to use a source of energy. They are: (1) Is it consistent with the company's philosophies? (2) Is it amoral? (3) Is it illegal? Beyond those three qualifications any decision by management to avoid the use of a potential source of energy becomes personal, and does not follow sound management principles. When management doesn't use all the qualified tools available, the probabilities are, their company's chances for success have been reduced. Spirituality is one more source of energy, albeit, not a common one, but one, if directed correctly, that will increase the probabilities for a company's success.

Back to our Workplace Values Survey—What about spiritual values? A majority of those surveyed acknowledged that they practiced some form of spiritual ritual—prayer, meditation, or services of some kind. A remarkable fifty-five percent claimed to have experienced a "personal transformation" or epiphany of some sort, mostly in the past five years. A report on this survey has been published by New Leaders Press. Dennis White authored the report, entitled the *International Workplace Values Survey Report.*

All of this suggests that, at least in the U.S., there is considerable interest in a return to "civility" and a renaissance of values in our society and in our workplaces. Thomas Moore (author of the bestselling *Care of the Soul*) refers to this quality as "conviviality." The hunger for this transformation is evident but still largely suppressed as it fights to overcome the strong consensus belief that philosophy does not belong in the business world. As an example, the vast majority of business people are still ardent followers of Adam Smith's "invisible hand." However, they have not yet realized that the social values of the mid-1700s (when Smith wrote the capitalist's "bible," *The Wealth of Nations*) were very different from those we live with today. The underlying assumptions of his day are nearly nonexistent today.

While a new economics will probably be born out of the huge social transformation that is presently underway, it is only one of the forces that keeps us locked into the Industrial Age mindset that wants everything compartmentalized and broken down scientifically. Nonscientific phenomena have a rough road to travel before they can gain mainstream acceptance, despite the documented testimonials and anecdotes that argue for the benefits of these so-called "soft" ideals.

In addition to his bestseller *Care of the Soul* and its sequel *Soul Mates,* Thomas Moore was a contributor to a 1995 New Leaders Press book which Bill DeFoore and I co-edited, *Rediscovering the Soul of Business.* In his essay, he writes:

> To us, "business spirituality" may sound like an oxymoron, but if the ancient insight that business has its own divine patronage is difficult for us to comprehend, it only shows us how far we have moved away from religion. Business has profound meaning and relevance to us as individuals and as a society, more profound than a secular mind might be capable of imagining.

Hints that this is true are to be found in the impact economics has on us. When business is faring well, the whole society prospers in every area of endeavor. When we go through an economic depression, we are truly depressed in soul. Money, business, and goods carry with them our thoughts, images, and feelings about life itself, about its bounty and its value, its delicate balances and its promises, its deep holes and its peak experiences.

Business is also the experience of community *par excellence.* In business we interact with each other, struggle and collaborate, love and hate. In business we make identities and careers, and also crush them and lose them. We see today how close business and government come to each other, to the point that one wonders if we are not ruled more by business than by government. Kings used to be divinely anointed. These days it seems that some business leaders consider themselves among the nobility, and some-times even seek out symbolic anointing through association with the clergy. This is a subtle indication of the profound role business plays in the lives of us all.

The relationship between business and community, whether local or global, is so serious as to touch upon ultimate values. The business person who seeks only to exploit that relationship for personal gain fails to perceive the theological roots of business, the fact that business is deeply involved in matters of ultimate meaning. Ethics in business is not a tangential con-cern, but speaks to the very heart of business life.

Sometimes when I speak to business people about the soul in their work, they ask anxiously about profit, the bottom line. My response is that there is a whole world, an underworld, beneath the so-called bottom line. If we make profit the ultimate concern of our work, then the soul has no recourse but to appear in negative ways—as low morale, symptoms among workers, conflict with society, and even poor quality of products.

Spiritual values, intuition, community, openness, trust,

love and caring, reflection, holistic or systems thinking—these ideals are all bridging gaps that have grown wider over the past couple of centuries. As bridges, they will help us reunite with those parts of ourselves that we have kept separate so we can begin to bring all of ourselves to work everyday. When this integration occurs, we will find renewed passion and meaning in our work.

At my invitation, Moore wrote the following response after reviewing the writings of Peters, George, and others in this debate:

In most debates, it seems to me, both sides have something important to say, but the debate format splits and divides our very thinking. In the matter of business and spirituality, I have strong feelings and a plethora of thoughts about discovering the sacred elements within business and the workplace. At the same time, I can appreciate anyone's effort to keep business secular.

Whenever I write about the sacred, which is all the time, I try to keep in mind the enigmatic words of Emily Dickinson: "There is so much that is tenderly profane in even the sacredest Human Life." Somehow, we have to pursue the sacred without splitting it off from the "tenderly profane." There is a difference between a secular life and secularism, the latter defending itself against the sacred and the spiritual.

So, yes, let's enter wholeheartedly into the secular life of business, enjoying the competition, the commercialism, and the strategies, but let's keep those secular pursuits "tender," tender enough to allow a spiritual dimension.

I believe that we are finally at a point in time when we may find radically new ways of being religious. The trouble is, today people tend to equate a spiritual life with naive and literalistic beliefs, moralism, authoritarianism, and sectarianism. But imagine a world in which each individual could cultivate an intelligent and comforting theological vision that would not only be tolerant of all other points of view, but would positively appreciate and gain from alternative convictions. This is what, in my book *Soul Mates,* I label "conviviality."

Imagine further a life which glimpses sacredness, infinite value and context, and what we might call divinity deep within every dimension of life. I believe that business has inherent spiritual values. It is a significant arena for the ongoing making of our world—a profoundly creative endeavor. It makes a major contribution to our life as a community. It influences our values and way of life fundamentally. It gives us much of our sense of meaning in life. These are all spiritual considerations.

To find the spiritual depths of business, we will have to re-imagine religion and spirituality radically, and we'll have to reconsider this culture's simplistic and cherished attachment to secularity. Both will have to find new ways of fitting into life, and both will have to undergo change.

Everything we do has greater depths than we perceive at first. In our life of business we are working out some profound issues, both as individuals and as a society. We would be less divided and alienated within ourselves if we acknowledged this deeper dimension. Psychology and the social sciences do not reach deep enough to deal adequately with these genuinely spiritual issues. Each in our own way, we have to find means of cultivating this spiritual depth, or we will continue to suffer the hubris and insensitivity of business narcissistically preoccupied with its own egotistic concerns.

This debate about whether or not the worlds of spirit and work can coexist is but a prelude to whether spirit and modern life can coexist. So, let's enter an honest dialogue about this and stand ready to learn, to grow, and to revel in the outcome. There is no other debate in which I'd rather be involved. Stay tuned.

## Part Two

# SPIRITUAL VALUES AND BUSINESS

### Chapter 5
### The Spiritual Workplace
Ken Blanchard

### Chapter 6
### Spiritual Entrepreneuring
Michael Scott Rankin

### Chapter 7
### Spirituality In Business
Perry Pascarella

### Chapter 8
### Consciousness, Caring, And Commerce
Joel Levey

**Ken Blanchard**, PhD, is the co-author of the best-selling book, *The One Minute Manager,* which sold more than seven million copies worldwide. He co-authored *The Power of Ethical Management,* with Dr. Norman Vincent Peale.

Blanchard is chairman of Blanchard Training and Development, Inc., a full-service management training and consulting company which he and his wife, Dr. Majorie Blanchard, founded in 1979 in San Diego, California. He is also a visiting lecturer at his alma mater, Cornell University, where he is a trustee emeritus of the Board of Trustees. He has received a multitude of awards and honors for his contributions in the field of management and leadership. In 1991 the National Speakers Association awarded him its highest honor, the "Council of Peers Award of Excellence." In 1992 Dr. Blanchard was inducted into the HRD Hall of Fame by *Training* magazine and Lakewood Conferences, and he also received the 1992 Golden Gavel Award from Toastmasters International.

**2**

# The Spiritual Workplace

## Ken Blanchard

During the 1994 Christmas Season I published a little gift book entitled *We Are the Beloved.* This book was originally written as a 1993 Christmas gift for the most important people in my life—my family and friends. It is through their urging that I agreed to share the story of my spiritual journey more widely.

I titled the book *We Are the Beloved* because I believe that we all are loved, with no strings attached.

The impetus for the book started a number of years ago when I began teaching the importance of self-esteem in my leadership and management seminars. I emphasized self-esteem because it had become clear to me that managers today could be more effective as coaches, counselors, and cheerleaders than as the judges, critics, and evaluators than they have been in the past.

Yet I realized that it is almost impossible for people who don't feel good about themselves to play these new roles. I began to wonder if effective :leadership doesn't begin on the inside and move out. After all, only people who genuinely like themselves can build the self-esteem of others without feeling it takes something away from themselves.

My concern with self-esteem coincided with my own renewed spiritual interest. In confronting my own spirituality

41

I began to sense that perhaps the quickest and most powerful way to significantly enhance one's self-esteem and make ourselves more loving is a spiritual awakening.

I say "awakening" because I have come to believe that all of us develop amnesia after we are born. We forget where we came from. I love Dan Millman's beautiful story about a little girl by the name of Sachi that Jack Canfield and Mark Victor Hansen included in their wonderful book, *Chicken Soup for the Soul:*

> The story is all about this amnesia. Soon after her brother was born, little Sachi began to ask her parents to leave her alone with the new baby. Her parents worried that, like most four-year-olds, she might want to hit or shake him, so they said, "No." But Sachi showed no signs of jealousy. She treated the baby with kindness, and her pleas to be left alone with him became more urgent. So they allowed it.
>
> Elated, she went into the baby's room and shut the door, but it opened a crack—enough for her curious parents to peek in and listen. They saw little Sachi walk quietly up to her baby brother, put her face close to his, and say, "Baby, tell me what God feels like. I'm starting to forget."

I know I am taking a risk with some of you when I mention God, but I think we can get ourselves into trouble if we believe there is nothing more powerful, knowledgeable, and loving than ourselves. My wife, Margie, and I were leading a seminar on Personal Excellence in the fall of 1994 at Yosemite National Park. One of the participants objected to my references to a higher power. Later on in the weekend we took people up to Glacier Point, a breathtaking summit 3,000 feet above the valley floor, to work on their mission statements. I noticed my unbelieving friend standing at the edge, looking thoughtfully at the gorgeous spectacle. I walked over to him, and the two of us stood there for a few moments taking it in. I said, "It's a beautiful accident, isn't it?" We both laughed.

As I've said many times, I think the most widespread addiction in the world is the human ego. Ego stands for Edging God Out. In *We Are the Beloved* I try to give people assistance in getting out of their own way with what I call the HELP model.

**H stands for humility.** In *The Power of Ethical Management*, Norman Vincent Peale and I said, "People with humility don't think less of themselves, they just think of themselves less." In other words, it's healthy to feel good about yourself, but don't get carried away. Humility helps you remember that there is someone more powerful, more loving, and more caring than you. I guarantee that getting in touch with your own vulnerability and centering yourself on a greater power will make you a better manager.

**E stands for excellence.** Most people think of excellence as being the best—better than anyone else. Unfortunately, there can only be one Number One. To think of excellence in this manner sets up life as a win-lose proposition, where the only person that matters to you is good old Number One. The kind of excellence that helps keep you on course is available to everyone. It is the process of rising up and becoming the very best you that you can be. This means balancing between achieving (accomplishing results), and connecting (maintaining important relationships).

**L stands for listening.** One of my favorite teachers used to say, "If God had wanted us to talk more than listen, He would have given us two mouths." One reason we have trouble staying out of our own way is that we don't take time to quiet ourselves and get centered. When fog settles in over the seaport, ships listen for the fog horn to know where the dangers are. The sound of the horn helps them stay on course. We, too, need to listen so that we don't stray off course. The old habit of charging hard through life leaves little time for listening to that voice that calls us to a more excellent way of living.

**P stands for praising.** Of all the concepts I have taught managers over the years, the most important has been the power of praising. Spencer Johnson and I emphasize in *The One Minute Manager* that the key to developing people is to catch them doing something right, so you can pat them on the back and recognize their performance. Nothing motivates people more than being caught in the act of doing something right. If you are to stay on course in your walk through life, you need to begin to catch *yourself* doing things right as well.

To me, our spirituality goes with us into the workplace. If we take and accept the love that is there for us, we can be so much better at caring for, listening to and helping others as well as ourselves.

**Michael Scott Rankin** has been a computer software designer and developer ever since college, starting his own software company ten years ago and consulting with a half dozen Fortune 500 companies. He met M. Scott Peck a decade ago and was in the first wave of leaders trained by him and The Foundation for Community Encouragement. He looks forward to extending his vision of community in the workplace with Kay Gilley and Intentional Leadership Systems.

His background includes the U.S. Air Force, aerospace, and consulting for the U.S. Navy. He holds a BS in math from Ohio State University and a MS in computer science from the University of Southern California.

# 3

# Spiritual Entrepreneuring

## Michael Scott Rankin

Bill Buckley calls it the "evanescence of the American ethos." The rabbi in a famous Scott Peck story observes "the spirit has gone out of the people." Perhaps this giant melting pot called America has done its job too well. Has it melted down our diversity of spirits leaving us with a spiritless society, replacing the Founding Fathers' indefatigable spirit and delight in diversity with a sated, self-conscious, listless despair? Has it produced an ascendancy of mediocrity and conformity in which we content ourselves with look-alike, interchangeable cars, houses, jobs, spouses, and lives? In just a few hundred years, have we managed throughout our land to breed a torpor of the spirit?

At a minimum, somewhere along the line we have lost interest in trying new experiments in expanding ourselves beyond what we learned as children or see in daily humdrum existence. We are too overburdened with unwanted or unplanned children, relationships, marriages and other responsibilities to find time to grow our own spirits. Instead we have staked out our home turf, erected our fences, and ensconced ourselves safely away from encounter with the new, different, and unusual. We have established those "lifestyle enclaves," as Robert Bellah so aptly put it, in which we feel safe, comfortable, secure, and unchallenged.

I know. I've been there.

A decade ago I had the opportunity to exit this alluring "safety of sameness" trap. In so doing I began, not knowing it at the time, to become a spiritual entrepreneur; I risked following spirit, not knowing where it might take me, naively hoping that it would be a better place than where I was.

It didn't look like an opportunity at the time. After five years with a small, rapidly growing company with which I thought I'd spend the rest of my working career, I got fired. I'd never failed big at something I really cared about before. I didn't know to handle it. Neither did anybody else. Very few of my former colleagues and friends at our "one big happy family" company ever bothered to call me again. My self-confidence was crushed: Was I incompetent in my chosen field, incapable of offering something of value to the business world? It was even worse since my father, source of so much wise counsel during my formative years, was one of the senior executives in the company and remained so until his retirement.

From my vantage point, ten years later, there was a good reason for my departure: I had aroused the ire of top management by spending just as much time listening, perhaps more, to the eighty rank-and-file members of the company as I had to the top dozen male officers for ideas on what the computer system I'd been hired to design and implement needed to provide. I viewed it as a long-range strategic investment worthy of everyone's input, not just the top people. They, all former senior military officers, viewed things more tactically on the order of here's what we want next week, and were not accustomed to waiting long for many things. I ignored warnings from employees that things were amiss, being too busy designing to have time for politics. Eventually, I was called in and told that my department was being handed over to another more responsive person. And respond he did. Thanks to his furtive campaigning I was shortly excised from the company altogether and, within short order, he embroiled them in a protracted multi-million-dollar lawsuit which apparently he enjoyed so much that, as I understand it, he became a lawyer. So much for my strategic planning.

Upon my departure from the company I interviewed for a new job with a few software development companies. Their bosses didn't have that much more experience and expertise than did I, so I thought. They had pulled off starting their own businesses, why couldn't I? I'd never gone without a regular paycheck since college. My severance funds would tide me over for a while, but would that be long enough to establish a viable business?

It was at this point, as I noted earlier, that I first moved in the direction of becoming a spiritual entrepreneur. Although my spirit was very low, something was happening inside me that was fundamentally different. Life seemed dark indeed, but then, as the saying goes, "faith sees best in the dark." Instead of going for the rational safety of a regular job, I chose to incubate my many doubts and uncertainties and see where they would lead me.

To help sort things out I headed for the familiar and friendly climes of the Rockies for the summer of 1985. While there, I decided to call a former girlfriend who had also told me recently to hit the road. I knew I shouldn't have called her and, indeed, she left no doubt about the demise of our relationship. But she did mention that the "Road Man" himself, M. Scott Peck, MD, author of *The Road Less Traveled,* was to be in our home town of Fort Worth in a few weeks.

## Building Community

I came home to hear Peck, who told us he would also be the guest speaker at a five-day retreat later that summer in North Carolina. I caught that as well. Each day at the retreat we spent an hour and a half in small groups of fifteen doing something called "community building," about which Peck gave us daily descriptive installments. One of my favorite memories of our daily group was that of a fourteen-year-old boy, asking a dour priest who was probably near his grandfather's age, "Thomas, we haven't heard from you in a while, what's going on in your life?"— a question most of us adults probably had on our minds as well but were too pusillanimous to ask.

I was profoundly touched by the community building in our small groups and its ability to move a diverse collection of people into a much more appreciative and closer connection with one another in a short time. Why had I never seen anything like this before? When would I see it again?

The leader of our small group was none other than the president of The Foundation for Community Encouragement (FCE), a nonprofit organization newly cofounded by Peck. As I talked with her more, I learned the Foundation needed a client-following, fundraising software system. As I had recent experience with small database development, I was able to sketch out such a system for her. When she approved it, the FCE became the founding client of my own company that is now stretching into its second decade. I had risked following my spirit and it was to nudge me into an unimaginably new and wondrous world of depth connection with other people, not the least of whom was my own self.

Within a few months I was invited to attend a formal Community Building Workshop (CBW) led by Peck himself. It was a singularly moving experience, with a visiting journalist's description of it being nominated for a Pulitzer Prize. Several of the attendees, I luckily among them, eventually became what was the FCE's first group of community building leaders or facilitators. Since our formation, we have done hundreds of CBWs and their variants all over the world.

My involvement at this time with the FCE marked a new awakening for me. It helped me clarify that I was looking too much to the secular world for guidance and control and not enough to the spiritual one. Encouraging signs of this source of guidance had appeared before. Ten years earlier, I had talked with a number of business associates about what master's degree they would recommend my working on. After hearing them unanimously recommend an MBA, I did listen to that inner voice and selected what spoke better to my curiosity and interest, computer science. I also remember a less satisfying choice in getting my first sports car, a Porsche. I studied the two versions available, the 911 and the 928. The latter was the new, scientifically designed one which was to redress the numerous problems with the 911 and had been scheduled to replace it altogether. Against my inner spirit but consistent with the experts, I bought the 928. Two years later, at some financial loss, I switched back to the 911. The 911 and its variants are now into their fourth decade of production and have never been better, while the 928 is soon to cease production.

Another aspect of my learning was that I have always been a better speaker than listener. That old Talmud adage, "I have two ears and one mouth so I can listen twice as much as I can speak," didn't make much sense to me. I remember years ago a lady friend saying she always enjoyed being with me because she never had to worry about thinking up anything to say. I stupidly took that as a compliment at the time, but now I try to remember a more important message in it for me. The same goes for my learning of the German language: because I was forever trying to speak it, my comprehension skills invariably trailed and I found myself fending off long questions a little too often with "es kommt darauf an" (it all depends).

After starting my little company, I risked following spirit once again in my second major endeavor into spiritual entrepreneuring: I resolved to share with others the delight I had found in our North Carolina community building and my facilitator training by cofounding a long-term community building group in Fort Worth in 1986. The group met every other week for over four years at my home until we started alternating our meeting locations. I learned a great deal from our group. We began utilizing some of the "dialogue" process which I learned about from some Catholic friends at the FCE. A typical initial question to the assembled attendees would be to share "what has touched you since our last meeting?" As part of our dialogue protocol we exercised three constraints: (1) speak no more than five minutes on a subject, (2) use "antecedent benevolence" (don't interrupt another who's speaking and take in to your maximum extent what he or she has to say), (3) don't feel obliged to speak on a topic if you don't care to.

Over the years we used a wide range of questions and remained reasonably free of those typical intellectual discussions into which so many other groups tend to drift. Attendance was always open to newcomers and we ranged from five to 29 attendees per meeting, making for an ever vibrant influx of views, experiences and personalities. Every six months to a year or so we would have a social event such as a potluck dinner or lake retreat.

My single biggest learning from our five and a half years of Fort Worth Community was that everybody has a piece of the truth that I am in need of hearing and learning from. I can't see myself very well and I immensely appreciated accurate reflections from others on how I impacted them. I tried to return the favor. One lady assuaged my lifetime of concern over others complaining about my "hyperactivity" and "nervous energy" by noting I had the "gift of delight." Some long-time attendees were able to gently, but firmly, communicate how several of my inattentions angered them. Another fellow said it was not until I forced off on him a hat someone had left behind from a previous meeting and that I was just trying to get rid of, that he really felt he belonged to the group! This leads into my second biggest learning from the group: Spirit works in strange ways; it is largely unimpressed with my controlling efforts to schedule or influence it. Not a single one of the half dozen or so times I brought a cake for a regular attendee's birthday did that person attend. Never when I prepared an initial question to address issues that were ripe between two or more participants did all requisite parties show up. The times I was most exhausted and least interested in going to the meeting invariably produced the best meetings for me. The times in which I most looked forward to the meetings, the worse they were.

## The LUCID Workshop

A couple of years after Fort Worth Community got going I met Dr. Margaret Pinder at a CBW, a wonderfully spirited counselor and professor at Amber University in Dallas. I visited and spoke with her college class and discovered she had more "community" in it than I had ever seen in the educational environment. Shortly thereafter, we determined that we would do a workshop to help people realize more community in their daily lives.

Based upon the principle of living in community daily, we called this the LUCID workshop. We did our first one in Glen Rose, Texas, in August, 1991. We began the workshop with a Kierkegaard passage from *The Sickness Unto Death* in which he purports that all people in varying measures have a despair or a "sickness of the spirit" and that the only way one can address it is to continually learn to "ground oneself transparently to the power that established it." Doing such transforms that despair, I surmised, into its opposite, a "healthiness of the spirit," or my favorite description for the "community" stage in the Peck community building model. We assembled several dozens of personal stories, poems, and other interesting items for attendees. Margaret or I would share one with the group, ask a question about it and then the group would break into dyads or triads where the question was addressed more intimately. The same guidelines noted earlier under the dialogue process were observed in the small groups. Such dialogue discipline gives participants a flavor of what "community" is like: unbiased, accepting, listening, noninterrupting, and invigorating.

We reassembled the small groups and offered any of them the opportunity to share any "ah-hahs" with the larger group.

By mid-afternoon of the first day, Margaret and I looked at each other and laughed with glee and amazement about how well our little experiment in structured dialogue was going. I am particularly pleased with the way it connects everybody to somebody early on, and then to other somebodys as the dyad and triad partners are changed. This addresses my frustration in workshops that exclusively just use a circle, which tends, by workshop end, to leave a few people feeling they have not really connected with anyone in the workshop.

Another venture into spiritual entrepreneuring occurred a couple of years after our first workshop when I received a call from the head psychologist in a federal prison camp while helping out at the FCE headquarters in Connecticut. They were interested in doing a CBW with the foundation. We eventually cleared some hurdles and planned on doing a conventional two-day workshop followed by some of the LUCID dialogue technology on the third day. The inmates were clever and humorous (one observed about the process: "you sure don't get this in *World Wrestling* magazine.) which made for lots of chaos and slow going.

After those first two days, we were still very far from any kind of "community" or a feeling of connectedness, trust, safety, respect, and acceptance pervading the psyche of the majority of those in attendance. On the third day, when we broke into LUCID-style dyads working much more one-on-one, I sensed a gradual slowing down and an improving level of communication. Gone was the nervous energy of trying to trick or out humor one another. Or so I thought. Immediately after a particularly moving and sensitive story by one of the inmates, a second straight-faced inmate attempted to return to earlier times of merriment by hoaxing the group with a sad, well-told tale ending with an amusing punch line. Upon feeling so completely ignored and unheard, the first inmate exploded. But this marked an important beginning and turning point for the group's valuing of "respect" for one another, an important weighty theme throughout the workshop.

I share these stories in which we have risked following spirit because I believe it is the essence of spiritual entrepreneuring and a main ingredient in impregnating business with renewed life. As near as I can tell, it happens one person at a time. For me, I needed to get blasted out of a secure, comfortable position in a company into a desert where I had no control. Lacking such, I was in a much better place to start listening to the spirit in others and myself. This is certainly something I have to keep on renewing: There are so many distractions to spend time with rather than my desert self.

I have noticed that our top FCE leaders continually risk working with new, challenging groups. They risk following spirit, often not fully knowing where it will be taking them. As noted earlier, this is very closely related to faith, the kind that Kierkegaard attributes to Abraham on his journey to Moriah to sacrifice Isaac. Kierkegaard says of Abraham, "He left one thing behind and took another with him. He left behind him his worldly understanding and took with him his faith."

A real test of this faith came to some leaders in the disturbing end to a workshop several years ago in California. In the final hour of closure a participant who had said nothing during the workshop suddenly opened up as with a verbal machine gun mowing down the workshop, leaders, and partici-pants in rapid order. He then proposed his going around the room to each participant and opining what their problem in life really was and how to solve it. The leaders and participants alike were in shock, except for one woman. After a few moments she walked quietly over to the "machine gunner," sat directly in front of him, looked into his eyes, and calmly asked him to start with her. He froze and the workshop closure was able to continue.

The reassuring thing about the inherent risk in spiritual entrepreneuring is, every time I seem to have risked something new, I have invariably received help from unexpected places, such as the woman just noted above. The theme is replete in Joseph Campbell's *The Hero with a Thousand Faces*. I hope it becomes replete in our lives as well.

**Perry Pascarella,** writer and speaker, is the former vice president–editor of Penton Publishing Co. and editor-in-chief of its flagship magazine *Industry Week*. He has written five books, the latest of which is *The Ten Commandments of the Workplace*.

He was an early crusader for humanistic and participative management and for corporate social responsibility. In 1992, he received the American Business Press' Crain Award for "outstanding career contributions to the development of editorial excellence in the business press."

# 4

# Spirituality In Business: The Bitter, The Sweet, The Imperative

## *Perry Pascarella*

In earlier times and in other places, man has regarded his animal or material needs as low or evil and his spiritual needs as supreme. Modern industrialized nations have turned that relationship upside down, regarding economic matters as essential and spiritual concerns as secondary if not out of bounds. Even so, more and more people seem to be feeling the pull of a spiritual attraction. This reality of the species surges through both old and new forms of expression in many aspects of our lives.

In business, we don't talk of spirituality in management meetings, and it's seldom the topic of conversations at the water cooler. Yet, spirituality lives on in people's hearts. For some, their spirituality shapes their daily lives. Spirituality haunts others as they turn their backs and behave as they think they must in the "business world."

In 1984, I wrote in *The New Achievers:* "The transcendental dimension to our work has been lost." Yet, I warned, "Work may have lost its spiritual aspect in the eyes of many, but people haven't lost their spiritual dimension."

Spirituality has been bubbling close to the surface in business during this past decade. We have seen a rush of books on spirit, love, and soul—even in the management department. Outside business we have experienced a ground swell of spiritu-

ality in secular forms and in churches—traditional and nontra-
ditional. As the pressure builds, we are coming to admit that we
live in material and spiritual dimensions simultaneously.

In business, an entire industry of consultants and writers
has emerged to convey techniques for managing just about
every aspect of the material realm. Unfortunately, no techniques for improving productivity or quality are truly effective
unless they are founded on an appreciation for, and an understanding of, people's spirituality.

When implemented and doing what they are supposed to
do, the best of techniques leave us feeling that something's
missing. For example:

- Involvement of employees in the decision-making
  process doesn't fully click unless each organization
  member wants to be part of a "unity" and be personally responsible for the welfare of others.

- Terms like "cooperation" and "teamwork" are merely
  slogans unless people genuinely feel a sense of unity
  and caring.

- Corporate purpose begins with the purpose an individual feels in his or her personal life. One corporate
  officer who devotes full time to defining the company's
  mission says he believes the final definition of the
  mission lies in the spiritual realm.

- Giving the customer what she wants amounts to no
  more than a device to serve some other end unless
  you love the customer as an end in herself. No
  amount of procedure or technique will substitute for
  an employee's serving out of genuine caring.

- Experts have studied leadership techniques and traits
  again and again, always leaving unexplained that
  intangible matter of the spirit between leader and
  follower.

## Conscious Of The Spirit

We are conscious of spiritual reality in many ways. First,
a sense of the existence of something other than this physical
world comes from somewhere deep inside many of us. We are
anguished by the mysteries of life beyond the physical world.
We turn over questions about who we are, what purpose exists
for us, how we should relate to other people.

Second, we search for linkages with some power and/or other people. We seek a oneness, a connection. Over the past quarter century, we have learned much from ecology about how relationships are critical to existence. We search, too, for significance in our lives—a relationship to something outside ourselves. Today, more and more people are insisting on finding significance in their work. In this quest for meaning and purpose they are examining their spiritual dimension.

Third, the world's religions and some of its philosophies regard the spirit as the seat of our morals. History has revealed to us universal truths to live by. These universal truths save us from our selfish destructive nature. From somewhere outside us or deep inside us come notions of fairness, honesty, and goodness. We know, for example, that decisions should be fair. The solution may be troublesome or elusive, but we know we must come as close as possible to what is right. We know there is a right even when we can't find it. These universal truths are wired into most of us, although we may debate who did the wiring or whether the circuits just happened to fall into place.

Fourth, it is less philosophically demanding to talk of spirit in terms of teams and that special, lively, magical sense of oneness that we might observe in a red hot hockey team; we cannot see it, prove it, or measure it, but we know it exists at times. There is also that spirit of determination like that which Margaret Thatcher describes in telling of Britain's war in the Falkland Islands. Creating and sending a naval force thousands of miles to engage in this battle without full plans and logistics preparation didn't make sense. A computer would have analyzed all the information on the situation and said, "Don't go." "But a computer couldn't gauge the spirit of the British people," she beams.

## Redefining Business—And People

There was no room in the corporation for spirituality when the corporation was defined simply in secular terms. Today, however, spirituality is leading people to redefine the corporation's reason for being and its methods of operation, laying down new measures of success. We saw it in environmentalism, in minority and women's rights, and in product safety. These are not isolated cases or issues. They represent a broad attack on the supremacy of materialism. They are responses to higher, universal values.

In our high-hassle world, more and more people are turning inward or outward for comfort and meaning. Technological and social conditions seem so bad that people feel they have to seek out higher standards and give meaning to their lives. At the same time, conditions are so good in some ways that some people have enough security and freedom to express their views. People are getting out of their boxes, erasing boundaries that they or others drew around them. They want to see their organizations directed by their values and playing by rules of a higher order. We will increasingly have to deal with their moral and spiritual dimension.

Inside the business organization, we have uncovered spirituality as we embraced worker participation and involvement. By seeking to learn what employees will commit to, we delve into their sense of purpose and their values. There we find ourselves facing the spiritual.

We have begun to recognize the whole person in our management processes. We once employed the body, then the brain, and now along comes the spirit which, if ignored, will cause the best of management techniques to fall short of their potential. Management tricks for measuring and improving productivity have built-in limits because they don't take into account the full dimensions of being human. Productivity is more than a measure of physical inputs and outputs; it reflects the stewardship of our talents, skills, inventiveness, and spirit. That's why efforts to win participation and commitment led us to the recent interest in corporate purpose, vision, and values statements.

Limiting our attention to only the physical world does not fully serve the individual and, because of that, fails to build organizations in which people operate at maximum effectiveness. So spirituality has crucial "business" implications. For that reason, business management will have to undergo the discomforts and uncertainties of dealing with spirituality in order to tap the full power of its people.

## Religion, Too

Those who dare to speak of spirituality in business generally stop short of religion. There are some who assert: "Spiritual leadership has nothing to do with church or religion." Try as we might, we cannot draw a line on what sort of spirituality comes into the workplace. It's already there. If my spirituality comes through my religion, religion enters the workplace with me.

It seems surprising, then, that American's conventional religion has scarcely become apparent in business thinking. Surveys indicate year after year that more than 90 percent of Americans say they believe in God. More than three fourths say they are Christians. One might expect, then, that the growing dynamic in American business would come from within the Christian community. Despite many laudable exceptions, this is not the case. Bringing Christianity into business is just not the thing to do. Yet, dozens of management books and hundreds of seminars have applied Eastern thinking to business management. Even Taoism or Buddhism seems to be quite acceptable.

Some aspects of the New Age emphasis on spirituality are very much in harmony with some of our traditional Judeo-Christian beliefs. In fact, they direct our attention back to core features of Western religions which have been buried under centuries of scientific materialism:

- The search for meaning
- The search for unity
- Dissatisfaction with materialism
- Favoring cooperation over competition
- Concern for oneness of mind and body
- The desire to be "in tune" with the universe

New Age thinking is challenging our culture and offering us alternative ways of living and thinking. We needed to open our eyes once again to the spiritual realm and put the physical realm into perspective. Perhaps New Age thinking will help us dislodge science from its pedestal as the only means of knowing. It can help us break out of the limited, scientific, rational view of the world which has made religious faith appear shabby and obsolete. In all its forms, spirituality forces us to view business in a broader context and consider a new corporate agenda.

## Holy And Unholy Ground

We tried to use our rationality to overcome human weaknesses and selfishness in the hope that it would create world harmony. The rational model is not adequate for completely understanding what we are all about, however. Our spiritual dimension is very real and has other things to teach us. Unfortunately, spirituality is not necessarily a unifying force. It can be divisive, even explosive. One person's spiritual journey may take him inward. In the extreme, he may misuse nonreligious or religious spiritual activity for self-gratification or self-development. Focused on self, he uses techniques to serve his physical and psychic needs in an effort to get ahead, to be "Number 1," to win. Some of these techniques are simply self-help efforts. Others are downright antisocial.

At the other end of the spectrum from this private belief system, people turn outward in a social religion centered on humility, love, and unity. Here, they see self-denial giving them freedom from cares about temporal matters.

At the fringe on either side, people can fall victim to exclusivity, elitism, judgmentalism, and self-righteousness. We have seen failures in business when a top executive attempts to drive his or her religious beliefs through the organization. On the other hand, numerous companies have succeeded in quite openly expressing, for example, a Christian mission, even offering Bible study or worship services before working hours, without offending people who choose not to participate. Trouble comes when people self-righteously attempt to get others to believe exactly as they do rather than trying to find commonalty and grounds for mutual respect.

The major religions call for the discipline of self. Far from being an "opiate of the masses," they are rigorous in their demands on the follower. In his book *The Revolt of the Elites and the Betrayal of Democracy*, Christopher Lasch asserts, "The spiritual discipline against self-righteousness is the very essence of religion. Because a secular society does not grasp the need for such a discipline, it misunderstands the nature of religion." Stephen Carter, in his 1993 book *The Culture of Disbelief*, points out that "it is the nature of [an] individual's faith, not the nature of *religion itself*, that dictates...exclusivity."

Essentially, all the major religions have taught honesty, humility, fairness, and justice. Who would object to the embodiment of these values in their business? Workers and customers want their business organizations to be moral. Why should they deny the source of their morality?

## New Rules

If rising spirituality leads us to rearrange our economic and noneconomic priorities once again, management will face dramatic change in people's attitudes toward the goods and services they consume and their role as producers. Managers will need to see people in their full measure if they are to understand where they are coming from and where they are going. The widespread response to transcendent values—things beyond this material world—is a fundamental truth too important for management to ignore.

People will approach their work, their interpersonal relationships, and their business organizations with different expectations from those we have seen in recent decades. As they respond to universal values, the traditional badges and bucks of our incentive systems, for example, may not work as effectively as in the past. That should be of little concern to the leader who recognizes the presence of an even greater set of motivators. Pushing the right buttons, however, may now mean reaching into the spiritual realm. To some degree, success in quality programs, for example, has been due to the tremendous energy released by people's being able to link their transcendent values to corporate goals. At last, they can openly strive for quality and service in keeping with their deepest wants.

We might ask: "What will spirituality do for the corporation?" Many people, however, are turning the question around: "How does this business and its methods fit with my view of the world, of my destiny?" We have been comfortable asking: "What and how much spirituality, if any, will business allow?" We will have to become more accustomed to seeing the other side of the coin: "What business will our spirituality allow?" As some would say: "Religion is a response not just to man's needs but to God's." The spirit does not exist to serve the corporation; quite the reverse is true.

Now that people are being recognized as whole persons, they will march to what they see as universal values for determining what business they're in and how they'll behave. The impact of our spirituality on business depends somewhat on whether business organizations rule it out, permit it, or encourage it. Remember, however, these structures don't create themselves. Society's expectations, customers' wants, and demands voiced by employees ultimately define business success.

The fruits of spirituality are tested in the material world's daily business. Since the business organization is the place to get things done, we are forced to find common cause, common interests, common values, and uncommon effort. We get things done not because we have no differences but because we find commonalty. Those universals that bring us together can generate untold power. The divisive elements—the bitter fruit—simply don't work there; when they prevail, the business fails.

The workplace is not a place for sermons but for the development of effective relationships. These relationships can be deepened and strengthened by the fruits of one's faith. Spirituality readies individuals for group activity not only through the values and sense of purpose it instills in them but by heightening the individual's accountability. In this era of teams and participation, we may think only of the togetherness factor and overlook the individual. We might fail to appreciate the fact that effective teamwork depends on the togetherness of strong, effective individuals, who know there are rights and wrongs, good and bad.

## Harvesting The Fruits

The new test for those who would lead or manage is more than a matter of whether a corporate leader himself or herself is spiritual. The critical question is: Is the leader sensitive to other people's spirituality? Without that, he or she will be unable to understand their followers' deepest values or anticipate what they will commit to.

Our management practices will have to be based on the recognition that we live in both the spiritual and material worlds. The motivation to be cooperative, to bear responsibility, and to serve in the business world is linked to what people bring from their spiritual world.

Business leaders have the opportunity to enjoy the fruits of spirituality. They can follow their own spirituality and that of others, letting it point the way to right and wrong and call attention to the fundamental fact that there are rights and wrongs. At the same time, they will have to be watchful of rituals and fringes that can be divisive. The years ahead won't be easy.

Those who believe there should be a barrier between religion and business have good reason for their fears. Under a hierarchical system, one's spirituality or religion can easily be imposed from above. To those below, creating a border would seem a good, although not always enforceable, idea. Also, we want to avoid the strife caused when a bazaar of beliefs breaks out into bickering about form rather than substance. We are fortunate today, however, that the openness, simplicity, and straightforwardness that are resulting from corporate renewal set entirely new conditions for expressing spirituality. Under our more participative, open, networking environment, influence moves up, down, and sideways; and it comes through dialogue rather than decree. Experience in group process is teaching people to appreciate the individual and to value differing skills and viewpoints; it does not value groupthink or dogma.

How, then, should we go about expressing our spirituality in business? From others, we would ask: "Demonstrate what your spirituality does for *me*. Don't just talk or try to sell me something or tell me how to behave. Don't force me to listen to your teacher; show me what you have learned about those things that are essential to all of us."

In turn, I must ask myself about my spirituality to test its genuineness and its value in the business place:

- Is it other-directed? Or does it simply help me serve myself?
- Does it enable me to serve others or does it aim at my own gratification?
- Is it people-building or is it people-using?
- Does it open inquiry or simply offer quick solutions?
- Do I respect—not merely tolerate—others' beliefs?
- Does it lead me to work on changing myself or changing others?
- Can I live with my inner values without wanting to bulldoze others into changing their values?
- Am I trying to serve God, or play God?
- Do I use my corporate position power to coerce others to believe what I believe?
- Do I try to politicize the organization, making it a special interest group?

In the years ahead, corporate managers will have to develop the ability to work with this critical new area of understanding. They cannot import spirituality as though it were just another management device for boosting sales or productivity. When it's present, however, they can welcome it and manage with it.

When all is said and done, there is little new regarding the debate about spirituality in business. What has changed is the fact that the forces for revealing and responding to spirituality are stronger than at any time in our recollection. We are expanding the borders of our business thinking. We are viewing business in a larger context. We are beginning to realize that the fruits of spirituality can take business well beyond its present limits.

**Joel Levey**, PhD, is co-founder of Seattle-based InnerWork Technologies, Inc., a firm that specializes in building and renewing organizational cultures in which team spirit, community, creative intelligence, and authentic leadership thrive. His clients include Hewlett-Packard, AT&T, Bell Labs, Du Pont, Weyerhaueser, Travelers Insurance, Petro-Canada, and NASA. His work was recognized by US Army West Point logisticians as "The most exquisite orchestration of human technology we have ever seen."

Joel and his wife Michelle are co-authors of *Quality of Mind: Tools for Self Mastery & Enhanced Performance* and Nightingale Conant's best-selling business audio program *The Focused Mindstate*. They are contributing authors for numerous works including *Learning Organizations: Developing Cultures for Tomorrow's Workplace; Community Building in Business: Renewing Spirit & Learning;* and *Rediscovering the Soul of Business.*

# 5

# Consciousness, Caring, And Commerce: Sustainable Values For The Global Marketplace

*Joel Levey*

> Without a global revolution in the sphere of hu-
> man consciousness, nothing will change for the
> better in the sphere of our being as humans, and
> the catastrophe towards which this world is
> headed—be it ecological, social, demographic or
> a general breakdown of civilization—will be
> unavoidable....The salvation of this human world
> lies nowhere else than in the human heart, in
> the human power to reflect, in human meekness
> and in human responsibility.
>> —Vaclav Havel, President of Czechoslovakia
>>         in his address to the U.S. Congress

To realize and sustain commercial success in a rapidly changing environment requires a high degree of consciousness and the knowledge of many disciplines. The breadth and depth of consciousness, the capacity for knowing, is determined by the scope of our mindful attention and our reasoning. As a whole, Western culture has devoted more attention and resources to developing outer technology than inner science. This imbalance of outer and inner development has created many problems in our world, and has left us without the insight or compassion to use our technological power wisely. Our challenge is to give business a heart and soul by giving permission, encouragement, rewards, even blessings for people to express their consciousness, caring, commitment and creativity through their work.

> The key to our inner resources is self-knowledge. Self-knowledge is gained by personal development—that is, by collecting experiences out of which new insights and wisdom are born. In fact, this come close to being the meaning of life. Consequently, the raison d'être for a company is to supply an environment in which personal development of human beings involved in the company can best take place... What a precious gift to humanity and our planet it would be if the remarkable knowledge we have achieved should be united with wisdom. Then our planet would be the paradise it is meant to be. Business life has the opportunity to bring that gift forward.
> —Rolf Osterberg, President,
> Svenski Filmindustri

The expanse of our consciousness, spiritual insight, and experience determines our worldview. Our worldview determines our values. Our values drive our actions and determine the quality of our relationships, our work, and our impact on others and the world around us (see Figure 1). Making our unconscious mental models, beliefs, and assumptions conscious is the greatest leverage point for initiating personal and organizational change.

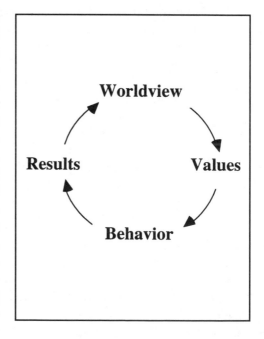

# In Search Of Wholeness

The most exciting breakthrough of the 21st
Century will occur not because of technology,
but because of an expanding concept of what it
means to be human.
>                —John Naisbitt, *Megatrends 2000*

We often hear people say that their wholeness as a human being is not welcome at work, and they are expected to leave their values, feelings, and physical needs at home. These comments are as common from executives as from blue collar workers. To ignore or deny any of our many dimensions is foolish, dangerous, and unfortunately quite common, especially in the institutions of our workaday world. What we ignore or disown we tend to waste or destroy.

Most dis-ease, be it physiological, sociological, or ecological, begins with "whispered" warning signs. Only if these are ignored do we find ourselves in trouble, as the whispers become "screams." Ignorance is the root of most disease. We are at a time when our ignorance has compromised the integrity of our ecosystem, when our social structures and families are collapsing, and when, in America, we are paying more than a trillion dollars each year for disease care, while 95 percent of all illness is due to our ignorance and unwise choices. This is more than the combined annual profits of all of the Fortune 500 companies, and business pays about 40 percent of the bill.

As living whole systems, we are endowed with miraculous capacities for sensory discovery of our world, creative physical movement and communication, a broad bandwidth of emotions, an inconceivable capability for creative imagination, intelligence and thinking, and a nervous system with an extraordinary ability for intuitive discernment of systems dynamics at a far greater breadth and depth than mere thinking or ordinary perception can ascertain.

At our heart and core, inseparable from the rest, is a quality of radiant and receptive presence, a creative and compassionate intelligence that defies description. In the English language we regard this as "consciousness" in the psychological sense, or "Spirit," the animating force within all things, if we take a more sacred view. Paradoxically, this illusive dimension of our deepest being is at the heart of our humanity, and being universal in proportions, it transcends the narrow confines of our personal identity. To say that there is no place for spirit or consciousness in business is as foolish as saying there is no place for our bodies and minds at work. Let's get real. We are multidimensional human beings and business, as all other arenas of human activity, is handicapped without drawing inspiration from the full spectrum of our humanity.

## Spirit And Systems Thinking

> My own working assumption is that we are here
> as local Universe information gatherers. We are
> given access to the divine design principles so
> that from them we can invent the tools that
> qualify us as problem solvers in support of the
> integrity of an eternally regenerative Universe.
>                              —R. Buckminster Fuller

At the heart of both business success and spiritual inquiry is the ability to think about and perceive our world in terms of whole systems. Both a systems view and a spiritual view of life and work invite a contemplation of interconnectedness across potentially limitless dimensions. For both disciplines, fruition is realized by discovering and applying our insights in ways that enable us to improve the quality of our lives. When applied to understanding our place in the universe, systems thinking reveals an ever-expanding and awe-inspiring panorama of complex and multidimensional interrelationships that span the farthest reaches of space-time, and weave all living beings into a web of profound interdependence within a seamless wholeness.

## Applied Systems Thinking

One of the most effective ways to hone our systems thinking and develop a spiritual view toward life and work is to view ourselves as inseparable from a vast network of interrelationships. In this world there is only one of you...and there are billions of others who share similar aspirations to yourself. Likewise, your business is one of millions trying to survive, and hopefully help, in a world desperately in need of help.

> The only ones among you who will be truly happy
> are those who have sought and found how to serve.
>                              —Albert Schweitzer

The "spiritual potency" of our individual and collective work increases as we expand our consciousness and thinking to embrace the whole system. This is determined by two factors:

- *Altruism.* How altruistic is our intent? Are we motivated by self-centered agendas or by a compassionate concern for others?

- *Sustainability.* Is our intention to bring short- or long-term benefit?

Native wisdom might express these criteria by asking:

- Is this good for "all my relations," (i.e., all living beings), and,

- Will this action or decision bring benefit for "seven generations?"

Taken to heart, and put to work, these two fierce criteria help us expand our thinking and awareness, and charge our actions with spiritual vitality.

With the proper motivation and presence of mind, any action can become an act of devotion or an expression of consciousness development.

Can you imagine yourself sitting at the center of your universe? Surrounding you are all your loved ones, family and friends, and all your co-workers, customers, suppliers, and stakeholders in your work—everyone whose efforts in some way enrich or influence your life and all those whom you influence directly or indirectly by your actions. Here are the members of your carpool, clubs, religious community, and basketball team....All living beings are here. All your ancestors and the future generations who will live with the impact of your decisions and actions are here surrounding you.

As you read this chapter or do your work today, are you inspired by an insight that enables you to help others? How many people's lives might you impact, directly or indirectly, over the course of the next year? Or, over the course of your lifetime? Remember, if you touch the heart of another human being, you change them forever!

We have found that pausing for a few moments of similar reflection will often expand, deepen, and inspire the quality of consciousness that we and the teams we work with bring to a day's work together.

## The "God Conversation"

Walking into the crowded meeting room at Bretton Woods, the first words I heard were, "Invoked or not, God is present." Surprised and delighted by the implications of this statement at a business conference, I pulled up a seat. Looking around, I found myself amidst more than two hundred of my colleagues in rapt attention as Peter Senge, Joe Jaworski, and Betty Sue Flowers engaged in a passionate and heartfelt "fishbowl" dialogue. The dialogue began with the opening question, "What sort of interesting conversations are you having with leaders in business these days?" The first reply, "How about the 'God Conversation'? It's a hot topic."

As Senge put it, "All this systems stuff has no meaning without understanding that we're part of something larger than ourselves." Knowing that we are all part of the web of life, a sacred reality, gives our lives a sense of roots and meaning. Any description of reality, be it modern or ancient, religious, mythological or scientific can only offer us a story, partial and incomplete about reality. The inquiry in business about building community, stewardship, core values, belonging, and spirit is about "real time, real stuff" that has profound implications for organizations serious about business success, learning, sustainability, competitive advantage, and retention of high caliber people in critical times.

## Data To Inspire Faith

> And I have felt a presence that disturbs me with
> the joy of elevated thoughts; a sense sublime of
> something far more deeply inter-fused, whose
> dwelling is the light of setting suns, and the
> round ocean and the living air, and the blue sky,
> and in the mind of man; a motion and a spirit,
> that impels all thinking things, all objects of all
> thought, and rolls through all things.
> —William Wordsworth

It was clear that those of us gathered at Bretton Woods were not alone when it came to an interest in spirit and business. Similar interest is reflected by articles related to spirit or soul at work in *Industry Week, Business Week, Fortune, Newsweek, The New Leaders, The New York Times,* and *Leaders* magazines in

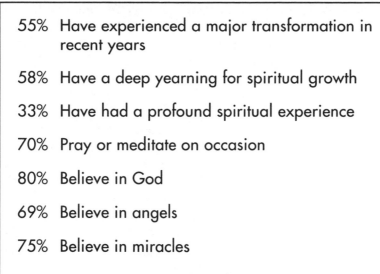

55%  Have experienced a major transformation in recent years

58%  Have a deep yearning for spiritual growth

33%  Have had a profound spiritual experience

70%  Pray or meditate on occasion

80%  Believe in God

69%  Believe in angels

75%  Believe in miracles

**Figure 2**
**Spiritual Presence In Our Lives**

recent times. In 1995 alone there were at least five major confer-ences for leaders in business that had a specific focus on integrat-ing more soul or spirit into business. Confirming these trends, the Institute for the Future launched a project to document the increasingly important role of spirituality in business.

Confirming trends are also indicated by a 1994 *Industry Week* survey, and by the *International Workplace Values Survey Report* which involved twelve hundred people in eighteen coun-tries. Fifty-five percent of those surveyed had experienced a "personal transformation" in recent years. Responses to the survey suggest that people in business feel a deep sense of isolation, and over two thirds of them, 69 percent, expressed an interest in having a greater sense of belonging in the workplace.

Imagine yourself at work, surrounded by all of your co-workers, partners, customers and suppliers. Now keep in mind that the polls say two out of three of these people have a deep yearning for spiritual growth. The polls also tell us that 80 percent of us believe in God, more than two out of three of us, 69 percent, believe in the presence of angels, and three out of four of us believe that unexplainable miracles are a reality in our lives.

In response, 70 percent of us reach out to the Sacred through prayer or meditation at least occasionally in our busy lives. Fully a third of us, our friends, family and co-workers, have had a profound, life altering religious or mystical experience. In reality, Spirit is as close to us as water is to waves, and may in a moment of grace reveal itself unexpectedly on the road to Damascus, or on the freeway driving to work.

There is considerable evidence suggesting that having a spiritual orientation toward life offers benefits for individuals and businesses. After five years of study in many leading corporations, Stanford University's pioneering Corporate Health Program project funded by the Rockefeller Foundation concluded that a spiritual orientation toward life increases our change resilience, and is one of five characteristics that are the basis for "optimal health." The *International Workplace Values Survey Report* tells us that interest in spiritual development ranks ahead of physical development in its importance to people in business, leading us to rethink the facilities and perks that may best reward our staffs. Clinical studies indicate that people who are sick are 75 percent more likely to become better if they have a spiritual view of life. In alcohol treatment, a "spiritual change" in a person is associated with a 93 percent permanent sobriety rate. Findings such as these inspire our faith that spirit is alive and well in business, even if it is seldom discussed; they are useful to seed conversations about the beliefs and core values at the heart of our work. These findings remind us that spiritual interests are a vital reality to many, and a presence that often "disturbs" our minds, and our worksite, "with the joy of elevated thoughts."

## The Path of Personal Mastery

The evidence of spirit at work is that people work with greater wisdom; they are kinder, more altruistic, less self-centered and more powerful; and they are mindful of their likely impact on others over time.

The foundation and fruition of spiritual values at work is realized in the quality of our relationships. We all know from experience that there is a direct relationship between the quality of our work, the quality of our relationships, and the quality of our inner state. (See Figure 3.) When there is discord in our relationships, our "mindbody" is filled with emotional turbulence, mental confusion, and physical tension. As a result, our health, peace of

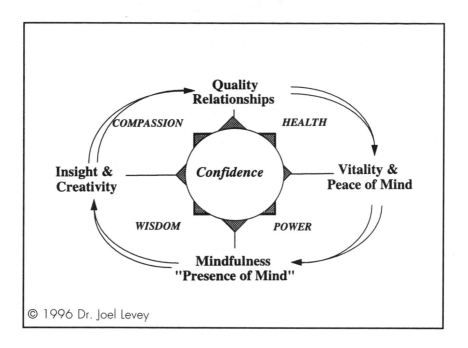

© 1996 Dr. Joel Levey

mind, mindfulness, wisdom, and effectiveness will be diminished. Yet, as we learn to bring greater harmony and balance to our relationships, release unnecessary physical and emotional tension, and strengthen our peace of mind, we develop the coherence of consciousness and the integrity of mindbody and spirit necessary to live and work with greater wisdom, compassion, and energy efficiency. As our relationships continue to improve, our inner qualities are more likely to improve, and this whole cycle builds upon itself, lifting our individual and collective capability, consciousness, and confidence to new heights. By understanding the dynamic interplay of these factors, we can leverage each factor and embark on a path of continuously expanding consciousness and caring.

## Control Follows Awareness

In business settings we have found a universal interest in the notion that "control follows awareness," or "we can only manage what we monitor." (See Figure 4.) People in business are quick to appreciate the value of mindfulness, the primary tool of consciousness. Mindfulness, the presence of mind that is aware of whatever is happening, only exists in the here and

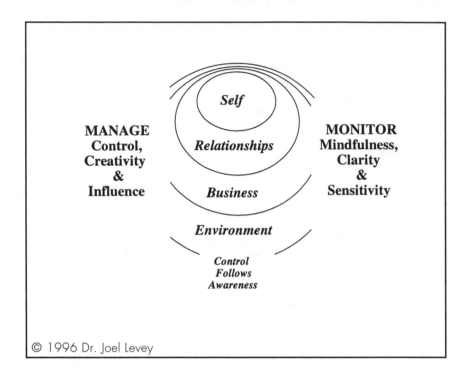

now—and it is only in this present moment that we have any power to control our life.

When we are mindful, we view current reality, outwardly and inwardly, with vivid clarity and objectivity. We recognize options and make wise decisions. Mindful awareness helps us communicate and act with precision, carefulness, and energy efficiency. Mindfulness is also the key to breakthroughs in creativity and intuition, as it assures the subtle presence of mind necessary to catch and develop emerging insights.

Mindfulness can be understood in contrast to "mindlessness," the all too familiar state of consciousness when we revert to the entropy of reactivity and habit. (See Figure 5). In moments of mindlessness we lose control of our lives. Mindfulness offers the ultimate protection from the problems of mindlessness such as: wasted time, effort, and resources; rework; missed opportunities; escalating problems; and dangerous accidents. By reclaiming the time wasted in mindlessness and rework, mindfulness can add years of quality experience to our lives.

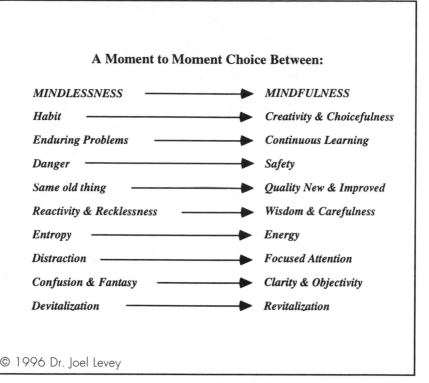

**A Moment to Moment Choice Between:**

| | | |
|---|---|---|
| *MINDLESSNESS* | ⟶ | *MINDFULNESS* |
| *Habit* | ⟶ | *Creativity & Choicefulness* |
| *Enduring Problems* | ⟶ | *Continuous Learning* |
| *Danger* | ⟶ | *Safety* |
| *Same old thing* | ⟶ | *Quality New & Improved* |
| *Reactivity & Recklessness* | ⟶ | *Wisdom & Carefulness* |
| *Entropy* | ⟶ | *Energy* |
| *Distraction* | ⟶ | *Focused Attention* |
| *Confusion & Fantasy* | ⟶ | *Clarity & Objectivity* |
| *Devitalization* | ⟶ | *Revitalization* |

© 1996 Dr. Joel Levey

Mindfulness is the foundational personal mastery skill and can be strengthened at any moment or during any activity. The key is simply to be conscious of what is true for you, moment to moment. With mindfulness, you are aware that you are seeing these words, and may even smile to yourself with delight as you know that you know. You are aware of the texture and weight of the book in your hands, or of the thoughts and associations triggered by reading these words.

Once we understand the value of mindfulness and practice the simple skills for cultivating it, we reclaim our life from the sink-hole of mindlessness. In numerous organizations, teams we have worked with have adopted a "wake up bell" or "bell of mindfulness" that chimes at odd times during the day as an invitation and reminder for people to wake up and refocus their mindful attention.

As mindfulness deepens, it matures into a heartfelt quality of caring, compassion, or appreciation. When mindfulness is perfected, we are free from distraction and have the peace, power, and presence of mind necessary to realize that consciousness, like space, is a boundless, all pervasive, and encompassing reality. In each moment of mindfulness, this universal reality makes itself known through our particular subjectivity. When our mindfulness is deep enough, we re-member ourselves as part of a larger, universal whole system of Consciousness—an unbroken continuity of presence that flows through time from moment to moment. Ultimately, this realization reaches an expanse that embraces all things in a unified, multidimensional field of knowing. In moments when this profound reality is recognized, we are free from what Einstein called the "optical delusion of consciousness," the illusion of being observers separate from what we observe. In this way, mindfulness opens the doorway to the limitless systems view of spiritual insight.

## Inspired Work: Visionary Research

> The most beautiful emotion we can experience is the mystical. It is the sower of all true art and science. He to whom this emotion is a stranger is as good as dead. To know that what is impenetrable to us really exists, manifesting itself as the highest wisdom and the most radiant beauty, which our dull faculties can comprehend only in the most primitive forms—this knowledge, this feeling, is at the center of true religiousness. In this sense and in this sense only, I belong to the ranks of devoutly religious men.
>
> —Albert Einstein

One of the most inspiring examples of systems thinking, expanding consciousness, and revealing the sacred dimensions of life through work, was our experience coaching the team of a pioneering two year "visionary research" project at Weyerhaeuser.

For two years the members of our cross-functional team met every other week to search for breakthrough ideas to the myriad of special research projects going on within various departments. The results were astonishing. We learned that the questions we held in our minds would organize our attention, and that the quality and scope of our individual and shared intention determined the bandwidth of possibilities and applications that were revealed through our inquiry.

"Our questions were at times like heartfelt prayers," one person said. "In the silence of our deep listening together, it was as though each of us had learned to push the pause button on the stories we keep telling ourselves about who we are. In this state of deep shared listening, we'd converge like islands meeting at their common roots deep under the surface of the sea, merging within a larger field of Presence in which we are both one and many. Though this experience was at times fleeting and difficult to describe, I have come to more deeply respect the meaning behind the words, 'where two or more are gathered in my name, there I am in the midst of you.'"

The answers to our questions were often surprising and unexpected. As one team member reminded us, quoting the respected Benedictine sage, Brother David Steindl-Rast: "Another name for God is surprise!" At times this notion rang so true that we were left stunned into a deeply reverent shared silence. Often we talked about what it would be like to focus these individual and collective skills toward addressing some of the really big challenges facing humanity. At times we sensed that our research work, this remarkable experiment in deep, shared intuitive inquiry, was creating a story that would offer inspiration, courage and guidance for other R&D teams for decades to come. Though the challenges were great, the Ocean of Wisdom seemed intent on splashing itself into our minds as a deeply intuitive knowing that would weave its way into our thinking and dreaming, providing business solutions that mere analysis could never have yielded.

## Leadership And Spirit At Work

Most often we are invited to work with an organization by a spirited leader. These people are generally the innovators and altruists in their organizations who really care about people and are committed to building a team or organization that brings out the best in them. Often these leaders express a spiritual yearning, though they aren't necessarily particularly religious. They are willing to think deeply, take risks, and act to get what they want for others.

In his dissertation, "Spirituality and Transformational Leadership in Secular Settings," Dr. Stephen E. Jacobsen, a former business entrepreneur and now ordained minister, observed that though leaders in business had a difficult time clearly defining "spirituality," they did believe and speak strongly about its importance in forming the values, ethics, and beliefs that they bring to work. This diverse group of business leaders of different genders, backgrounds, organizational settings, and locations shared a common belief that spirituality is at the heart of their business activity. They regarded "spirituality" as a means of integrating self and the world, and affirmed that life is a seamless whole system with an absence of boundaries between what is "spiritual" and what is "secular."

Spirited leaders live with deep questions, often catalyzed by major breakdowns or breakthroughs in their life. Their heartbreaks, heart attacks, or near-to-death experiences expanded their consciousness and offered glimpses of a larger, sacred reality. Many have fought for their freedom or health, others for human rights, or for sobriety, and are willing to take a strong stand to help others. They are often people of strong faith and determination, whose personal epiphanies and tragedies have cracked open their hearts and souls to the sacred presence and grace at the heart of humanity. As a result, their life is dedicated to helping others discover their own potential, and their work becomes a vehicle to fulfill this purpose. Having hit the wall and broken through, they are willing to take risks and create opportunities for their people to work in ways that affirm and respect the integrity of their health, dignity, and spiritual wholeness.

## Beyond The Dow To The Tao
## of Business

As the world becomes more of a global village, the sustainable values of consciousness and caring increase in immediacy and urgency. The changeless human spirit in an ever changing environment is a reality that challenges us to expand our view of "profit" beyond the limited confines of a financial index, to encompass the totality and intricate interweaving of our universal interdependence. Understanding the impact of this larger balance sheet, and expressing it through our commerce in the global marketplace, is the Tao of business.

This master blend of commerce and consciousness recognizes the wholeness and integrity of the human spirit in all its endeavors and interrelationships. This awareness allows us to sustain and build upon the systems integrity of the "divine design principles" to create a world in which the highest potentials of people can unfold in an unbridled, joyful, creative, and compassionate way. To do this implies a global responsibility to make business decisions and act in ways that respect and support basic human rights.

Consciousness of whole systems is the wisdom aspect of spirit in business. But to activate this wisdom and actualize it into sustained business success requires bringing whole systems awareness alive and into action by bringing our whole person—mindbody and spirit—to work. To be effective, we need not only eyes, but also limbs and a responsive heart. The eyes, in this case, are our wisdom—our ability to see and perceive whole systems. Our limbs represent how we reach out to others in the quality of our interactions. When our actions are guided by our wisdom and our caring heart, then we have moved beyond systems *thinking* to full blown systems *living*.

# Part Two

# BEING HUMAN:
# STARTING WITH THE HEART

**Angeles Arrien** is an anthropologist, educator, award-winning author, and corporate consultant. She lectures nationally and internationally, and conducts workshops that bridge cultural anthropology, psychology, and comparative religions. She teaches the universal components of communication, leadership skills, education, and health care. Her work reveals how indigenous wisdoms are relevant in our families, professional lives, and our relationship with the Earth. She is president and founder of the Foundation for Cross-Cultural Education and Research.

Arrien is the author of *The Four Fold Way: Walking the Paths of the Warrior, Teacher, Healer, and Visionary*, and *Signs of Life: The Five Universal Shapes and How to Use Them* (winner of the 1993 Benjamin Franklin Award).

# 6

# Shape-Shifting The Work Experience

## *Angeles Arrien*

*Let the beauty of what you love, be what
you do.*

—Rumi

### Remembering The Beauty Way

Best-selling author Marianne Williamson eloquently expresses the challenge that all human beings face in the 21st Century. Her words are a compelling call to the human spirit in this decade, relevant in all those places in our lives where we find ourselves creatively engaged and wanting to make a contribution:

> Our deepest fear is not that we are inadequate.
> Our deepest fear is that we are powerful be-
> yond measure. It is our Light, not our Dark-
> ness, that most frightens us. We ask ourselves,
> who am I to be brilliant, gorgeous, talented,
> fabulous? Actually, who are you NOT to be?
> You are a child of God. Your playing small
> does not serve the World. There is nothing
> enlightened about shrinking so that other
> people won't feel insecure around you. We were
> born to make manifest the glory of God that is

within us. It is not just in some of us, it is in
everyone. And as we let our light shine, we
unconsciously give other people permission to do
the same. As we are liberated from our own fear,
our presence automatically liberates others.

To answer these questions and to meet Williamson's
challenge, it is necessary to take a look at the collective
illusions generated from fears that foster "*shrinking*" and "*playing small*" rather than "*manifesting the glory*" of who we are.
Whether or not we are happy with our current circumstances,
we cannot afford to be less than who we are.

The majority of indigenous peoples believe the work of our
time is to heal the Split Lodgepole (a place where we are divided
or duplicitous in our nature) and to mend the Rainbow Hoop (a
place to honor and include diversity). It's also a time to reclaim
our authentic nature and restore the vision of the Braided Way
(a place where there is space for what is old and what is new to
come together to create a creative third option). The questions
remain—how to heal soul loss at home and in the workplace,
and how to sustain the values of courage, integrity, creativity,
humor, responsibility, wisdom, and love.

## The Eight Lies

In the Lakota tradition, according to Billy Mills in his
book *Wokini,* there are eight lies of Iktumi (the trickster or liar
figure) that have the ability to jeopardize happiness and ruin a
person's life. These are Iktumi's ancient invitations to *play
small:*

- If only I were rich, then I would be happy.
- If only I were famous, then I would be happy.
- If only I could find the right person to marry, then I
  would be happy.
- If only I had more friends, then I would be happy.
- If only I were more attractive, then I would be happy.
- If only I weren't physically handicapped in any way,
  then I would be happy.
- If only someone close to me hadn't died, then I would
  be happy.
- If only the world were a better place, then I would be
  happy.

None of these illusions are true in relationship to our happiness. At work and at home, we obsessively strive for as many of the eight illusions as we can, things Iktumi tells us will make us happy. Once these goals are attained, we are often stunned to find ourselves still without satisfaction, meaning, or happiness. We can meet Williamson's challenge by consciously removing these Iktumi lies from our lives. Ceasing to strive for happiness and meaning in this way allows us to open and become *"liberated from our own fear"* and false attachments.

Gandhi reminds us of an important leadership principle that can serve us well in staying liberated and fully expressive in a meaningful way in all sectors of our life. He states that:

> Power, privilege, and position are great re-
> sources. Use them well. Do not become at-
> tached to them; for when we do, we begin to
> loose our moral fiber.

Regardless of where we find ourselves making a contribution or being connected to our creative fire, nothing will be accomplished that has meaning unless the lies of Iktumi are dismantled, and the priority of happiness is connected to values that support our moral fiber and reinstate the right use of power, privilege, and position.

## Cross-Cultural Ways Of Caring For The Soul In Life Situations

How do we do all of these things? How do we stay balanced, unattached, and open and still function? Cross-culturally, I have found the following principles that help care for the soul in life situations: The first is the four rivers of life; the second is the three universal life processes; the third is the four universal archetypes; and the fourth is the braided way.

### Reflecting On The Four Rivers Of Life

Many indigenous societies have not only outer tracking devices, but also internal tracking devices. An internal device used to identify the quality of life experience and determine if one is "still alive, or walking the procession of the living dead," is the indigenous concept of the four rivers of life: The River of Inspiration, the River of Challenge, the River of Surprise, and the River of Love. Whether we are at home or in the workplace, tracking the four rivers of life becomes an invaluable means of seeing how connected or unconnected we are to our life dream. When we stay connected to the gift of life and fully participate, we are still in our power and not experiencing soul loss.

The following questions allow us to reflect on the four rivers of life:

**The River of Inspiration: Where are we most inspired?** Sources of inspiration reveal where we are still connected to our creative fire or life dream. Anywhere that we experience expansion or uplift marks the presence of creativity. Who or what inspires us at this time serves to remind us that we are still alive and refusing to "walk the procession of the living dead." Where we are not inspired may well signal the presence of Iktumi or overattachment to the resources of power, privilege, and position.

**The River of Challenge: Where are we most challenged?** Who or what is challenging or testing us at this time? The meaning of the word *challenge* is an invitation to grow again, to move beyond the familiar and the knowable. To be challenged is to be stretched and moved beyond our established comfort zones. The River of Challenge reminds us to remember Williamson's quote that "we are powerful beyond measure." Native Americans of the Southwest say, "Bless those who challenge us, for they reopen the doors to remembering who we really are."

**The River of Surprise: Where are we surprised and delighted by the unexpected?** How we handle the unexpected in favorable ways indicates the presence of spontaneity and a connection to wonder, awe, and curiosity. The adventurer, the explorer, and the discoverer remain healthy and strong within our nature when we are delighted by surprise. Where we are not delighted by surprise or remain inflexible to the unexpected is where we have become rigid, controlling, attached, and have lost our sense of humor—again, an announcement of Iktumi's presence in our lives.

**The River of Love: Where are we deeply touched and moved by life's experience?** In Africa when one is deeply touched or moved, they say "Oh the Great Spirit's finger has come in and rearranged your heart." Wherever we have the capacity of being touched or moved indicates a place where we are open hearted. If we are not touched or moved on a daily basis, it signals closed heartedness and announces that we have become part of the "procession of the living dead." Where are we half-hearted rather than full-hearted, weak-hearted rather than strong-hearted, close-hearted rather than open-hearted, and carrying doubt or confusion rather than clear heartedness?

Tracking the four rivers on a daily basis, at work and at home, cares for the soul, enriches quality living, and increases creativity and production wherever we refuse to consciously "walk the procession of the living dead." Being aware of our sources of inspiration, challenge, surprise, and moments of being deeply touched, helps us manifest what Williamson calls *"the glory of who we are."*

This begins to heal the Split Lodgepole or to mend the Rainbow Hoop, and to restore the vision of the Braided Way— all needed to support the realm of Spirit or Mystery in all aspects of our lives. Vice-President Al Gore, while addressing the Elmwood Institute, spoke of this same need when he said, "The more deeply I search for the root of the global environmental crisis, the more I am convinced that it is an outer manifestation of an inner crisis that is, for lack of a better word, spiritual."

As we move into the 21st Century, it is the work of all human beings to attend to the health of both our "inner" and "outer" houses: our inner house, the limitless world within; and the outer house of the world in which we live our daily lives. Many people in contemporary society feel little or no connection between those two worlds. This is a state that the indigenous, land-based peoples of the earth, whose cultures reach back thousands of years, would find not only sad but incomprehensible.

### Tracking The Three Universal Life Processes

There are three universal processes that we are involved with on a daily basis. Being cognizant of these processes allows us to know what our daily work truly is: work with self, work with one other, and work in groups. What is my current work with self—both internally and externally? Many tribal peoples call this work with self "Morning Star" work. How is this being reflected back to me in my life at this time?

What is my work with significant others? Some indigenous societies refer to one-to-one work as "Rainbow Hoop" work. This work is a training in intimacy, commitment, and people skills, whether it's with a loved one, friend, or colleague.

What is my group or collective work at this time? How can I be a creative change agent or healing catalyst within organizations, teams, and family settings? Native Americans call group work "Medicine Wheel" work; some Asian societies refer to group work as "Bamboo Reed" work, where we learn how to be both firm and yielding.

Indigenous peoples state that a mark of a healthy person is one who is comfortable and effective in all three areas of self, other, and collective. Which of these processes is your current strength, and which of these is the least developed at this time? Bringing all three universal processes to equal power allows one to experience increased self-esteem and effectiveness in the world.

## Balancing And Unifying The Four Universal Archetypes

No matter what world we live in now, we are all people of the earth, connected to one another by our mutual humanity. When we listen to land-based peoples, we are listening to our oldest selves. Indigenous cultures have developed practices to re-balance and draw upon our own inner wisdom base.

They believe we also have access to four blueprints for human behavior, or four archetypes that can assist us in manifesting who we really are. These four archetypes are the Warrior/Leader (leadership), the Healer, the Visionary, and the Teacher. Because each archetype draws on the roots of our deepest mythic humanity, we too can tap into their wisdom and remember who we really are. When we learn to live these archetypes within ourselves, we begin to heal ourselves and our fragmented world.

Based on my research, these four principles comprise the heart of indigenous values about how to live life simply and well. I call these principles the Four-Fold Way, a method for incorporating indigenous wisdoms into contemporary times.

1. *Show up, or choose to be present.* Being present allows us to access the human resources of right use of power, presence, and communication. This the way of the Warrior/Leader.

2. *Pay attention to what has heart and meaning.* Paying attention opens us to the human resources of love, gratitude, acknowledgment, and validation. This is the way of the Healer.

3. *Tell the truth without blame or judgment.* Nonjudgmental truthfulness maintains our authenticity, and develops our inner vision and creativity. This is the way of the Visionary.

4. *Be open to outcome, not attached to outcome.* Openness and nonattachment help us recover the human resources of wisdom and objectivity. This is the way of the Teacher.

When we understand these universal experiences, we are better able to respect the diverse ways in which these shared themes are expressed by all people. Even though these four archetypes are emphasized in most indigenous traditions, it is important to understand that they are universal and available to all humankind, regardless of context, culture, structure, and practice. In our society, we express the way of the Warrior in our leadership ability. We express the way of the Healer through our attitudes toward maintaining our own health and the health of our environment. We express the way of the Visionary through our personal creativity, and through our ability to bring our life dreams and visions into the world. We express the way of the Teacher through our constructive communication and informational skills.

William Blake may have been inspired by all four archetypes to write:

> "I in a fourfold vision see
> And fourfold vision is given me
> Fourfold is my supreme delight..."

## Supporting the Braided Way by Being a Creative Catalyst

During cycles of change and challenge, we can become more effective by holding the vision and possibility of a Braided Way. A braid can be a symbol for unifying polarities of any kind, thus creating a third option. For example, one portion of the braid could represent the new, one portion the old. The third portion of the braid is where the old and the new are equally honored, creating a neutral ground where similarities and differences can coexist and support one another.

Native peoples of the world hold the belief that we are all original medicine, nowhere else duplicated in the world. In these times of change, we are being called on to employ our creative fire and to bring forward our life's dreams. It is very important for us to take our place, to shift the shape of our

reality or our experience, and to build new worlds both internally and externally.

An example of this occurred at Clinton's Economic Summit in 1993. A Navajo elder, who was the spokesperson for all
the native peoples on reservations, came forward to speak. He
came to talk about the plight of those living on the reservations
in this country. He acknowledged first, with gratitude, all of the
people who were there. He then proceeded to describe what was
working on the reservations. After that he acknowledged what
was not working. He concluded by saying, "I regret that I have
only three creative solutions to offer."

What a healing experience it would be for all of us to use
this model of communication in our families, in our professional lives, and in our spiritual explorations. If we could start
with acknowledging those present, and then say what is working; the next step would be to address what isn't working.
Finally the last step would be to generate at least three creative
solutions to the problem; not just one solution to which we
have become attached.

It is very easy to complain—and it is important to acknowledge what is not working. However it is time for us to
become creative catalysts and healing agents. By caring for the
soul in the workplace and becoming creative catalysts in our
communities, we bring balance to our personal and professional lives. As catalysts, we need to bring forward creative
solutions and to master what native peoples of the world call
"shape-shifting"; a commitment through creativity to shift the
shape of our experience and honor the vision of integration, the
Braided Way. Williamson reminds us of the power of shape-
shifting:

> And as we let our light shine, we uncon-
> sciously give other people permission to do the
> same. As we are liberated from our own fear,
> our presence automatically liberates others.

When we are open to being powerful, loving, creative, and
wise with self, other, and collectives, we experience the world
and ourselves as the many splendored things that we are. We
rise to Williamson's challenge, honor Gandhi's principle of
leadership, and release Iktumi's eight lies. This is the essence
of Spirit expressed in all aspects of our lives.

**Kymn Harvin Rutigliano**, PhD, has spent the past 30 years conveying a singular vision: Life is all about love. During the course of her distinguished career, she has worked as a journalist, political speech writer, corporate change champion, relationship coach, management consultant, speaker, and author. She is internationally known for her groundbreaking work at AT&T and with other Fortune 100 companies committed to nurturing the hearts and spirits—as well as minds and bodies—of their employees. Her work provides a "wake up call" for her clients to discover and integrate into their professional lives their own inner resources of love, clarity, and spiritual expression.

This essay, featuring Rutigliano's work with AT&T Senior Vice President Ken Bertaccini, is an excerpt from her current book project of the same name.

**7**

# Bringing LOVE Back Into Business

*Kymn Harvin Rutigliano*

Pick up just about any business book on the market, flip through the pages, look at the table of contents, the index, even the chapter subtitles and, in nearly all cases, you won't find what I consider to be the most important element of business success: LOVE.

"Love? Really? Does she really mean *love?*"

Yes, I do.

L-O-V-E, that four-letter word that is seldom uttered in the carpeted halls of American business. L-O-V-E, that baggage-laden word that women and men alike generally do not associate with business. L-O-V-E, the purview of romantics, families, shrinks, and poets but certainly not fodder for the board room, supervisors' trainings, or staff meetings...or is it?

Maybe, just maybe, love is the key to business success, especially in the 21st Century. Let me tell you why I—a former journalist, political speech-writer, corporate publicist, training executive, and now management consultant—believe this so strongly.

**Love is the most healing power in all the world.** And boy, do we need healing. Each of us. Each of the companies we work for and work with. There is no person or place, no business or organization, that could not benefit from love's healing touch.

93

**Love is the universal language.** As we become more global in our approach to business, markets, and natural resources, love is essential to building bridges instead of walls. Love unites, spans cultures, creates common ground.

**Love is the heart of service.** Observe those who truly model "excellent customer service" and they will epitomize two things: loving what they do and loving people—and people are who they serve. They might never say the "L word" but there is that sense about them. And this "sense" adds up to big dollars and cents, competitive advantage, customer loyalty, high employee morale—in short, business success.

**Love is the truest expression of who we are—spiritual human beings.** The foundation of most of the world's major religions is love. Even the staunchest atheist can admit that love is what people crave.

How can it be, then, that business, which is comprised of people in various partnerships of exchange, does not see or have love as its core? How can it be that something so central, so key, has been ignored for so long? How can it be that love most often is considered an oxymoron with business?

The reasons are many. Though love is one of the most studied, researched, and written about phenomena in life, it is also one of the most misunderstood. In part because the English language is very imprecise in connoting the many different types of love, this four-letter word has been all but forbidden in the business world where mental and physical prowess has ruled. However, this does not mean love has not been present, has not been experienced, or has not been at work in our corporations, our businesses, our enterprises.

Love has been there all along, just waiting—patiently—to be discovered for the power that it is—not just in our families, with friends, between lovers—but in corporate life as well. An "awakening" is happening all across our world—the paradigm shifts, the growing sense that there is more to life than acquiring, the burgeoning appreciation of ourselves and others not simply as mortal human beings but also immortal spiritual beings. This awakening demands that we look deep into our work lives, deep into the fabric of our organizations, deep into the fundamentals of truly living to find what has been there all along as a driving force, just out of our line of vision, just beyond our present consciousness...love.

Now you'll notice I haven't defined the "L word." This is intentional. Love is beyond definition, beyond classification, beyond the limits of our current language. Yet, we crave discrete definitions, labels and parameters—in part because they give us the illusion of safety or understanding. So, what is love in a business context?

I agree with Jim Autry who, in his best-selling book *Love and Profit,* says: "Good management is largely a matter of love. Or if you're uncomfortable with that word, call it caring, because proper management involves caring for people, not manipulating them."

I agree with international consultant Sabina Spencer: "I know what you mean by love in business. Can I put any words on exactly what it means? No way. Can I speak to completely describe it? No way. It's not about words, it's about experience. Once you start describing love, it's now not the experience but the description of it."

I agree with AT&T Senior Vice President and Chief Quality Officer Ken Bertaccini who said, back in 1989, "Love has a legitimate place in business. Using love in this context is a bold step, but I think we're ready to put love in our business." Stressing the importance of understanding this definition of love, he explained, "We're talking about love in the context of 'love your neighbor as you love yourself,' and treat others as you would like to be treated. We don't hold to the scenarios that there's no room for love in business. We all need to love one another to exist individually and collectively, whether it's on a personal or business level."

I agree with best-selling author and professor Leo Buscaglia who writes in *Living, Learning, Loving:* "I have always hesitated to define love because I see love as limitless, and as you become bigger and more beautiful and more expansive, so does love. And so to limit it by a definition seemed really bad. I like St. Exupery's definition...'Perhaps love is the process of my leading you gently back to yourself.' Maybe that is what teaching is."

Maybe that is what work is—the process not only by which we earn a living, but learn to live as well. Learning to live means learning to love, not using people for our own gain.

I agree with *The Seat of the Soul* author Gary Zukav who says, "The days of success through maximizing return on investment to shareholders, of exploiting fellow souls and the earth are over. If you choose to continue to behave this way, you will create certain consequences—painful and destructive ones."

Because love is what life is about at its core, what the human journey is about, what we all want to give and receive, then love, in my view, is also what business, at its core, is about and needs to be about more directly, more consciously. Now I know all about profits, policies, procedures. For eons we have been duped—or have duped ourselves—into believing that this is what makes business work—focusing on making money and using people in the process.

We've been wrong.

Business, when at its best, focuses on "making people" and using money in the process. Gee, what a novel idea! If people truly are the heart of business (how could it be otherwise since without people there is NO business), and love is the heart of people, then doesn't it stand to reason that love does have a place—a central place—in business?

Once we realize this, we can unlock enormous capabilities to have people in business, people served by business THRIVE—and our world, our businesses, organizations, communities, and families will THRIVE also.

For "living proof" just ask Bertaccini. He was the first executive in the company of 300,000 people to publicly take a stand for legitimizing the "L Word" in business. Back in 1989, when he was President and CEO of AT&T Consumer Products (the residential telephone division), Ken altered his

AT&T Consumer Products' Shared Values Pyramid

organization's platform of values which was called "Shared Values." He inserted "LOVE" in the center of the foundation row (along with Caring, Trust, Integrity and Respect).

In a front-page announcement via an AT&T Consumer Products newsletter reaching 13,000 people, Ken said:

> Using love in this context is a bold step, but I think we're ready to legitimize the "L word" and put love in our business....We're talking about love in the context of love your neighbor as you love yourself, and treat others as you would like to be treated. We don't hold to the scenario that there's no room for love in business. We all need to love one another to exist individually and collectively whether it's on a personal or a business level.

> Adding love to our Shared Values challenges us to own and live our personal values of caring, trust and respect. Certainly these are all definitions of love. You can't care for someone, trust or respect them if you don't love them. And putting love in our Shared Values Pyramid sends a message to our people and to everybody, inside and outside of AT&T, who looks at Consumer Products that we really do care about each other.

> What we need is to increase our individual commitment to *owning* and *living* our values. Certainly anything of this magnitude and something so near and dear to all of us is going to require some understanding and some communication. I believe we've clearly established the Shared Values as the foundation of our business. And now we are making a very provocative statement by adding a word not typically used in business to our business and to our pyramid. Our Shared Values are, and will continue to be, the source of our strength and our success. They enable us to be the best for our owners, our customers, and our people.

So what led Bertaccini to make such a courageous move?

There are many answers to that question, depending on who you ask. I offer a very personal one based on the years I spent serving in Ken's Consumer Products organization (1985-1988) and the time I spent interviewing Ken in early 1995.

Simply stated, something had happened to Ken that had changed his life. That "something" was cancer.

In 1987 Ken was diagnosed with a rare form of head and neck cancer. Over ninety percent of the time, this kind of cancer was inoperable and terminal. It rarely responded to chemotherapy or radiation. The prognosis was bleak. No one was more stunned than Ken himself. A picture of health, vibrant, alive, full of energy, Ken had seldom been sick. He juggled an enormous workload as well as family responsibilities with aplomb. Not only was he shocked by the diagnosis, but the 13,000 people in his organization were shocked as well. And they rallied to his side in amazing ways. They demanded another miracle.

Two years before, in 1985, Consumer Products had been the least profitable division of AT&T. Ken had been given an ultimatum to either turn the business around within two years or AT&T would exit the residential telephone business and 13,000 people would lose their jobs. In the face of such an ultimatum, Ken gathered his top 300 managers together and asked: "Do you believe in miracles?" He went on to spell out the dilemma facing the organization and asked everyone to join with him in creating a "miracle"—the turnaround of Consumer Products.

From that point forward, a spirit of "miracle creating" permeated the organization. A variety of initiatives were begun, including one I was privileged to create and head, known as "Project Miracles." This was a training program designed, at its fundamental level, to show people they have the power to create extraordinary results in their lives, both on and off the job. Though I could not publicly state it at the time—even to Ken—the program truly was "all about love." I had already learned that the best way to help people deal with change and to empower them to produce miraculous results was to encourage them to love themselves and others more fully by giving them the tools with which to build healthy, lasting relationships. And that's what Project Miracles was about.

Ken funded the program and made it possible for 13,000

people to spend three to five days off the job, focusing on living life at 100%—with honesty, integrity, commitment, and caring...with love. The result of this initiative—and the many others underway in Consumer Products at the same time—was that Consumer Products became one of the most profitable divisions of AT&T and had the highest morale by 1987—months before the two-year deadline.

And so, when word spread that Ken Bertaccini had cancer, the outpouring of love and support for him was incredible. Cards, letters, presents, and phone calls flooded his office daily. People wrote of how he had given them the gift of "Project Miracles" and now it was time for him to have a miracle in his own life. Prayer meetings were held, moments of silence preceded staff meetings, quiet words of support were murmured in hallways. Ken Bertaccini was not going to die if his team of "spotters" (as Project Miracles graduates called themselves) had anything to say about it. And die he did not.

Against nearly all odds, Ken beat the cancer. He is cancer-free to this day, nearly seven years later. He's once again the picture of health, though he no longer has taste buds or a sense of smell (side effects of the radiation). He credits four things with his miraculous cure: his faith, the unconditional support of his family, the miracle of modern medicine coupled with the care of his doctors, and the outpouring of love from his friends and AT&T colleagues.

I concur. And while I am confident of the first three—his faith, his family and modern medicine—I have firsthand experience with the latter. The people of Consumer Products did not want to see their leader die. They had received much from him in the way of "Project Miracles" —among other initiatives—and they wanted to return something back. And even though the workplace became "safe" for expressions of caring like "Check 13" (a hug), and the "Seat of Honor" feedback sessions (affirming the qualities valued in another), "love" still was talked about only in hushed tones. But when word spread that Ken had cancer, it was as if the dam broke and all the love that had been "bottled up" began to be expressed...not just to Ken, but throughout the organization.

The possibility of their leader's death, in my view at least, reminded people of their own mortality and the importance of expressing their love and care now, not later. So people started speaking and expressing what was already present but hereto-fore largely unspoken—messages of love, support, caring, prayers, faith, belief in miracles. Ken's illness had catalyzed another miracle in the workplace—full self-expression of one's deepest held feelings.

AT&T—for many years a leader in technology, innovation, and management—now leads the way once again. The story of Ken Bertaccini and AT&T Consumer Products is living proof of the power of love—not just in family and social life, but in business life as well.

I invite you to join Ken and me—and countless others—who fully believe love has a rightful place in our workplaces, in our businesses, in our organizations. Let us open our hearts, our spirits as well as our minds and voices and express what is already there at the core—LOVE. Let us take the risk. Let us love one another...

Yes, even at work.

**Jacqueline Haessly,** BA, BS, MSEd, authored *Learning to Live Together*, and contributed to *When the Canary Stops Singing: Women's Perspectives for Transforming Business*, *The New Entrepreneurs: Business Visionaries for the 21st Century*, and *Rediscovering the Soul of Business*. Her latest chapters appear in *Families as Educators for Global Citizenship*.

Haessly directs Peacemaking Associates—a training and consulting company—and is pursuing doctoral work in peace studies. Her biographic entries appear in *Who's Who in Women of the World*, *Business and Professional Women*, *Women of the Americas*, and *International Leaders* for her work in the field of peace and global awareness education. With her husband, Dr. Daniel Di Domizio, she shares in the nurturing and homemaking tasks associated with the fun, love, tears, and laughter of busy family life.

# 8

# Transformation And The World Of Commerce

## Jacqueline Haessly

The world around us is hurting, crying out in anguish for relief. The news media overflows with the sounds of this pain and affliction. We hear parents crying for the loss of their children due to gang or drug-related gunfire in Bogota or Detroit, bombings and terrorist attacks in Oklahoma City or Bosnia, or starvation in San Antonio or Somalia. We hear young ones whimpering from too many beatings, too many drugs, too little food, and too few playgrounds on which to renew their spirits. We hear women, men, and children yelling in fear from domestic abuse. We hear the elderly and the disabled weeping in loneliness, deserted by those they love. We hear the homeless moaning as they lie shivering in the night. We hear women and men in offices, universities, factories, and the streets of our cities calling out against sexual and gender abuse. We hear children sobbing in shame from the exploitation of their young bodies. We hear lovers howling for partners maimed or dead in someone's war. We hear prisoners in war-torn countries screaming in agony from battering and political torture.

### Becoming Conscious

As corporate leaders, managers, workers, and ordinary citizens, we grieve at this pain and at the pollution and desecration of this planet which we know sustains us. We agonize about these abuses and the complexity of the problems that confront us in this world, in this space, and in this time. In one way or another, we want to stop the pain and bring an end to the suffering.

In the midst of this suffering we ask ourselves two questions: (1) How is this suffering related to spirituality and, specifically, spirituality and business, and (2) what, if anything, is our role as business people in addressing this suffering? To phrase these questions in another way, what does this suffering have to do with commerce, and the work of our lives?

Commerce, according to *Webster's New International Dictionary* (1989), has to do with trade, with the free and mutual interchange of goods, property, and services in a way that is *mutually beneficial* [emphasis added] to all parties, and which is based on a pattern of reciprocal communication. This is also the position advanced by those who advocate the "Invisible Hand" theory attributed to Adam Smith, linking the free enterprise dimension of commerce with benefits to society.

Even a glance at news reports of current social, economic, and political situations in the United States and around the globe will show that commerce, as defined above, does not always work. The theory of the Invisible Hand does not work. It is hard to engage in the *interchange* of most forms of commerce in communities racked by gunfire or other acts of violence or terrorism. It is impossible to engage in the *mutual* exchange of goods, property, or services when one is destitute and one's children are starving. And it would be a travesty to think that children, torn from their families and forced against their will to engage in practices that benefit a growing sex industry, are willing participants in any form of *reciprocal communication*. Commerce, in such situations, may benefit the few, but where, in all of this, do we find the elusive Invisible Hand which is supposed to benefit society and its people? So we see, in a significant way, the answer to the question we raise above is that this suffering, and our ability as business people to address it, has everything to do with commerce and the work of our lives!

The theme of this book, "blending consciousness with commerce," suggests another connection between these questions and the work of our lives. According to *Webster's New International Dictionary* (1989), consciousness is defined as "knowing what is happening around one." Consciousness affects "the totality of one's thoughts, feelings and impressions."

The suffering of this world touches all our lives. How deeply we allow this suffering to penetrate our consciousness in our work world will affect how well we use our power as business decision makers to address it.

How can we, as business leaders, attempt to blend commerce with consciousness in a way that brings both healing and wholeness to a hurting world? What does it mean to use our corporate power for the good of our society? To transform it for the benefit and well-being of the whole of humanity?

To address these questions we begin with an exploration of power and its relationship to soul. For this we will draw upon the wisdom and experience of a group of people not usually associated with the world of commerce—feminist theologians and spiritual leaders from diverse cultures and continents who not only address the question of soul, but who also offer examples which express soul in commerce. These women cross cultures and reflect the religious, economic, political, and social experiences of women from widely differing geographical regions of the world: Africa, Asia, Australia, Europe, India, the Pacific Islands, Central, North and South America. Each has contributed significantly to a discussion of power in the community and corporate setting. Each has given voice to the ways that business leaders use their power to help heal a hurting world.

## Power and Spirit:
## Links To Empowerment

### Reclaiming Our Power

What is power? How do we understand it? How do we use power in our personal life? In our professional and public life? How do we use power in our business? How is the use of power experienced by others in our corporation? What is our corporate culture in regard to power?

Few words in the English language evoke such strong, complex, and often contradictory emotions as the word *power.* Some fear it; others embrace it eagerly. Kings, presidents, religious leaders, gang leaders, rebels, even corporate leaders have killed for it. Administrators, managers, and ordinary citizens distrust it. Politicians want it. Communities want it. Nations want it. Today we hear the raised voices of the poor and the dispossessed who want it. Each voice touches our emotions, adding to

our fear, our distrust, our anger, our determination, our anticipation, or our joy!

Reflect for a moment on the variety of connective words
associated with the word *power*. Power, at times, is understood as
a positive concept. Consider the joyous celebrations of farmers,
factory workers, and homemakers who awaited the coming of
electrical power across the rural areas of our countries. Worldwide, electric power has long been understood as a positive force
for good. When linked to such other common words as *gas, horse,
hydro, solar*, and *wind*, these phrases express positive images of
power put to use for individual and community well-being. Power
also can be understood as a negative concept. For example,
phrases such as *satanic power, exploitative power, manipulative
power, authoritarian power*, and *dictatorial power* evoke a sense of
fear and trembling for many.

Then there are those words which, when linked to power,
generate in one either a sense of pride or a sense of fear,
depending upon where one stands in a given life experience.
Read the following phrases slowly. Note your own emotional
response to each pair of words. Jot your responses down on a
sheet of paper if you wish.

| | | | |
|---|---|---|---|
| *Black* Power | *Colonial* Power | *Corporate* Power | *Economic* Power |
| *Feminist* Power | *Financial* Power | *German* Power | *Hispanic* Power |
| *Indian* Power | *Industrial* Power | *Intellectual* Power | *Irish* Power |
| *Japanese* Power | *Military* Power | *Native* Power | *Nuclear* Power |
| *People* Power | *Polish* Power | *Political* Power | *Religious* Power |
| *Soviet* Power | *Student* Power | *Super*power | *White* Power |

What thoughts and experiences did these words evoke in
you? What emotions? For those who share membership in a
group, these terms speak of personal or group identity, pride of
heritage, and personal, group, or national success. Group pride
motivates members to act together for a common cause. For those
who stand on the outside of the group, either by choice or by
exclusion, such phases may call forth experiences of injustice,
oppression, and loss of home, land, and life. Such phrases can
induce feelings of discomfort and, at times, fear for one's very life.

Thus, for some, such phrases are a battle cry to be feared and negated.

It is important to understand that the emotional responses to phrases such as these depend entirely upon the place we are standing, the shoes we are wearing when we speak or hear such words. It is our emotional reaction to these terms, to our own understanding of these concepts of power, that keep us—as a people and as a world—disconnected, hurting, and in fear of each other. Unless we recognize "the place where we stand" and "the place where the other stands" it is difficult, if not almost impossible, to comprehend the experience of the self or the other in relationship to these concepts of power.

Our perception of *power* is formed by our personal and collective experiences of power *as it is used. Power,* itself, is really a neutral term, meaning simply to be able; to have potential. It is only when the word *power* is linked to other words that it takes on specific meanings. It has the potential to stir up a wide array of emotions in the human spirit.

Much of our understanding of power comes from personal and social experiences with political or economic power. Some feminist theologians, describing past or current cultural, economic, political, religious, and social relationships between women and men, or between different groups within or among societies, refer to the writings of others who link power to control and domination. Let us listen to their words.

Joan Chittister explores concepts of power in the writings of Max Weber, Karl Marx, and Rollo May and finds them all related to concepts of control. Betty A. Mottinger explores the evolving concepts of power as used in business and government leadership. For the most part, these definitions also have less to do with ability or potential than they have to do with control and dominance.

*Webster's New International Dictionary* reflects the ambiguity associated with this word. First, it describes power simply thus: to be able; an ability to act; the capacity to perform. However, by the fourth of more than twenty definitions, the concept of the word changes from one of ability and potential to a Machiavellian interpretation of force, control, and domination over another.

For centuries, Machiavelli's thesis has formed a basis of training for government, military, and corporate leadership. Equating power with control, Machiavelli urged the Prince to act in ways that limited the freedom of others and to acquire that which was not properly his. In this paradigm, neither the prince—whose need for dominance over his subjects led to all manner of manipulative behavior, nor his subjects—who were left without the freedom to make decisions affecting their very lives—were free to reach their own full potential, the very essence of the word *power.* Indeed, under the model suggested by Machiavelli, the Prince must live in a state of perpetual distrust and fear lest he be overtaken by enemies seeking conquest.

In the world of commerce, a corporate culture based on a Machiavellian model of dominance and control can lead to mistrust and suspicion between workers and managers, foster internal competitiveness between workers and departments, and drain energy which could be directed toward achieving corporate goals. Communities, corporations and governments that follow this model find themselves faced with widespread dissension and even rebellion as citizens and workers seek to exercise a voice in the workings of their life.

Business leaders who want to succeed in today's business environment know they need a different understanding of power. They acknowledge that when control is imposed from without, workers are less likely to sustain personal effort to achieve quality in either performance or service. They recognize that when power comes from within, it is reflected in an individual and group commitment to quality in achieving both personal and corporate work goals. They understand that today's corporate setting requires a new leadership style, one based on cooperation, team building, and openness to shared decision making.

## Embracing Our Spirituality

It is my thesis that there is a different concept of power, one that has nothing to do with control and dominance. Women theologians from all continents are in the forefront of those who challenge us to consider alternative models of power, models which are based on deeply held spiritual values. They challenge us to reclaim power for what it is: *to have the ability, the potential, the capacity to do or to make something, to be.* Yong Ting Jin suggests that alternative models of power are necessary to "shape and build up a new community of women and men" based on equality and justice. Ada Maria Isari-Diaz reminds us that 'power liberates all people—women and men—

"to become the most they themselves can be." Jin adds: "Power is the *blessing for one to live in love, in peace with justice, in community* [emphasis added]. This power is never violent or destructive, ego-centered, or domineering. This power is understood, motivated, and exercised by one's set of values. It serves to foster, enhance, and nurture all of life."

This is a power grounded in a spirituality that sees a connectedness between oneself and all others who share life with us on this small planet we each call home. Such a spirituality affirms the diverse ways that women and men express their sense of connection to each other, to their universe and to the Spirit-God force Who gives life meaning. But what, we may ask, is spirituality, and how is it related to power, or to corporate culture and the world of commerce?

Sandra Schneiders writes that "spirituality in the broadest sense defies definition. It refers to whatever human experience is alive and intentional, *conscious of itself and responsive to others*" [emphasis added]. Can it be that the very concept of consciousness calls us to be responsive to others? Schneiders goes on to suggest that there is an increased interest in spirituality today because "spirituality represents, on the whole, a profound and authentic desire of [late] 20th Century humanity for wholeness in the midst of fragmentation, for community in the face of isolation and loneliness, for liberating transcendence, for meaning in life [and] for values that endure."

It is this awareness that gives rise to spirituality programs in the workplace. People hunger for a sense of connection with a Spirit Being higher than themselves. They also long for a sense of connection to others and for a way to address the complex issues that impact on life as we move forward together toward the 21st Century. Spirituality, especially a global spirituality that affirms the diverse ways that people express this interconnection with each other and to a Higher Spirit or Power, satisfies this hunger and generates the spiritual power necessary to transform the world.

Spiritual power is soulpower, the very heart of our being. Power generates. Spiritual power generates a life-giving commitment to create good in the world. Power energizes. It energizes a machine, a movement, or a people. Spiritual power energizes a person, a people, and even a corporation to sustain the effort in times of struggle and times of doubt. Spiritual power brings forth the joy that dwells within and creates a transformed world.

According to Mottinger, spiritual power is a gift from One known by many names which allows "the Spirit's intended purposes to be worked out in the lives of those involved in relationship [because] spiritual power is always expressed within relationships." Both liberation theologians and feminist theologians describe spiritual power as power in relationship with another. Marta Benavides states it in very simple yet profound terms: "My mother's definition of the spiritual was to care and act on behalf of life, to keep people alive."

## Liberation Theology

Liberation theology, according to Mary Jo Weaver is "a belief that...God's primary passion is to free humans from oppressive situations, and God's self-disclosure occurs when we recognize and accept God's summons to us to participate in the historical struggle for liberation." Liberation theology draws us into the experience of God suffering with and for all of humanity who still live in poverty, suffer political oppression, economic exploitation, or cultural, racial, religious, ethnic, national, gender, ability, or age discrimination. In its fullest manifestation, liberation theology "directs our attention to where God dwells."

Liberation theologians search the scriptures for stories that proclaim God's liberating action for all. Through prayerful reflection and discussions with peasants, shop keepers, business leaders, and landowners, they discover common themes between the scriptures and the stories of their own lives. Through this process, liberation theologians raise awareness, deepen consciousness, and share the message of God's liberating action in the context of people's lives today. For those responding to the challenges of liberation theology, spiritual power can be described as an expression of our personal commitment to make a difference in the lives of people who are in pain.

Feminist theologians, who also ground their work in a theology of liberation, go far beyond this. They believe that, in the past, most liberation theologians tended to address economic and political oppression of male workers but did not identify conditions leading to the economic, political and social oppression of women and children or the suppression of cultures. They believe that most male theologians failed to identify the basic structures and systems of a patriarchal heritage which for millennia has discounted, disclaimed, and dishonored women. Today, this is changing as both women's and men's voices are raised across the continents calling for a more holistic, experiential, empowering theology directed at the liberation of the whole of the human community.

## Empowering Our Selves, And Others

Drawing on feminist experience, liberating theological reflection, and a sense of global spirituality, we have seen that women everywhere are rejecting definitions of power that imply control or dominance over another and are moving towards empowerment for themselves and their communities.

Diane L. Eck, writing about empowerment, expresses this move thusly: "Women's power begins at home, with work to change and to free ourselves, then extends to local and national networks for change, and finally to international, global efforts for change." According to Eck, power does not begin at the international level, but rather is dependent upon organization at the local level. She adds that women "must be able to see the linkages between other oppressions, in the bedroom, [in their places of work, in their communities] in the nation, and in the international scene, and must work together to generate power."

Empowerment can be defined as "an ongoing process through which people achieve self-reliance, participate in, and contribute to the larger society. It is holistic; it includes a balancing of mind, body, spirit or soul, relationships, lifestyle choices, environmental concerns, and social responsibility" (taken from the Empowerment statement of SET Ministry, Milwaukee, WI, 1992). Empowerment is grounded in an awareness that all power comes from a Spirit source Who, in our diverse religious traditions, goes by many names. Empowerment allows us to be part of the human process of liberation from our own exploitation as well as from our participation, however unknowingly or unwillingly, in the exploitation of others.

Empowerment implies a willingness to share power in relationship with others based on attitudes and values of genuine respect, compassion, mutual support, cooperation, and a commitment to the common good. Empowerment occurs when there is an awareness of options, an exchange of ideas, a sharing of resources, a commitment to bring forth change in oneself and others, and a willingness to act responsibly for the good of the whole of humanity. It includes a recognition that empowerment means to act "with" others, not "for" others.

Diane Loy Ferri suggests that in the corporate setting, empowerment leads to mutual ownership of ideas and shared responsibility to implement them. It is here that leaders and decision makers can best affirm themselves and others as people who are empowered to act. Understanding that empowerment of self and others is grounded in an understanding of Spirit and soul—both necessary to heal our hurting world— empowered people address abuses and effect change, transforming both the business environment and the broader society.

Spirit—and soul—are about the personal, inner life of a person, while power is about the outward, political expression of one's inner vision. Eleanor Rae describes the link between Spirit and power this way: "What do spirituality and politics [the personal and the political] have in common? Both politics and spirituality have to do with change. Politics may be regarded as the *what* of the process of change, while spirituality is the *how* of the process."

Spirituality emphasizes unity and connectedness, while politics emphasizes our separateness. According to Rae, in any process of change there are three interwoven dimensions: (1) an analysis of the situation which needs to change (the political); (2) a vision of what can be, coupled with a belief that change is possible (the spiritual); and (3) a concrete plan of action which, when implemented, leads to the empowerment of individuals and the community (linking the spiritual with the political). In other words, the content of change is political while the process is spiritual. Rae adds, "Both spirituality and politics share a common ground in that both are concerned with power; that is, power created, maintained and utilized in the alignment with a particular view of life." She goes on: "we must proceed in a way that is based on and acts out of the unity of the spiritual and the political."

Spirituality, according to Rae, focuses from society to the individual, emphasizing the uniqueness of the individual as well as our unity and connectedness to each other while politics focuses from the individual to the society, emphasizing the communal aspects of society as well as our separateness.

If spirituality is about connectedness and politics is about change, they intersect where the lives of people are involved in relationship. As we have seen, spiritual power is, first and foremost, about relationships. Therefore, we must examine the "who" of those relationships and the qualities that support those relationships. Feminist theologians are united in identifying the "who" of power relationships: women and men, poor and rich, aged and youth, the illiterate and the literate, laborers and managers, peasants and politicians, tinkers and teachers, clergy and lay, black, brown, yellow and white, all joined together in a commitment to create a just and peaceful world where equality and compassion reign.

## Vision And Action:
## Links To Transformation

### Daring To Vision

Feminist theologians are also united in identifying the qualities of power relationships. They believe that one cannot have a transformed and empowered self unless one also has a transformed and empowered society. They are at the forefront, then, to articulate a vision of a world where all people are treated with dignity and respect. They recognize the need to work with both women and men to create a society where participation in decision making that affects one's life in the home, the workplace and the world is full and equal, where values of mutuality, response-ability, compassion, consensus, cooperation, inclusion, reciprocity, interdependence, and openness to the ideas and experiences of others are treasured and where human rights, affirmation for the common good, and full human liberation are espoused and practiced.

Mary Jo Weaver reminds us that a feminist theology of liberation is, above all, "widely interdisciplinary and cooperative; it begins with the everyday experience of [people in their own communities] and then claims power of solidarity with victims of oppression everywhere." She adds, "In this light our understanding of power begins in those places most common and also most sacred to us—in our reflections on our experiences of power as shaped by home and family." I add the neighborhoods, fields, factories, and offices where we gather to share our dreams as we work to earn our daily bread.

In our vision of a renewed society, relationships are based on inclusiveness, full and equal participation in decision making that affects one's life, and response-ability is both mutual and life-giving. Collegiality, collaboration, and consensus decision making replace hierarchical structures in both religious and secular society. Cooperative ventures replace competitive. Acknowledging the diverse gifts of the members of the community, leadership tasks are shared. Recognizing that political, environmental and economic issues cross local, national and regional borders, decision making which respects our global interdependence is both affirmed and celebrated. The structure that emerges is that of community which Carter Heyward describes as "an inclusive, nonauthoritarian body of interdependent members whose lives *literally are bound up one in another* and who share a common commitment to justice" She adds: "The power of community is sparked among persons who come together and is embodied in mutual engagement." We do this for the common good of all humanity.

We each need to see ourselves as co-creators with a Spirit force in our lives if we want to bring our vision to reality. According to Eleanor Rae, "In every age, the Spirit, who is embodied love, calls a people to act with Her on those issues that are most critical. In our own time, the...Spirit seems to be centering Her presence and activity in areas where unjust structures are being challenged and, ultimately, transformed in the core of the earth."

We have seen that the exercise of spiritual power is based upon an articulated vision of the kind of society which will best meet the needs of all of humanity as lived out in the diverse places we each call home. According to Rosemary Radford Rather such a vision recognizes that "the creation of a just self and a just society cannot be separated." This power, according to Jin, is "dynamic and constructive because it has to do with caring, inclusiveness, peace with justice as against racism, sexism, classism and militarism."

This is not an easy, risk-free task, as Ada Maria Isari-Diaz reminds us. "The changes we are advocating will change the world radically....[We] need to begin to live out those changes so that our vision does become a reality. The only way we can move ahead is by living the reality we envision." I would add that we need to do this in our personal, professional and public life, within our families, our communities, our workplaces, and our nations and our world. For our efforts, Isari-Diaz reminds us, we may incur ridicule, rejection and even life-threatening danger. Still, even acknowledging the risks we face, she joins with the voices of others from across the continents calling for a more holistic, experiential, empowering theology and a new understanding of power, one which empowers all of us to act for the liberation of the whole of the human community.

## Creating Personal, Community And Global Transformation

What then, we might ask, are the conditions for the expression of spiritual power? Can this, will this, lead to personal, community and global transformation?

Recognizing that current economic and political structures and systems are, in many cases, energy-draining and lead to widespread inequalities in relations with others, those embracing spiritual power will seek to create structures and systems that are life-enhancing. Eleanor Rae goes so far as to say that our understanding of power demands that we work incessantly to create the political, economic, and social conditions needed for the self-realization of all persons. It also requires establishing relational structures and operational modes in all spheres of life which facilitate and promote the self-realization of all persons. Finally, our understanding of power requires promotion of the creativity of all persons so that they can contribute efficaciously to the common good.

Mottinger suggests that spiritual power is not only a gift *from* One known by many names. It is also reflected in a person's behavior as their *gift to the community* [emphasis added]. Spiritual power is given freely that we may each be co-creators in bringing forth the promise of the garden where all shall dwell in peace and harmony. Moreover, she reminds us, spiritual power is used "to influence people towards God's purposes," not our own. She states that all the world's religions hold to this understanding of spiritual power.

The question becomes, then, one of response. When others attempt to control or dominate, what is the response of the person deeply grounded in spirituality? What response will most effectively lead to empowerment, both for oneself and for one's people, as well as for one's oppressor?

Through our groundedness in our own spiritual traditions, according to Mottinger, we are each called to exhort—to call to task those who use authority and privilege to foster dissonance and disharmony in the world; to prophesy—to announce consequences for unjust actions and to proclaim an image of what can be if we allow the Spirit to breathe freely through us; to minister—to tend to the wounded of body and spirit, to care for the needy, the forgotten, the disenfranchised, to lead the community in celebration; and to teach—to show people new ways of living and being in relationship with our God, each other, and this world we deeply love.

How does this translate into the world of commerce? Business, labor, and political leaders who seek areas of agreement regarding plant locations, wages, use of resources, or care for the environment, are reducing dissonance. Consumers who seek legal and political redress for faulty and unsafe products are announcing consequences for illegal or unethical business practices. Owners of companies who operate in ways that are socially, economically and politically just to their workers, their investors, their community, and all other stakeholders, and who do so in ways that honor the earth and its biosphere, are already proclaiming their image of what can be. Corporate sponsorship of community programs addressing illiteracy, hunger, homelessness, and recreation all reflect a commitment to care for and to minister to those with needs. Those companies, who risk cooperating and partnering with others for the good of the corporation and the community, model new ways of living and being with others in this world. All this is gift of the Spirit.

Grounded in spirituality, let us return to the places of our work with a renewed respect for each other and a renewed commitment to use resources sparingly, manufacture products safely, treat workers and the communities in which they reside justly, engage in the process of decision making openly, distribute wealth equitably, and resolve disputes peacefully.

## Rejoicing In The Transforming Process

We have heard the call for a renewed definition of power, authority, and leadership. We have explored the multiple dimensions of spiritual power. We have seen that a foundation for spiritual power is based upon an articulated vision of the kind of society which will best meet the needs of all of humanity as lived out in the diverse places we each call home. We have seen how people from across the globe are reclaiming power for what it rightfully is—Potential. We have identified those qualities necessary for the effective expression of a power which will bond us to each other as together we face the challenges of everyday and everywhere life.

We have listened to the voices of women who call for the empowerment of people, the formation of community, and the transformation of society. Now, we face what Marjorie Tuite called "The Burden of Knowing." Once we are conscious of the pain in the world, and know the possibilities for wholeness, we must choose. Knowing that the Spirit Who dwells within unites each to the other, will we chose, along with Marta Benavides' mother, "to care and act on behalf of life, to keep people alive"? Grounded in the Spirit, we shape a community with others, one where each person in community can call upon a deeply grounded spirituality to empower us to choose wisely and to sustain commitment when energy saps. Here in this life-giving place called community, the full range of human emotions and human experiences will be honored and treasured.

Let us join that community of people who sees the sacredness and connectedness of all of life, those who are already using their own spiritual power to heal and transform a hurting world. Let us join in the process of transforming our own world—our world of family and neighborhood, and our world of work—our own trouble spots of the world. Let us join with others in the struggle to heal the world still in pain. Let us embrace the possibilities of a world at peace. Remembering our spiritual connections, let us celebrate our vision and our actions in song and dance. Let us rejoice!

Part Four

# WORK—A JOURNEY OF SELF-DISCOVERY

Chapter 9
**Responding To The Call Of The Soul**
Rae Thompson

Chapter 10
**Money—A Unique Tool For Self-Discovery**
David Schwerin

Chapter 11
**Organizational Soulwork: Creating Profit**
Margaret Molinari

Chapter 12
**Searching For Home In The Marketplace**
Sajeela Moskowitz Ramsey

Chapter 13
**Succeeding From The Inside Out**
Barbara and Randy Powers

**Rae Thompson** is a writer, editor, and consultant. Her company, Heartswork, is founded upon her belief that organizational change occurs one person at a time, and that true transformation begins with the change agent. She has 25 years of experience designing, developing, and documenting innovative programs related to organizational change. She specializes in promoting "conscious communication," creating written materials and designing seminars that synthesize and translate concepts into practical methods and personal experiences.

Thompson's formal education is in applied psychology and organization development. She is the cofounder of Organizational Mastery, a systematic approach for creating and sustaining healthy productive companies and empowering the individuals within those companies. Her clients include the Smithsonian Institution, National Institutes of Health, Detroit Edison Company, EARTH Day USA, Unity Church, Professional Resources, Inc., and Integrated Human Dynamics.

# 9

# Responding To The Call Of The Soul

## Rae Thompson

Finding the right work is like discovering your
own soul in the world.
　　　　　　—Thomas Moore, *Care of the Soul*

On December 31, 1992, I walked away from my secure
middle management position at a well-known institution. My
job had been to build partnerships and identify common ground
among departments with diverse interests. Each measure of
my success occurred in the context of struggle, characterized
by the fierce determination of many key players to preserve
their autonomy at the expense of the whole organization. After
eight years, I felt exhausted by their resistance, and knew that
my resistance only exacerbated the tension we all experienced.
I also knew something was missing. For two years prior to
leaving I had felt increasingly unfulfilled at work. My behavior
began to change. I smiled less, hesitated to express myself
openly, and took less initiative to promote programs in which I
believed. My sense of who I truly was and the person I had
become at work were out of sync. I had begun to separate my
"life" from my work.

## First Response

As I made my transition to self-employment, I was determined to create a business that allowed, even depended upon,
my expression of my "whole self," no holding back. Filled with a
sense of adventure and the anticipation of destiny fulfilling itself,
I started my own consulting business. My mission was to work
with organizations that invited change, practiced partnership,
and valued personal empowerment. With a friend and colleague,
I co-created Organizational Mastery, a systematic method for
facilitating and sustaining healthy productive organizations. We
trained others in OM and consulted with small companies, large
government agencies, and private corporations. While I enjoyed
seeing the positive results of my work, there was still something
missing, out of sync. I continued to struggle. At times I overlooked
my own sense of purpose, or relied on clients and colleagues to
tell me how well I was doing. Searching for what seemed to elude
me, I began to nurture the "still small voice" within.

Through networking, I met many people who had left
government organizations and even thriving companies to
become self-employed. Others had been down-sized, right-
sized, merged, or reorganized out of their jobs. Reevaluating
what we chose to do with our lives, many of us were finding out
who we truly were in the process. I came to believe that the
impetus driving many of us was the desire to be authentic, to
behave in our work with integrity. Compelled to reassess our
cultural norms, learned behaviors, attitudes and beliefs, we
were finding what was true for us personally. We longed to
satisfy a deep desire to feel connected—first with ourselves,
then with others, and ultimately with something much bigger
than ourselves. We were drawn to find what was missing in our
lives and to make ourselves whole. Integrating our personal
and professional lives, we were reshaping our personal values
and applying them in our work. Being anything other than our
authentic complete selves depleted us, and we demanded to be
treated with dignity as whole persons in our jobs, to express
our feelings, feel fulfilled, and have meaning in our work.

## An Urgent Message

With the unexpected death of my father in November
1994, I had the opportunity to discover what was missing in my

work. Sitting at his bedside after his open heart surgery, I felt his frustration at not being able to talk because of the tubes in his throat, and watched him labor for each breath, even with the help of a respirator. I saw both fear and love in his eyes at different times: fear, when he spelled out "it's scary" on a paper where I had written the alphabet to help him communicate; love, when he silently formed the words "I love you" with his lips. Seeing and feeling a lot of love in those last days with him, I began to sense there was a message for me in this experience. Sharing his pain, I knew I did not want to face my death having something to say that I could not communicate or that remained unsaid. I wanted to know that I had done something fulfilling with my life; that I had not held back...my desires, my talents, my willingness to achieve my dreams. I believe my father was at peace when he passed away. He had loved life; was always laughing, enjoying his friends, talking with people he had just met, being radiantly alive. He shared as much of himself as he was able to share.

Learning to receive my father's nonverbal communication helped me strengthen my connection to my own voice within. Experiencing the depths of my grief for him opened up vast new territory for me and gave me an expanded awareness of myself. In the ensuing weeks and months, I asked myself, "Am I sharing as much of me as I can? Am I willing to risk failure or rejection to speak my truths, to do what my heart would have me do? What is in my heart? What would make my work and my life fulfilling? What's missing?" Answers to these questions came from deep within me, faintly at first, and then with increasing power.

I discovered that what had been missing in my work was my own fully authentic response to my soul and my willingness to completely trust what I knew from within. At that time, my soul captured my imagination and promised to fulfill my heart's desires if I would listen to and follow its guidance. My soul helped me learn that I felt fully alive when I let myself feel and express my emotions. I recognized that my struggle came, in part, from working with clients who fought against their own souls' calling, as I had. I understood the importance of accepting work with clients I trusted and with whom it was easy to trust myself, i.e., clients who nourished their own souls. My soul infused me with passion for writing and teaching others to communicate their passions. I knew that I would write about my own experiences and the work of others who were helping to transform businesses into healthy soul-filled places of work. My soul also revealed my deep-seated fears of exposing myself, being outcast, having nothing worthwhile to say. It was the sense of urgency to fully express myself that surfaced during my farewell to my father that compelled me to face my fears and move forward.

## Fine Tuning: An Ongoing Process

I put my consulting partnership on hold and refocused my business on writing, editing, and communication-related consulting. By being aware of and taking responsibility for expressing my true self, I believed I was becoming my soul's proprietor. I claimed ownership of my soul and accepted responsibility for its care. Then I wondered whether I could actually own my soul. Perhaps the greater truth was that I was beginning to accept my soul's ownership of me. Finally, I realized that neither was true. My experience was not about ownership. It was about reuniting with something meaningful and fulfilling that lived deep within me, as well as beyond me. By listening and responding to my soul, I was satisfying my desire to be authentic.

## Personal Insights And Observations

As I continue to explore and refine my own choices about my life's work, it is helpful to contemplate what I have learned so far, and to consider how my experience may reflect what is happening in businesses and organizations nationwide. Based on my personal process, research, and work with clients, I have distilled the following insights and observations:

1. **It is increasingly difficult to ignore my soul's call to renew itself.** Five years ago, I experienced my soul's urging as a feeling of uneasiness and a vague sense that I would leave my job. In the first years of my business, I developed a heightened sensitivity to what felt "right" and what truly engaged me. Since making a commitment to write, I have had strong indications of being on the right or wrong track. For example, I recently agreed to meet with a potential client, even though the proposed consulting work would have conflicted with my newly received guidance. On the flight out of town, I became physically ill with all the symptoms of the flu. The meeting went badly. When I returned to my writing 24 hours later, I suddenly and completely "recovered." Within days, I received notice that my potential client was

choosing to work with another consultant. I noticed that as I learned to pay attention and accept direction from within, "magic" did happen. Within six months of shifting my business focus, I submitted an essay for this book, began writing a book based on OM, received two client contracts for writing with a third in the works, and completed the editing of a book I had been collaborating on for five years.

2. **As I respond to my soul's calling, I begin to shift the way I experience the world.** In my old way of thinking, I valued having security more than following my dreams, and believed that a steady job gave me control of my life. In business for myself, I realized that my security came from being aligned with my true self, and acting with integrity in who I was and what I did. My control, or power, came from within me. In my old consciousness, I believed that there were only so many jobs and limited money, so I needed to be first, beat out somebody else, and accumulate a lot of things to prove my success. As my thinking shifted, I learned to balance this "scarcity" view with one of abundance, a perspective which, for me, required (and still requires) considerable trust. Additionally, I began to balance logic and ideas with intuition and feelings, and to replace my need to know every detail in advance with faith in the process and myself. I practiced being in the flow of my life.

As I reviewed and changed my assumptions, beliefs, and attitudes, I experienced a greater ease in my life; a sense of fulfillment and contentment that was new for me. For example, early in my consulting business, I had felt vulnerable each time I presented myself to potential clients. My ideas and approaches often contradicted traditional business practices, and I witnessed the significant investment in the status quo held by some leaders and managers. So, I looked closely at my own "status quo." I had always seen myself as the outsider, encountering resistance on a mission to transform others. I was attempting to sell them something outside myself, an approach or technique. When I became aligned with who I truly was, I could believe that mutually fulfilling partnerships with clients were possible. For the first time I knew what it felt like to feel fulfilled because I was fulfilling myself from within. When I acted from my new beliefs, and when I acknowledged and valued my true self, I began to attract clients who were right for me and for whom I was well-suited. As I restructured my assumptions and beliefs about

| | |
|---|---|
| PARADIGM | The filter of assumptions through which we experience our world and define our reality. |
| PARADIGM SHIFT | The transfer or change from viewing the world based on one set of assumptions to viewing the world based on another set of assumptions; having a paradigm shift implies having an old paradigm and a new paradigm. |

what was real, my actual experience of the world changed.

3. **New paradigm values are gaining momentum and bringing balance and wholeness to businesses and organizations.** I soon discovered that many of my friends and colleagues were experiencing similar paradigm shifts in their lives and organizations. Some of my clients had also recognized what did not work in their old paradigm, and were making conscious choices to embrace new paradigm values. I had been fascinated for years by the concept of paradigms. Preparing for our OM training in 1993, I synthesized my understanding of old and new paradigm characteristics and assumptions in the context of organizations.

**Example 1.** Businesses operating in the old paradigm are characterized by competition and the scarcity model. There is never enough. Someone has to lose. Employees are treated as separate entities at work, unconnected to anything larger, functioning in their area of expertise, and often kept in a vacuum, receiving minimal information at the discretion of someone with power over them. Individual talents and objectives are often overridden for the sake of the company. People strive to become the best, fittest, or most successful in the context of their specific business and job assignment. Employees at all levels are overworked and overtired, often sacrificing their health, marriages, and families for the sake of profit.

**Example 2.** Businesses operating in the new
paradigm emphasize the importance of relationships and reverence for the interconnectedness
of all life. They focus on cooperation and collaboration, drawing on the model of abundance and
creating ways for each player to win. The playing
field is expanded and includes families, communities, and the environment. Employees are
viewed as whole beings with multifaceted lives
and talents and are supported in developing to
their full potential. Power over others is replaced
by shared power and power from within. In the
new paradigm, businesses honor their own
members and each other, and value the open
flow of information, personal feelings, and intuition.

Reviewing my initial synthesis of old and new paradigm
characteristics, I recognized that even the distinctions of "old"
and "new" implied a dichotomy that was indicative of the old
paradigm, with its either/or perspective. I surmised that a
paradigm shift was not a pure transition from one distinct
condition to another. Rather it was (and is) the blending or
merging of the old and the new into a "integrative wholeness,"
a composite synthesis of each paradigm, woven together in a
way that reflects the whole and, by its very nature, brings
about balance and harmony. Each paradigm, in its own time,
contains essential elements required for successful businesses
and healthy lives. The objective is to integrate and balance the
two over time. I expected that few individuals and businesses
would achieve such balance easily. Most of us would likely find
our pendulum of experience swinging far into new paradigm
values. We would choose to place considerable emphasis on
characteristics such as cooperation, sustainable development,
and spiritual growth to offset the extreme effects of our long-
standing focus on the consciousness of the old paradigm's
competitiveness, unlimited expansion and material growth. I
redesigned the results of my synthesis into a continuum,
which better represented the relationship between the two
paradigms. An excerpt from my new synthesis is shown on the
following page.

| OLD PARADIGM | STATEMENT OF BELIEF | NEW PARADIGM |
|---|---|---|
| Competition; survival of fittest | ← LIFE EVOLVES BY → | Cooperation toward maturity of whole |
| Studying parts to understand whole; reductionism | ← PROBLEMS SOLVED BY → | Observing and experiencing relationships and patterns |
| Enemy | ← CHANGE IS → | Natural |
| Quantitative | ← WORTH IS → | Qualitative |
| Material growth | ← SUCCESS MEASURED BY → | Spiritual development and well-being |
| Unlimited expansion | ← IDEAL GROWTH AS → | Sustainable development |
| Scarcity | ← ECONOMICS OF → | Abundance |
| Exclusive by nature; *either/or* mentality | ← PERSPECTIVE IS → | Inclusive by nature; *and* mentality |
| Bestowed or earned by doing | ← HUMAN VALUE IS → | Intrinsic and inherent in being |
| Rational analysis | ← KNOWLEDGE COMES FROM → | Intuition |
| External; by control over | ← POWER IS → | Internal; through alignment with |
| Dominance and control; hierarchy network | ← RELATIONSHIPS ESTABLISHED THROUGH → | Equality and empowerment; |
| Exploited | ← NATURE IS → | Revered |
| Structure | ← ORGANIZATIONS EMPHASIZE → | Process and flow |
| Thoughts, ideas, concepts | ← BUSINESS VALUES EXPRESSION OF → | Feelings, emotions, experiences |

## Figure 1
## Continuum of Paradigm Assumptions And Characteristics

Those of us choosing to bring wholeness into our lives are reevaluating what is important to us and learning to act on it, and from it, with love. We are asking and answering tough questions for ourselves and our businesses. Where can I balance competition with cooperation? In what ways can I enhance the quality of my life? At what point does making money give way to my spiritual development and well-being? What can I do personally to be inclusive, empower others, and express my deepest feelings? Are these values important to me? What am I willing to do to demonstrate my commitment to these values?

4. **The transformation, or paradigm shift, taking place in many businesses and organizations is related to the search for "soul" undertaken by individual members.** In *Care of the Soul*, Thomas Moore says that soul is the dimension of our experience of life and ourselves, and that soul displays relatedness, heart, and personal substance. My experience of the call of my soul was filled with raw emotion, intuitive guidance, strong images, my recognition of lifelong patterns, and opportunities to experience the natural flow of my life. In response, I drew from and built upon loving relationships and strived to remain aligned with my soul's purpose. As I became increasingly familiar with my soul, it unveiled its qualities, and I noted their strong resemblance to the characteristics associated with the new paradigm. I wondered if our collective identification of old and new paradigms was a recognition of our desire for soul? Could it be that the old paradigm ignored or suppressed the soul? Was it possible that the characteristics ascribed to the new paradigm were indicative of our longing for the qualities of soul? By making paradigm shifts in our workplaces and business activities, creating work that fulfilled and satisfied our desires to be authentic and act with integrity, were we truly responding to the call of our souls?

Looking now at what many of my colleagues and I were (and are) seeking in our lives and our work, I see many of the characteristics ascribed to soul. I believe that the integration of the new paradigm qualities of soul into the workplace is required for businesses to prosper and thrive, now and in the years to come. The depths of our passions are being called forth to compensate and balance the heights attained by our intellect. Intuition is being summoned from within to create harmony with our well-developed rational thinking capabilities. Focus on the quality of our lives is gaining momentum over emphasis on how many and how much. We can call this transformative process spirituality, religion, personal empowerment, or integrative wholeness. Whatever its name, what transforms our work and our lives is each of us coming into alignment with our true self; being in relationship with each other and revering all life; and acting from our new "soul" consciousness in our families, businesses, and communities.

5. **Making a paradigm shift requires imagination, commitment, and compassion.** Getting there from here is not always easy. Old paradigm attitudes and behaviors tend to beget more of the same. Einstein said, "The world will not evolve past its current crisis by using the same thinking that created the situation." Can a model for the emerging paradigm be devised by old paradigm consciousness? Most likely, no. In my experience a true paradigm shift requires a leap of faith into what is unknown to my intellect. It requires imagination and my full belief in the experience I imagine. My inspiration for imagining came from studying the collected works of Neville, a native of Barbados whose insights about the power of imagination were popularized during the second quarter of this century. My personal and professional application of imagination came from my OM co-founder Robert Stevens, who developed a structured imagination process, based, in part, on the work of Neville. We integrated this powerful process in each stage of our work. We used it to identify the future desired by our clients and to help them, and us, recognize when we were acting out of the consciousness of the "old" and "new" paradigms.

> The ideal you seek and hope to attain will not
> manifest itself, will not be realized by you, until
> you have imagined that you are already that ideal.
> —Neville, *The Power of Awareness*

As businesses navigate their passage into the emerging paradigm, I believe it is essential that they create ways to involve employees in vision or imagination sessions of their desired future. Giving employees the opportunity to align their personal goals and values with those of the company helps ensure its long-term success. Each member can be asked, "What are your desired outcomes for this organization? What do you personally choose to have, to do, to be?" Together, employees and management can define the corporate "soul" that provides them with whole-ness, meaning, and fulfillment.

Even with the use of imagination, making a true paradigm shift requires a continual recommitment to embody the con-sciousness, (beliefs, assumptions, and behaviors) that we choose. For me, making a shift also requires a commitment to strengthen both my ability to hear my soul's call and the authenticity or purity of my response to that call. The message of my soul is always available. Sometimes I hear it plainly and respond auto-matically, while sometimes I hear it and fail to respond. When I focus on what is outside of me, the "static" interferes completely with the voice of my soul. When I remain committed to the voice within me, I open the channel of communication.

In businesses and organizations, each executive and em-ployee has the opportunity to open up channels of communica-tion, first within themselves and then with each other. When we are willing to share what is true for us personally, we begin to make connections with others who are finding and acting from their souls' purpose. We begin to embrace our whole selves, our feelings and our passions, and become genuine with each other. We begin to feel fully alive and fulfilled.

While our continued commitment is essential to changing our lives, it does not guarantee that we will always follow through as we desire. As humans, we make mistakes and experience doubts. Achieving a true paradigm shift requires having compas-sion for ourselves and each other as we learn to listen consistently and respond with integrity to the messages of our souls. Both the new paradigm and the soul demand patience and trust in the process. In touch with my soul, I experienced a full range of emotions, from the exhilaration of finding my soul's purpose to the grief of recognizing that I had failed to fully or persistently follow its path. As I am compassionate with myself, I develop a growing capacity to love and feel compassion for others. It is imperative for leaders in businesses and organizations moving into the new paradigm to nurture their compassion for the unfolding of individual souls, and for the earth. By trusting the timing and rhythm of the soul, each of us can find the timing and rhythm of our lives and our work.

## Answering The Call

I believe it is time for us to understand and respond to our souls' urgings. It is time to recognize our interdependence as humans on this planet and our connection with all life, a paramount message of the new paradigm. Listening and responding to the call of our own souls is the first step in reestablishing connection with others and our environment. We can then acknowledge that in our global economy, when anyone loses, we all lose. Such new awareness can appear to shut down the game of competitive commerce. Or it can spur us on to face and meet the challenges of our times. I believe we can honor our true selves, our souls, in our work. We can make it "good business" to activate the qualities of soul, such as spiritual growth, intuition, and authenticity, in ourselves, our employees and our clients. If soul is the true essence of life and we do anything other than cultivate that essence, for ourselves and in business, we are shutting the door on our own evolution.

**David A. Schwerin** began his investment career in 1968 and founded D J Investment Advisors Inc. in 1976, where he currently serves as president. He has had numerous articles published, has given expert witness testimony and has been widely quoted in the press. Schwerin has an MBA in finance, a PhD in religious studies, and has taught economics on the college level.

For the past few years he has been doing research, in conjunction with a book he is writing, on the groundbreaking changes occurring in the business world. As a student of the "Perennial Philosophy" for over 25 years, he sees the teachings of ageless wisdom forming a cornerstone for many of the transformative shifts taking hold in the workplace. This article is a chapter from his forthcoming book.

# 10

# Money—A Unique Tool For Self-Discovery

## David A. Schwerin

When coinage was first invented it was usually administered by the priestly class. The earliest coins often bore a religious symbol on one side and a secular symbol on the other. Money was intended to facilitate human interactions in the material world, while helping man remember his dependence on God and the laws of nature. Today, money has too frequently become one-sided; a symbol for power, security and control. As such it has value almost exclusively on the material level. When the desire for financial independence grows excessive, it can give rise to the illusion of self-sufficiency and a belief in the primacy of money's power. While the takeover binge of the 1980s provided innumerable examples of how excessive greed and lust for power eventually led to much disillusionment and despair, it does not have to be that way. In fact, money can serve a very useful purpose, not only as a medium of exchange, but as an instrument for enlightenment as well. To quote philosopher Jacob Needleman:

> Money in the modern era is a purely secular force,
> reflecting the lower nature of man. Cut off from
> any relation to spiritual aspiration, it has become
> the most obvious example of a fire raging out of
> control. Our challenge is to bring money back to
> the place where it belongs in human life....And

> that place is secondary. Our aim is to understand
> what it means to make money *secondary* in life. As
> a principal representative of the lower nature, the
> outward, physical body of man, money must
> become secondary, as the body must become
> secondary....And if money is to be secondary in our
> lives, it can only mean that money serve the aim of
> self-knowledge.

I have been fortunate to have been professionally involved in the business of managing money for a period spanning four decades. While not all experiences have been pleasant or fruitful, they have been enormously helpful in clarifying a number of important issues about life's most fundamental questions. The securities markets represent the hopes and fears, loves and hates of a vast cross-section of humanity; it evokes the full gamut of emotional reactions. Dealing with money forces one to come to grips with aspects of the self that are too often avoided.

## If Anyone Really Knows He Can't Tell

Needleman's admonition that the key to enlightenment is to "know thyself" is but an echo of Ageless Wisdom, the perennial philosophy of the sages. No one else can answer the really important questions. It is a task we each must undertake by ourselves. The best technique for obtaining valuable insights is self-observation. This simply means paying close attention to everything; being open-minded, curious, and detached. In other words, one must make a commitment to observe and remember everything that occurs regardless of one's beliefs, preferences or fears. It is hard to do and takes a great deal of practice. Because the investment business provides instant feedback about the judgments one is constantly required to make, the person who analyzes his or her emotions and personality quirks carefully and objectively has a much better chance of reducing future mistakes. While other professions also provide opportunities for mistakes, it is unlikely the feedback is as instantaneous or as frequent as it is in the goldfish bowl environment of the investment business. To quote Edward C. Johnson II, one of the deans of Wall Street and the long-time head of the Fidelity mutual fund complex:

> Because the conscious and subconscious human
> mind is so vast—the stock market, by the way, is

just a bunch of minds—that there is no science, no IBM machine, no anything of that sort, that can tame it. What this means to us in practical affairs is that if we are able to do the thing that Americans find very hard to do—that is, *understand ourselves* (emphasis added) to some degree—we have a chance of becoming effective stock operators. That is a hard thing and a rare thing.

## To Err Is Human; To Be Conscious Divine

It does not take long for anyone involved in the investment world to realize they are going to make an embarrassingly large number of errors. While money managers are generally rational, well educated and motivated, they are affected by the same emotional hang-ups and ego attachments that afflict most of humanity. According to an article by Charles D. Ellis, the author of numerous books on finance and investing:

> Most of the people in the investment business are "winners" who have won all their lives by being bright, articulate, disciplined, and willing to work hard. They are so accustomed to succeeding by trying harder and are so used to believing that failure to succeed is the failure's own fault that they may take it personally when they see that the average professionally managed fund cannot keep pace with the market any more than John Henry could beat the steam drill.

More specifically, Jeffrey Shames, who has supervised portfolio managers for large financial institutions, was quoted in *Investor's Daily* as saying:

> It's my job to foster an environment where people are able to make mistakes. Anybody who's not making mistakes is not doing his job. Even if you're great at picking stocks, you're still going to be wrong four times out of ten. You have to be able to adjust to the emotional aspects of being wrong. When you pick losers, it affects your mood. It's a humbling job.

Looking back, this profession, with its frequent opportunities for making mistakes, is ideal for learning some of life's most important lessons. As a portfolio manager, I discovered more about myself from a few investments that did embarrassingly poorly than from all of my correct decisions combined. When humbled one is forced to look deeply inside to understand what motivated his decision and why the choice did not turn out as expected. Perhaps too much faith was put in another person's analysis or judgment. If so, confidence may be enhanced to the point where greater reliance is placed on one's own innate ability. Or perhaps the decision was based on what was popular at the time. Such realization may give one courage to take a more skeptical view about whatever the majority believes. Alternatively, it may have been a failure to give adequate consideration to the changes taking place in a particular company, industry, or sector of the economy. The more important a concept of reality is to someone's self-esteem and sense of worth, the more tenacious he or she will be in holding to the old idea and the greater the rejection of evidence that conflicts with his current belief system. Acknowledging fallibility, one becomes more accepting of the mistakes of others. Compassion for the human predicament, wherein all imperfect souls are here to learn their lessons, is greatly enhanced.

Our greatest progress is made under the prodding of pain and discomfort. Ageless Wisdom tells us that success and failure are two sides of the same coin; i.e., instructive experiences. Failure is by far the more effective for ensuring receptivity to new insights and differing points of view. Thus mistakes help to deflate the ego, enhance appreciation for the perfection of imperfection, and redouble the effort made in searching for the meaning of life's experiences.

## All Generalizations Are False
## Except This One

Making mistakes may be inevitable, but there is nothing wrong with trying to minimize their frequency. Doing so sharpens our powers of discrimination. Life forces each of us to make choices everyday, providing the opportunity to hone reasoning and intuitive faculties and, thereby, make choices that are in harmony with our very distinct personalities and the universal laws of nature. When one makes choices where the outcome is at risk, one learns one's capacities and, over time, how to expand them. Success in risk taking enriches self confidence and failure teaches humility and discrimination, producing a win-win situation. Certainly, the money management profession provides ample opportunities for risk taking.

Before undertaking any action where the outcome is unknown, it is wise to ascertain one's specific tolerance for risk. In the financial sphere, this means scrutinizing financial and psychological limitations. Does one prefer to eat well or sleep well? This is not as easy a decision as it sounds since the emotions of greed and fear cloud most investors' perceptions. Many times, clients who come to us with the unequivocal desire to minimize risk will want to change their objectives and invest more aggressively when the investment climate has been unusually hospitable for a period of time. Assuming their circumstances have not changed, we discourage any deviation from their plan as it is not only counter to their original, more dispassionately determined desires but, more times than not, the wrong time to be taking increased risks. In fact, this has proven to be an excellent guide to an impending change in market direction; investors inevitably want to buy at market tops and sell when their securities have fared poorly, that is, at or near lows. It is amazing how reasonable people, who buy as many of their material goods as possible on sale, want to buy securities at full price and shy away from purchasing them when they are at a discount to their intrinsic value. Anyone who does not have the financial capacity and emotional stability to maintain a long-term perspective should be using only the safest of investments and not deviating from this course. Investors must constantly guard against getting caught up in the herd mentality of the mass mind. If one does not know what makes him or her tick or is too easily swayed by popular opinion, the stock market is an expensive place to learn. The problems encountered in the investment business require one to continually fine tune their reasoning ability and become receptive to intuitive or gut feelings and then find the proper balance between the two.

A specific example that shows how I applied and misapplied some of these concepts may be helpful. Interest rates reached far into double digits in the inflation-ridden early 1980s, then declined into the early 1990s, falling, in 1993, to well less than half their former peak. This was not a favorable development for those individuals who are dependent on their investment income, particularly those who imprudently based their standard of living on unsustainably high interest rates. As investments matured, or were called away by the issuer, the money had to be reinvested at much lower rates of return. In many cases, this required an adjustment in spending patterns or, at a minimum, less of a cushion for emergencies. This is a difficult situation for a money manager, who, while counseling clients against increasingly un-realistic income expectations, is nevertheless, a handy scapegoat. In an attempt to mitigate the situation, we were forced to look for investment alternatives that would minimize any loss of income without sacrificing quality. While we have learned the hard way that there is no free lunch, we believed that higher-yielding mortgage backed bonds were a reasonable place to invest such income-oriented funds. These securities were considered to be of very high quality and the interest rates available at that time exceeded those of similar quality bonds by several percentage points. The one drawback was that the life of these bonds was uncertain and could vary from a relatively short period of time to as long as thirty years. The determining factor was the speed at which the underlying mortgages were paid off; this in turn a function of where interest rates would settle in the ensuing years. In an attempt to be conservative, we assumed rates would increase moderately over the next several years and the mortgage paydowns would, therefore, slow down. Under what we believed to be very reasonable assumptions, the bonds we were buying were likely to provide a superior return relative to alternative securities of the same quality and duration. The likelihood that we were not conservative enough in our assumptions was thought to be very small. The competitive global environment was ex-pected to keep inflation under control and the real rate of return of the bonds we purchased was historically attractive even if inflation moved somewhat higher than anticipated.

Despite what appeared to be a very rational evaluation of the situation, something bothered me about these investments. I could not figure out why I was uneasy but something was gnawing at me. Numerous hours were spent awake at night looking at all the possible things that could go wrong with our analysis. In less than a year, our miscalculation became obvious. Interest rates moved much higher than we, or most other econo-mists, had expected and considerably higher than the fundamen-tals justified. In fact, we experienced the worst bond market in 50 years. (As Mark Twain is alleged to have said, "The art of prophesy is very difficult, especially with respect to the future.")

Because of this rise in interest rates, the speed at which the underlying mortgages were paid off began to slow dramatically. Therefore, the maturity of the bonds we had purchased were assumed by the market to be much longer than previously expected and the market price dropped accordingly. Fortunately, we had avoided the more exotic and riskier securities that were projected, at the time, to provide higher returns than the mundane bonds we purchased. Being patient has turned out to be a correct course of action as the price of the bonds returned to about where they started, while the interest payments have provided good returns in the interim. There was an opportunity cost involved, however, as it would have been most advantageous to remain in very short-term investments until interest rates neared their peak and then buy longer term issues. As may be discerned from the last comment, I still have a perfectionist streak in me.

I am convinced that my intuition was trying to warn me that a major change in interest rates—one much greater than the reasoning side of my brain would have been able to accept given the data available—was about to take place. In a world characterized by a minimum of change analytic skills are quite satisfactory. But as Bennett W. Goodspeed, author of *The Tao Jones Averages*, says, "to deal with change, one has to rely on skills of the nonanalytic or intuitive mode." Significant changes can not be analyzed until after they occur. It is not easy, particularly for those in the scientifically-oriented Western culture, to rely on soft or partial information especially when such decisions require one to go out on a limb relative to the consensus. As discussed in a February 13, 1995, *Business Week* article entitled "Why Investors Stampede," people usually follow the behavior of their peers whether choosing a doctor, restaurant, or investment. If individuals learn that their contemporaries favor something, even when it is counter to their own opinion, they tend to go with the herd rationalizing that the majority must know what they are doing. This lemming-like behavior is understandable as it takes a great deal of self confidence to stand up to a wave of opposing opinion.

While arguably a generalization, I have repeatedly seen that if I had placed greater reliance on my intuition rather than my reason, I would have been better off in both the investment realm and the more significant arena of life.

## Don't Sweat The Small Stuff—
## It's All Small Stuff

Through the pursuit of worldly goals—using money as the prime facilitator—we experience emotions that range from exhilaration to depression. In fact, everything we think or do swings us to and fro around a central tendency or core. In this sense, the securities markets are a metaphor for life with prices continually moving from overvalued to undervalued as the levels of optimism and pessimism rise and fall. Those who can learn to lean against the wind, buying when blood is running in the streets and selling when euphoria is rampant have excellent long term results. Taking a position that is contrary to the majority's is usually successful; not only in the field of investing, but in most of our day-to-day activities. As mentioned above, this is not easy to do as the crowd tends to entice others to its way of thinking; mass opinion creates a snowball effect. In 1929, stocks had advanced for many years but the nearly universal opinion was that they would inevitably go higher. The 1929 financial panic illustrates the principle that when opinion becomes so one-sided, it is usually wrong. The same thing happened on a smaller scale in the 1980s as "everyone" was sure that real estate prices had nowhere to go but up. After all, "no one is making any more land" and prices had been going up for as long as most people cared to remember. Eventually the crowd is proven wrong and the experience that results from following the majority is not pleasant.

How does the majority view our current state of affairs? As widely reported in the press, our problems—crime, pollution, education, poverty and job security—seem overwhelming if not insoluble. Political corruption and incompetence make the situation appear even more desperate. As immense as our problems seem, they are not new with regard to either type or magnitude. An October 10, 1847 editorial in *Harper's* magazine described the situation as follows:

> It is a gloomy moment in the history of our country. Not in the lifetime of most men has there been so much grave and deep apprehension; never has the future seemed so incalculable as at this time. The domestic economic situation is in chaos. Our dollar is weak throughout the world. Prices are so high as to be utterly impossible. The political

cauldron seethes and bubbles with uncertainty.
Russia hangs, as usual, like a cloud, dark and
silent, upon the horizon. It is a solemn moment. Of
our troubles no man can see the end.

In fact, periods of adversity have always provided fertile
ground for planting seeds of renewal. Beneath the surface there
is, not only a growing awareness of our problems, but an increasing desire to get on with the task at hand. Once critical mass is
achieved—the hundredth monkey effect—our insurmountable
problems will be attacked and, in time, seem more like an exciting
challenge than a daunting crisis. To a professional money manager, who must keep on top of unfolding events worldwide, the
recognition of our interdependence is unassailable. As television,
computers, faxes, and wireless telephony imprint this awareness on all inhabitants of the globe, we will have to take
responsibility for the problems we have created if only because
their consequences affect everyone intimately and almost in-
stantaneously.

The Mexican financial crisis of 1994 points up the extent of
our interconnectedness. Most investors were caught by surprise
and securities markets from Brazil to Hong Kong were sent into a
tailspin. In today's global economy there are virtually no barriers
to the free flow of capital. The combined stock market capitaliza-
tion of Latin America, Asia, and Africa has grown from around
$100 billion ten years ago to over $2 trillion in 1995. Investors are
from all regions of the world and include private individuals,
many of whom invest through mutual funds, and institutional
investors. The latter are often managing the retirement funds of
not only the affluent but much less well off pensioners as well.
Thus when a crisis, real or imagined, develops, everyone is
affected regardless of nationality or ability to sustain loss. The
same holds true when lax pollution detection or enforcement
permits harmful emissions in the air or water. Neither geographical nor political borders are able to inhibit the free flow of
information or pollution.

Worn down by many years, if not incarnations, of excesses,
we are inexorably forced to focus our attention on our motives and
priorities as the pendulum swings from one extreme to the other.
In order to attain a semblance of equilibrium, we must determine
what it is that we truly want. After several decades of watching
how I, as well as hundreds of my clients, react to fluctuations in

the value of financial assets, it is quite clear that there is little correlation between the amount of money one has and one's sense of happiness or fulfillment. Some clients who live on the relatively modest income derived from assets of several hundred thousand dollars often lead a more carefree and meaningful life than those with ten times as much in assets and income. Likewise, those who have inherited enough money to enable them to indulge themselves with an multitude of material comforts are often in a constant state of turmoil and discontent. According to billionaire Ross Perot,

> The most overrated thing in the world is money.
> I've lived pretty much all across the economic
> spectrum, and I'm no more happy and no less
> happy than when my wife and I first drove into
> Dallas with everything we owned in the back of our
> car... Money is just the by-product of building a
> company that delivers a better service, serves its
> stockholders, and deals fairly with its employees.

When we find that material goods are not providing the peace and contentment we desire, we are forced to look elsewhere. While the external material world is the proper arena for learning our lessons, the internal, spiritual world is the place we find our ultimate satisfaction. Sir John Templeton, legendary pioneer of the Templeton Mutual Funds, was quoted as saying: "I think all careers are more successful and satisfying if you use spiritual principles. I can't think of a single exception."

As we move into the 21st Century, signs of renewal, based on the perennial philosophy of the ages that we are all truly interconnected and dependent, are appearing, raising the consciousness of many business organizations. Restructuring, downsizing, and outsourcing strategies force companies to rethink their objectives and become more discriminating with regard to their prejudices and priorities. Sometimes the new spirit descends from boardroom initiatives and sometimes it emanates from employees at the grass roots level. As someone whose job it is to speak to corporate executives and who regularly reads hundreds of annual reports and other corporate communications, it is clear to me that there is a transformation taking place. A few excerpts from a variety of sources are cited below:

> Diversity is much more than a program or legal
> requirement at HP; it is a business priority...a

culture that fosters respect for and appreciation of differences among people clearly helps teamwork, productivity and morale.

—1994 Annual Report,
Hewlett-Packard Corporation

To achieve a fulfilled contribution, we need a better understanding both of what motivates and concerns our employees at all levels and of their ambitions.

—1994 Annual Review, Unilever Group

We celebrate mistakes as part of the learning process.

—James Burge, Vice President
Motorola Corporation,
August 4, 1994, *The Wall Street Journal*

We continue to demand of ourselves the strongest possible commitment to environmental excellence in all our operations worldwide. This steadfast commitment is an absolute necessity as we strive to meet society's expectations, achieve our business goals and live up to our long-held values of environmental stewardship and good corporate citizenship.

—1993 Polaroid Corporation,
Report on the Environment

Right now I feel like I imagine pro basketball players feel—they're doing exactly what they like to do, and getting paid for it. That's the way it is at Saturn: People depending on one another. People pulling in the same direction. It feels good.

—Kevin Hawkins in *Powertrain Assembly*,
The 1994 Saturn Homecoming
Commemorative Magazine

While not yet pervasive, and in some cases motivated by public relations considerations, uplifting mission statements, reflecting values based on inclusion and cooperation, are beginning to be wholeheartedly incorporated into the workplace. The pattern is unmistakable and seemingly irreversible. As this trend continues, money will again be seen as a two-sided object with its material side taking an important but "small stuff" role to its much loftier function as an educating instrument and a reminder of man's spiritual needs and aspirations.

**Margaret Molinari**, PhD, is a change agent and organizational consultant. She is a people strategist with a long-standing interest in creating customer responsive, soul-filled organizations. This focus has emerged from her work with traditional bureaucracies seeking to renew themselves in the face of complex change and global competition. She began her consulting in union/management Quality of Work Life Projects in the early 1970s, and has worked with a wide range of systems including federal and state government, Cummins Engine Company, General Motors, family-owned companies, and education.

She received her PhD in Social-Clinical Psychology in 1977 from the Wright Institute in Berkeley, California. Her current consulting and writing focuses on developing organizational soul within a traditional workplace in order to create a strategic market advantage.

# 11

# Organizational Soulwork: Creating Profit

## Margaret Molinari

In the middle of a lecture at the workshop, a participant interrupted the presenter with a powerful, emotion laden rebuke. She said, "Unless you go out to nature, you will not be able to know spirit. You must go out to the woods, put your face down on the earth, taste the dirt, hear the song of nature and then you will know the rhythm of this earth and God!" I listened, fascinated by the intensity of the feeling. My first response was agreement—of course we must go to nature. But then I wondered what would happen if I interrupted the lecture and said, "Unless you go into a stamping plant you will not be able to know spirit. You must go into the factory, put your face down on the concrete floor, taste the oil, feel the pounding of the huge stamping machines as they shape metal, and then you will know the rhythm of this earth and God!" I could imagine the men in the white coats who would be called to come after me.

—Corporate Executive

Organizational soulwork by its very nature is profitable because it grows the individual and the system in both spirit and resources. This is a controversial statement in today's business and one that we are not accustomed to making. We generally do not mix the worlds of the sacred and the profane, preferring to say that they are necessarily separate and cannot be combined. We can understand a profit of spirit, of increased morale, of better employee relations, but increasing the bottom line? Can we dare to blend the worlds we have kept separate for so long? Or, more to the point—with the chaos and turbulence that we are experiencing in our organizations, can we dare to ignore the question?

Our times call for a return to a wholeness of spirit. We are more than the physical reality of our bodies or the cognitive skills of our minds. The same is true of our organizations. Each system has a purpose far deeper than simply as a collection of paid employees who work in concrete structures, shuffle papers or operate equipment. Rigid mechanical solutions that have solved some problems in the past are now causing us pain as they constrict our potential to grow and be profitable. Both individuals and organizations find themselves isolated and alienated from the intricate web of connection to everyone and everything else on this planet. Without recognizing that individuals have the ability to link themselves in spirit, we turn to the illusion of control and our organizations suffer from inflexible processes, systems, and structures. The bottom line suffers, our special heroes fall and Wall Street pushes for quick fixes and technocratic responses, sustaining a downward spiral.

Organizations are living, pulsating organic bodies that develop a soul of their own beyond mortar and concrete, above the bottom line and processed data, and despite the organization chart and company mission statement. Human systems are made up of people who come together for some purpose. In business it is making a profit through providing some product or service for a satisfied customer. Our paradigm is changing: Our systems have a living soul that we must nurture. This soul is sized to the dimensions of the system, no matter how big it may become, no matter how complex its work, no matter how much control we would like to have.

We call soul that indefinable quality that makes a person whole, that brings us nearer to wisdom. Soul links each individual to the larger circle of spirit to give meaning and coherence to life. Traditionally we have acknowledged that individuals have souls and each spiritual path defines the process to its development and fulfillment. To say that an organization or institution has a soul beyond its technology, profit and loss, and production system, recognizes the subtlety and dynamism of living systems. It is the strongest tool that we have to respond to the paradoxes and complexities of our times.

In his 1989 book *Managing as a Performing Art*, Peter Vaill aptly uses the phrase "permanent white water" to describe today's business experience. This certainly gives us a visceral image of what our mechanical institutions are confronting. Since he published the phrase, the complexity has multiplied itself and it may now be too simple an image.

Picture a boat in white water: You are not familiar with the river since its rock-bed and shape changes every time a boat navigates it. So you cannot go to anyone else for advice. The equipment you use is new. Even the crew may be "virtual" because people are constantly moving around the organization for development and promotion.

You are left with only one fact that you can depend on: yourself with all of your strengths and weaknesses. Self-knowledge allows you to develop the technical and social skills needed to create a team to respond instantly to any problem. It doesn't matter whether you are the captain or a crew member, because each person in the boat is a leader and plays a vital role. You can help your team function as an integrated whole in order to discover a way through the white water. You and your team are constantly adjusting your actions based on what you observe and experience in the immediate present.

When you don't make it, you start over again the next day, using what you have learned. With today's experience you set up new responses. This is the basis of your operations. Everything else changes all of the time. The crew must learn to act, as Kathy Dannemiller states, with many hands and many feet, yet one heart and one head in supercharged water turbulence. It must develop a soul.

The leaders who can navigate these waters are embarking on the spiritual journey of the hero. It is every bit as soul-filled, harrowing, dramatic, and real as any ancient story. Hundreds of cultures tell the universal tale of the Hero's Journey where the individual is called to depths of the underworld, struggles with the dark night of the soul, learns from the inner realms, and returns to the ordinary world to share and implement the new awareness while waiting for the next call. And like ancient sagas, each person is called to the path, no matter their role, their level within society, or their occupation. We are all called to the Hero's Journey because the stakes are high—we can no longer afford "special" heroes to tell us what to do. We are all heroes and heroines, called to do organizational soul work in order to survive and prosper.

The core dynamic is recognizing that everything that occurs is an important piece of information. Each scenario is integrated into a larger pattern. When we ask the question of how something is integrated, it is possible to find the answer. If we don't ask we will not find the soul linkages and patterns that provide the needed data and understanding. It is the role of leadership to find and navigate the patterns that will bring about the purpose of the system. Leaders are the pattern makers and pattern keepers of our organizations.

## Pattern Makers And Pattern Keepers

Why patterns? Large systems are like the proverbial elephant that is touched by three blind men at the same time. Each thinks that he knows what an elephant is like from a limited perspective and generalizes to the whole from the snake-like tail, the wall-like side, and the tree-like trunk. Each person experiences something different because the size allows only a limited perspective from one spot. What is not told in the story is that the blind man can sense the enormous size, can smell the distinctive odor, can touch the quality of the skin, can feel its life force and heart beat, and can hear the sounds made by the animal. Although many things are different, many things are the same no matter what your perspective. The task in modern organizations is very similar. We are all blind when it comes to the fuller picture of a very large system. We can compensate for our limited sight by sitting down and discussing our experience of the elephant with each other.

Only when we take the time to combine all of our sense experiences, all of our intuitive observations, all of our technical training, all of our kinesthetic knowledge, all of what we can possibly pull together as aware and conscious human beings, will we begin to understand this creature called an elephant. It is then that we will be able to get the best picture possible. It won't ever be a full picture that we can hold on to because it is constantly changing. There are many ways in which the analogy of being blind is appropriate to the current leadership situation. An individual cannot see what is going on in our organizations, especially our very large ones. We cannot be everywhere at once. We can't know every person. Our leaders are lonely and isolated because of the size and nature of their role. We are not bright enough to carry all the information in our heads, no matter our cognitive abilities. We are not powerful enough to control everything as systems get bigger. Frequently we are not well versed in weaving our five sense data with the many expanding senses of spirit and intuition. It is almost as if we were recently blinded, and haven't yet developed other skills to compensate for our loss. Our old ways did work until yesterday and sometimes they still work today—but they don't always work.

Chaos theory has indicated that the varying scope of fractal patterns is key to understanding what appears random. We can find the patterns, repeatable and remarkably consistent, throughout a system if we keep in mind that they will be distinctive at each level or slice. Since we know that this is how a system operates, leadership can begin to manage what seems uncontrollable with the very same knowledge: we can invent and implement the patterns that we want.

## The Hero's Journey

Let us look at four guideposts for developing soul in an organization. They give us clues to existing and needed patterns. The Hero's Journey can begin with a crisis in any one of them, touching off a round of learning where each aspect of the entire spiral is made clearer. Because they are inextricably woven together, there is no "right" first question or place to begin, only the assurance that when a paradox, shadow or contradiction emerges, it is "right" to follow it in its natural cycle. It spirals onward, continuously deepening our understanding and widening our view.

### Guidepost #1: From Vision To Purpose

We have developed what I call a corporate icon—
Through people we design, manufacture, engineer,
and service our product for customer satisfaction.
The planners are uncomfortable with this, talking

> about machines and dollars. All of that is impor-
> tant but it is only achieved through people. A
> leader has to be focused on people and then the
> rest comes. I've found that when you name the
> task first and let people play around with it, you
> can eventually ask how it is going to get done.
> People do it. The group can then focus on the
> people challenges to getting the task done. You
> avoid the resistance to talking about soul as fuzzy.
> You let people get grease under their nails first
> where they are comfortable, and then you talk
> about how people do it. It works and comes out
> fabulous.
>
> —Corporate Financial Executive

Shaping a vision is a crucial role of leadership. It creates the framework for what is possible within the organization. A vision is a snapshot showing how things will look at some future point. A vision is one depiction demonstrating the core purpose of an organization. Purpose is something that gets deeper—closer to soul—as it is made more explicit. It captures the spirit or soul reason for what we do in this world.

The call to the Hero's Journey from visionary purpose often focuses on a discrepancy between intention and action. We aren't doing what we think we are doing or what we want to do. Or we are doing what satisfies us as individuals and not what the organization needs. This discrepancy may emerge in the form of surprising customer feedback, lower quality than was predicted, or an inability to get a new product out on time. The "right answers" that allowed us to be successful before are not providing the results that we currently need. We are like an orchestra of brilliant solo performers who create only mediocre music together because each plays his own interpretation of the music. We have come to accept "right answers" in different arenas that are contradictory and can cancel each other out or confuse. There is no commonly held visionary purpose which clarifies and helps us align our own individual purpose.

## Guidepost #2: From Relationship To SpiritWeaving

> If you get into a business that is not viable, you
> have to get the soul of the organization. It is hard
> to improve an organization when the people are
> dead and the systems are mechanical. This organi-

zation had a lot of process stuff going on. They did all the right things—vision, principles, etc. But it had no heart. There weren't even any footprints in the sand when I came. They had all the technical capability but it had gotten to the point where everything had to be made an assignment if it was to get done. No one did anything on their own.

—Corporate Executive

Human beings require relationships to exist. We cannot live in isolation without food, clothing, tools, and people. The weaving of spirit is the next step in relationship where we acknowledge something or someone in our environment and then honor its spirit. SpiritWeaving is the very nurturance of the soul's existence, the focal point for its being in time. The soul needs stimulation, intensity, and the differences of life in order to clarify itself. It demands the contrasts, paradoxes, shadows, and correspondences of the whole. It is found in bridging the spaces between one individual and another. As the body suffers when cut off from all stimulus and the mind goes mad, the soul will wither and become pruned without connections with other living beings.

SpiritWeaving is not a new or radical concept in organizations. We use the idea everyday when we speak of team spirit and school spirit, high or low morale, national honor, or company pride. How people relate and bond to each other usually reflects the patterns of dis-ease that precipitate the call of the Hero's Journey. It could be provoked by a chance meeting with someone who questions your vision. It can come observing the personnel patterns of disruption caused by office arguments, lawsuits, firings for insubordination, low morale, unethical behavior by employees, internal competition, suboptimization by functional groups, product design problems, and introduction delays. It can come outside the organization from major stakeholders who are dissatisfied, by customer alienation, lack of awareness of market trends, ignoring environmental considerations, and rising negative public opinion. The leader may observe stress in one area or in multiple arenas, frustrated that things just aren't working right. Perhaps individuals are repeating some behavior like getting sick, divorcing their spouses, drinking, or gaining weight. Or the top leadership spends most of its time and energy in continual conflict and competition. The patterns emerge: The organization is experiencing some confusion or contradiction in its relationships within itself and with its stakeholders.

It can be a loud call, hard to miss in its insistence, or a quiet call, subtle in its implications. Unfortunately, we will miss the opportunities to create something new and be responsive when we are not able to hear or see what is happening around us because we have not developed the ability to relate to others. Intuitive senses, often ignored or distrusted, are key to experiencing and acknowledging people dynamics. Empathy, sensing energy, seeing the whole picture, and a keen sense of timing are examples of this type of intuitive knowing.

SpiritWeaving for the individual is using all parts of ourselves in unison. SpiritWeaving for the organization is bonding and blending all of the people necessary to a system's success into a whole so that they work together. Using all of the capabilities of each member, the organization achieves more as a productive, organic being, creative and responsive to its environment.

### Guidepost #3: From Integration To Integrity

> After months of effort, a team consisting of representatives of two unions and engineering presented its shop floor problem-solving approach to the visiting dignitary. Steeped in collaboration and participation, the leader of the group asked, "How could we improve the process?" Tactfully, the reply from the Japanese training executive was, "Very good Quality Circle approach. Very good." Again the leader asked how to improve the process. The Japanese executive's eyes engaged the leader for the first time. He asked, "And where do the problems come from that are worked on?" "Oh, from the shop floor—these are the problems that bother the workers the most." The Japanese manager smiled and said, "Ah, they should come from the top of the plant, from the management, in order to point out what is important to fix. Otherwise the workers will not know what is important."
>
> —Organizational Consultant

As a system identifies its purpose and how it wants its people to relate, it must integrate its operational parts in order to achieve its aim. The internal and external systems, processes and structures work together in harmony for the organization to function well. The soul-filled organization operates as one complete, organic body with coherent integrity. The goal is that each job and the system as a whole function in total connection and with alignment.

Operational problems, such as an inability to make a quality product because of a lack of fit between design and manufacturing processes, often indicate that an organization is out of integrity. Redundancy and fixing quality at the end of a process are wasted efforts that cost a system. Internal competition between functions and a scrambling for scarce resources focus employees attention within a system and lead to large gaps with the customer and market. The call to the Hero's Journey from integrity is when the various functions within a system can do their jobs, yet the whole doesn't work together smoothly.

## Guidepost #4: From Improvement To Continuous Improvement At An Ever-Increasing Rate

> An American company that was proud of its innovation in its new plants in the US, was hosting a Japanese training executive. After spending all day at an innovative plant noted for its team structures and extensive training program, the plant manager asked, "What did you think of the operation and its training programs?" The Japanese leader replied, "Very nice plant. Very good training programs." He paused a few seconds before adding, "You in America do a very good job of teaching people to do their work. We in Japan teach people how to improve their work."
>
> —American Executive

Continuous improvement focuses on the many ways of looking at the quality of what an organization does, not only on its quantity or size attributes. Novel concepts, innovative approaches, different perspectives, and creative responses are encouraged. Rupert Sheldrake posits that we create something called a "morphogenetic field" with each new idea. This is a field of energy that is accessible to everyone. Putting it another way, he is offering the radical concept that the natural spiritweave of humanity allows ideas to be shared on some basic human level. It is the reason why, he says, that new discoveries are often simultaneously announced. The new knowledge in fact changes everything around it making what had not been real or feasible before now possible. Thus both the quality and rate of change brought about by a new concept becomes exponential, as in the story of the hundredth monkey. It is a way of saying that new ideas create new reality.

Sporadic, crisis-oriented improvements are possible without clear purpose, spiritweave and systemic integrity, but they will not last and do not lead to continuous improvement over time. Rather a culture of the "program of the month" becomes the norm with employees learning to cynically ride out the latest push from the top. Ideas are stale, processes, rigid and responses predictable. Those people who are different and see variances are made uncomfortable and excluded. Without "human" or "soul" homework, organizations are not able to continuously improve themselves because there is no infrastructure to support odd, unusual and radical changes.

## Responding To The Call Of The Hero's Journey

The call of the Hero's Journey is most often resisted when it comes. "It's just a temporary setback." Or there is a renewal of old efforts and programs. It may be seen as a fluctuation in the market, to be restored at an upturn. For many leaders, it feels like a personal indictment of their management abilities to acknowledge that the organization is confused. They judge themselves as inadequate and thus become paralyzed in the current situation. So answering the call for them is tantamount to admitting that they have been poor leaders.

A shame/hubris paradox emerges. Shame places the blame on oneself, while hubris finds others to indict. Blaming is a result of thinking that a system is a rigid machine and controllable through proscribed action. It assumes a static situation which is predictable and manageable. It focuses on the details of the current situation rather than the overall system and its patterns. In some ways it is a relief from the unending complexity. It is clear and concise, not muddy and dark. Once blame is fixed, it appears that you can move onward and that you can avoid the call to the Hero's Journey.

Unfortunately as neat and clean as this may be rationally, it is not true. The call will repeat itself in deeper and more profound ways if the total system is not addressed.

To the observant leader, the pattern persists. It nags. It itches. It annoys. It doesn't go away. The fractals repeat themselves with growing intensity and more severe crises. What was only a problem in production is now a problem in engineering, or the design department. The new marketing approach has not solved everything. Profits can be adjusted for several quarters, but the well is going dry. We can continue to look as though we are successful, but somehow it is not right.

The call asks us to experience pain and confusion, accept shadow, and not run away. It requires self-examination as well as organizational listening. It means going to and living where there is no either/or, no right or wrong, no good or bad. It demands accepting the call to inner work and exploring realities that are uncomfortable and paradoxical. It is not the pathology of depression but the growth of ingression as we delve into the hidden dynamics inside our organization.

In mythology, the period of three days is a common part of the story: Jonah was in the belly of the whale for three days, Christ was resurrected after three days, and Inanna spent three days in the underworld. Something important is being said here— it takes time to go through the transformation necessary for the hero to find his or her deepening. It is not immediate, with quick answers and sure solutions to be found on the shelf. Buying the latest management guru's program won't do it. The dark night of the soul and its work for a system is difficult, time consuming, intense, and demands a commitment away from the regular work of living one's ordinary life.

Not having an answer right away is awkward for traditional managers who have been rewarded for knowing what to do in any emergency or crisis. Waiting, leaving answers uncertain, living with contradictions, and keeping an open mind are experienced with shaky and queasy feelings. Yet the time gives us the opportunity to confront ourselves as whole, confusing and contradictory beings and systems. From this we learn that we are flawed and incomplete and striving to reach for some core goodness.

We connect with a new knowledge and a larger picture that clarifies and guides. We recognize some key in the symmetry. We can reconcile the paradoxes with sharper insight. We see the spirit at work enriching bottom line possibilities. We are ready to come out of the void and back into the light. Yet we resist again. We don't want to go back and be faced with actually changing our world. It is easier to stay in the abstract world of spirit and not find practical, bottom-line applications. Besides, who else will understand that the spirit and the flesh are one? We finally go. We take what we learn, cherishing its richness, its clarity, its sympathy and wonder, back to the everyday world, and find ways to adjust to our new sense of who we are.

We look for allies to help us. In some situations this may mean active participation; In others—consultation with our colleagues and employees. It may mean months or years of discussions or an intensive event to explore its implementation. It may be addressing an old product that is outdated. It may be developing a set of operating principles. It may mean investigating new markets. It may be "none of the above" and based on some unique local needs. What is important is that we translate our knowing into a clear, recognizable, understood pattern that everyone in the organization is familiar with and can apply. We become the instrument for the organization to achieve something new.

Once the knowledge is brought back and put into implementation, the process doesn't stop. We have added a new understanding which helps us in the immediate moment. Yet tomorrow we know we will have other situations, other forces, other ingredients in the stew of organizational life. The spiral demands that we await the next call, and it is more likely to be sooner than later.

The Hero's Journey to the inner world is a way letting go of all that we have learned, all of our old paradigms. They have not been bad or wrong paradigms, since they have served us well up to this point. The fact is that they are no longer appropriate for the speed and style of the world around us today. When we let go, a sense of potential is created that allows us to re-member and re-create our purpose. Soul work is a leap into the great unknown to become vibrant, pulsating, evolving human beings and systems.

Leadership is the art of always keeping the larger story of the reconciliation of the practical and the abstract, the sacred and the profane, the soul and the bottom line in mind to continuously move forward. It is the process of finding and implementing the great patterns of life as they weave about us. Jean Houston calls it keeping ourselves open "for the news of the universe." When we don't pathologize our mistakes, our less-than-wise efforts, we can find their source and re-mind ourselves of what we are all about. We can nurture ourselves into the possible.

# Summary

Leaders today are being asked to do what was impossible yesterday. Tomorrow they will be asked to do what is unthinkable today. The skills and abilities that sustain this rate of change and improvement must move at an equal—if not increased— rate simply to keep up. The soulwork of the Hero's Journey is a critical concept for profitability and sustained growth because it reminds us that individually we are more than we ever dared to dream ourselves to be and that organizationally we weave best to-gether—to compete, survive and create bottom line results. Clear and full in ourselves and participating in profoundly woven partnerships, we can improve our world.

**Sajeela Moskowitz Ramsey** is the founder and director of CORE Consulting (Center for Organizational Renewal and Effectivenss) offering Aesthetic Interventions™ and visionary leadership development for organizations and communities. She has over 20 years experience in training, speaking, and consulting. She holds a BA in Communications and the Expressive Arts, as well as certificates in somatic counseling, biokinisiology, and organization transformation. She is an avid interdisciplinarian, and has purused the healing, fine, performing, and media arts over a 20-year span. Her World Bank keynote talk, called "Lead with Art and Soul," was published in Steve Covey's *Executive Excellence* magazine in 1994. She is also a published poet. Ramsey considers herself to be an entrepreneur of transformation, fostering an awareness that we are all stakeholders in the planetary eco-social system. Moving the soul of the world with poetic vision is her opus.

# 12

# Searching For Home In The Marketplace: The Art Of Organizational Well-being

*Sajeela Moskowitz Ramsey*

Recently I saw a client who makes a six-figure salary. He spends all his time doing busines-related travel. He joked with me, asking if I knew what the richest and the poorest people in this country have in common. I thought about it a moment, and couldn't guess what spans these polarities of the social spectrum. My client's answer was clever: they're both homeless! I laughed at his joke at the time, but almost immediately I was struck by a poignant and utterly universal question:

Where indeed is our home?

In today's work world many of us are spiritually hungry and homeless, as impoverished and desperate as any beggar on the street.

We spend most of our waking hours at, or commuting to and from our jobs; a literal paragon of never being at home! We're just as literally not "home" in spirit at the workplace. We take no time to daydream, to attend to the imaginative side of life. The psyche becomes starved, and we're left with a deficit of creative energy. This extends into our cultural well-being, demonstrating a widespread crisis organizations and the people who inhabit them.

How many of you can think of times when you were exhausted and uninspired at the end of your workday? How many of you catch yourself daydreaming on the job, and wish you could just do that for a spell? Could daydreaming be a natural biological response to a waning psyche in need of refueling?

An executive who's been with a world class company for over ten years summed it up when he referred to his workplace as his "golden cage." His remark reminded me of a Mexican folk saying: A cage made of gold is still just a cage, but never a home.

All of us have witnessed the 1990 as a platform for corporate upheaval. This pervasive displacement in the workforce brings up primary processes, particularly fear and apathy. We can all name current trends in organizations that speak to this turmoil. Examples include downsizing, reengineering, flattening, reinventing, outsourcing, and so on.

The common tendril among these is change. These all conjure up familiar entropic images of structural disintegration, and an accompanied sense of loss. We're approaching a critical juncture in the marketplace and in our lives. The forces of change are a wake-up call, provoking in us a yearning that's a cultural search to find a way home.

As a contractor at a major upscale hotel, I became aware that my lifestyle as an artistic free spirit seemed fascinating to those I met, and drew many clients to me. My pursuit of the metaphysical, healing, fine, media, and performance arts, along with extensive travel, had a certain appeal for people who were locked into business world bottom lines. I've always done what I wanted to do. My life has been relatively free-flowing and spontaneous, even chaotic at times.

My experience has been richly creative, and very adventurous. I've managed to unwittingly nourish the psyche at every turn by leading a poetic life. I think that's what draws clients, because it feeds and sparks their imaginations! It gives their business world psyches a sorely needed jump start.

Working in a 1990 business climate has exposed to me the issues of corporate "homelessness." In the context of organizations in flux I recognized the chaotic life paths I chose prepared me for working with the change process! But how to translate the crazy wisdom from my experiences into something meaningful for the marketplace? The answer came by seeing my life as an ongoing journey in search of "home." And the way home for me was the path of "aesthetic intervention."

Can you recall a moment in your life when something suddenly seized you, stopped you dead in your tracks? Maybe you responsible, and they have the authority to control and coordinate their own work. Responsibility is located where the work is done, not in levels above. Instead of wasting valuable time and resources by looking up and out to the manager for answers, they are able to take ownership of the work, which allows them to be flexible and adapt to changing market requirements.

In contrast, a bureaucratic structure is not built to adapt quickly. Workers operate in a narrow band of specialization and control, which hinders organizational adaptability and sustainability. It also weakens morale. Merrelyn Emery tells about a major aircraft manufacturer where a whole unit was given the afternoon off because of the successful completion of a new aircraft. Two women workers were walking by the hanger where the brand new plane was sitting and one commented to the other, "What a gorgeous plane. I wish that I would get to work on something that beautiful." The sad and ironic thing is that both of these women had worked on the plane! Only they never knew it, because they only worked on a narrow piece of process.

Participative design deserves serious consideration, if for no other reason than that it makes financial sense. The strategy yields faster and less costly redesign for increased flexibility and adaptability. At the core of participative design are the human needs for productive work. We must not fall back into bureaucracy in disguise. At its core, bureaucratic design fosters dependency. It discourages people from taking the risks needed to improve business. The participative design model creates an environment that encourages people to take appropriate risks that pay off in competitive advantages. Bureacratic machinations of heightened command and control, traditional reengineering, and forced ranking all diminish the human spirit. The human spirit expands, however, when people feel valued, when they participate, when they feel engaged in the decisions that affect the success of their daily work.

Democratic systems allow people to attend to the human spirit, creating joy, enhanced health, creativity, motivation, commitment, and a willingness to take responsibility. Albert Einstein never thought of separating his spirit from his work. The Austrian physicist Godel said of Einstein: "His theology and his science were inextricably tied together; it was unthinkable to him that they could exist separately."

**Karen D. Lundquist** is the CEO and a principal consultant for Creative Breakthroughs, Inc. (CBI) which she cofounded in 1994 with Magaly d. Rodriguez and Carol Ann Cappuzzo. Lundquist holds a Bachelors and Master's degree in chemical engineering from the University of Nebraska. Before CBI, she was employed for fifteen years by a major global chemical company. As a plant manager, she implemented disciplined business systems along with Rapid Change Technologies™ to rebuild spirit and community which resulted in an unprecedented performance turnaround in less than a year.

CBI's mission is to speed appropriate action toward far-reaching goals by applying practical tools and technologies for business and personal growth.

Rapid Change Technologies™ is a protected trademark owned by Creative Breakthroughs, Inc.

$\boxed{16}$

# 16

# Pioneering New Frontiers For Profitability

## Karen D. Lundquist

**Big Question:** *What is it that can re-energize people to want to contribute their best efforts at work after they have reached career level, top pay or have just become sick and tired of their jobs?*

Silently seeking the answer to this question, I began a fifteen-year search in corporate America. Now that I found it, my career is dedicated to helping people improve their lives, jobs, and businesses.

What follows is a story about releasing trapped energy for personal and organizational transformation. It's about people in the depths of despair who miraculously breathed new life into a manufacturing site destined for closure.

By materializing the intangible human spirit into conscious use of practical tools for self knowledge and interpersonal skills, a business turnaround worth tens of millions of dollars was achieved in less than a year. In 1993 I left the site and the company. I am still delighted to receive reports of continued growth and improvement.

## Getting My Wish

"Ha-Ha," my soon-to-be ex-boss teased, "They're picketing at your plant today, and there's a big management visit." He left my office very light on his feet, almost skipping, as if he was proud of the new challenge he had just presented. In a few days, I was leaving the plush nest at headquarters to become the plant manager at a 330-person facility in the Midwest. Now, adding to my already high anxiety, thousands of questions raced through my mind about what could be going on out there. This *was* an important career stepping stone on the way to the top...which was what everyone wanted. Right?

My dream was finally coming true! My wish had been granted! After years of studying concepts and theories from the great masters of business improvement, I longed for the chance to put these teachings to work. The principles I'd learned rang true. I wanted to prove them right, by leading an organization of empowered employees toward high performance. In addition, it didn't hurt that a plant manager was traditionally viewed as the local seat of power representing the corporation. These jobs were saved as grooming experiences for top flight management positions. Being a woman with only 13 years of corporate experience, and with outspoken ideas about diversity and employee empowerment, I had not considered myself eligible.

Ambivalence ruled as I considered the new plant manager assignment versus staying in my comfortable position at headquarters. These were exciting times. The company was reengineering and right-sizing for the most effective and efficient service to customers. Stock prices were sure to soar. My job was safe and secure. Additionally, I could hear about, and possibly influence, any new corporate initiatives. I knew what power was, and this was it...or close to it.

Manufacturing was known for being out in the sticks, the trenches, the first place hit by cost reductions and the last to know about it. It meant managing the nitty-gritty issues: safety and environmental, labor and personnel, customer satisfaction, technical, cost, scheduling, product quality, and community relations. Manufacturing is what happens between customer orders and sales revenues, between the proverbial rock and a hard place—a catch-all for blame in the supply chain.

One well-meaning engineering director informed me that in the past twenty-five years only two plant managers in our company had been promoted out of that position, and he was one of them. "You can manage nine out of ten areas above their expectations, and they'll shoot you down for not delivering the tenth," he warned. Still the urge to lead an organization possessed me.

Although I didn't fully recognize it at the time, I was blessed with a boss who wasn't stuck in the corporate paradigm of what a plant manger should look like. He could see the possibilities of my convictions. After offering me the new assignment, he gave that extra little encouragement I needed when I hesitated. I told him that I was enjoying my life here at headquarters and my established support network, so I would take the weekend to consider his offer. He let me know, in no uncertain terms, that it would be best to develop a new support network in this new business.

In corporate terms, the reassignment had been made. I had been given a privileged opportunity as a plant manager and charged with the not-so-well-defined goal of "Make change!" with an implied "Or else!" The message was loud and clear that I was entering a hotbed of labor unrest and unsatisfied customer demands, signaling that my days as a "corporate princess" were over. Suddenly, the old adage "you must be careful what you wish for because you might get it" was ringing in my ears.

## The Big Secret

This plant was one of the best kept secrets in the corporation. It was an old facility built in the early 1930s, but not started up until after World War II. The local economy of the small, Midwestern town depended on the plant for jobs and other service requirements it created.

In the 1970s, they were known as the "Can-Do Plant." Over the past decade, the people had been through a series of emotional ups and downs which tracked the patterns of layoffs and rehiring (appearing to employees as union-busting activities). The employees saw management decisions as unconnected and arbitrary, and I learned that very little business information had been shared with them. The company's business people detested dealing with the site's remoteness and hostility, avoiding it at all cost. Consequently, new maintenance and improvement funding, products, and technologies were awarded to other plants.

The terrible reputation spread far and wide. I had heard stories and rumors about it...driving a forklift off the dock (not once, but twice!), flash fires, and one of the worst safety records in the company; environmental nightmares galore; and most of all, the labor union that plagued the management and was reported to block any improvements in performance and managing systems. "Just look, they picketed during a senior management visit," I was told by my new bosses at headquarters!

This sort of worker uprising is viewed at headquarters as a heinous crime committed by employees and a serious black-eye for management who must not be doing their job to keep the peace. When I asked what the employees had to say that would cause them to picket, I was met with blank stares and vague, evasive explanations.

At the time of my transfer to the so-called western frontiers of the corporate holdings, the movie "Dances with Wolves" was at its peak of popularity. You can imagine the parallels and metaphors available to my colleagues who poked fun at my new assignment. "You're being sent out there to handle the uprising." "How will you learn to speak the language?" "Will you socialize with the native people?" However, it also provided a framework for me to consider the cause of the unspeakable truth which kept people playing games and bound in dysfunctional roles.

The rumors were true. The situation was horrifying. The big secret was that each employee, both management and labor, was reacting out of fear for their survival. In my naiveté, I was sure that my new manufacturing systems technologies and leadership training would calm their fears so we could get on with it. Things were sure to change around here, and fast. It was just a matter of tracking what was really going on and making the prescribed interventions.

## Stepping Into The Fray

When I arrived at the plant to take the reins, I spent a couple hours with my predecessor in which he confirmed all the rumors, and then disappeared. This had obviously been a stressful situation, and my guess was that he had participated from the sidelines in a pain avoidance mode. He was emotionally relieved and made no ceremonial comments or gestures otherwise. He was not about to take a final tour of the facility, shake hands and say good-byes, or purport to miss one element of his grueling six-year experience.

Next, I met with the superintendents. They were enthusiastic and energized by the recent management change and increasing production demands. The story unfolded that another plant belonging to the company in the neighboring state had been closed. Many of the products and people were transferred into this plant with the orders to "produce!"

The plant had few systems in place that could handle the doubled production. People were not trained to carry out their new assignments since two thirds of all jobs had been changed to accommodate the seniority system. At this point there was no time for training, I was told, because production demand was too high. Perhaps it could happen when things slowed down...they thought.

Massive overtime on the shop floor, which often reached summertime temperatures of 110°F, was the only solution to getting the product shipped. Meeting customer performance requirements was a distant dream. Because of the panic, the place was operating in a command and control mode. Tempers flared, and public "whippings" were common. No wonder there were 385 formal grievances on file! At a time when spirits should be high with the anticipation of increased production, people were miserable.

Then there was safety. The superintendents blamed the poor record on the fact that people just didn't care about following the safety rules, preferring short cuts. After all, I was told that the union leaders' declared seniority was considered to be more important than safety.

The truly dedicated superintendents were obviously working to the point of exhaustion. To bolster their spirits, headquarters told them this plant had a long life ahead of it. However, they saw that a plant shutdown was inevitable, attributing it to the unruly labor situation and their failure to do their jobs properly.

## Fear And Frustration

The story continued to unfold as I spoke with the other managers and supervisors who were depressed and tormented. They were enraged about the unfair demands they had been handed, not the least of which was the corporate mandate to not make waves in the labor pool, effectively tying their hands in dealing with performance.

Fear was the supervisors' driver. They were working harder and putting in longer hours than ever before to do more of what they knew how to do. Some improvements were surfacing, but not fast enough to keep management off their backs. It was common for them to keep a low profile in order to avoid public humiliation.

The hostility toward management was generally shared by

the shop floor crews. They were tired of dictated directives to meet production deadlines, and of being told they were deadbeats when equipment wouldn't work or they didn't have proper training. One crew delivered a frustrated and threatening message to me, "If something isn't done about our supervisor, you will find him dead in a trash dumpster some morning after midnight shift!"

Feeling battered and bloody after each tour of the manufacturing area, my objective was to respond to the cries for help by listening carefully, acknowledging their issues, then asking for time and their cooperation to address the situations they presented. Reactions were mixed with very few wanting to get involved, feeling that this was all management's problem. Most were willing to wait and see the changes I might bring about. At least, I was listening.

## Prayers, Principles, And Plans

At this point my prayers were simple: Help us work through the night and next day without injury and please help people find joy in their work. Profitability was a distant possibility.

First things first: The management team held many safety meetings to impart the message that safety was more important than production. We initiated a safety system which would involve employees in technologies and responsibility for safety monitoring and improvements. Safety seemed to improve for a while, as long as supervision was policing it. But production suffered.

Next came a vision and mission to ensure that everyone knew where the plant was headed and how we would work together to get there. The management team constructed the vision and mission in lengthy sessions where we all demonstrated our knowledge of the business and how our plant needed to function to meet those needs. Then, we took this message to each of the crews, and we were met with apathy. How could they be so disinterested with this exciting stuff?

Of course! Everyone wants to be a contributor on a winning team, so we had to define the game and give people the rules to win. To do this we planned to inform people about the business performance measurements, the competition, customer requirements and our stewardship of millions of dollars of sales and investment. Once again, these meetings were met with lukewarm response. Halfway through the series, I began one crew meeting by asking what they had heard this meeting was about. The blasé response was, "About two hours."

Similar efforts fell flat while introducing new technologies in the areas of continuous flow manufacturing, quality, leadership, environmental, maintenance, and operational training. A few teams were forming reluctantly, but it was evident we could only do one thing well at a time and everything else would suffer. We desperately needed everyone taking responsibility because there was just too much to do. Meanwhile, the rallying cry in the plant was, "This too shall pass." The employees were uninvolved.

## Falling Into The Depths

I dreaded the abusive meetings with the business team who blamed this plant for most customer complaints. When my six-month performance review rolled around and I had not yet delivered the requested improvements, my performance rating plummeted. Gulp! It was easy to fall into the victim mode of, "Oh great, now this plant is ruining my career, too. What a cheap shot, the other guy was there for six years and they expect me to turn things around in six months?"

*Woe is us.* What was missing? All our efforts had followed the prescribed principles of a high performance organization, yet most employees avoided working in teams or taking on improvement responsibility. During the annual visit by the business director, operators scowled and waved him off to avoid talking with him. He was incensed and declared that he would never allow a customer to tour this site.

As if times weren't rough enough, we narrowly avoided a contract termination by the union which would have opened up the site to the possibility of a strike. It was a mere technicality that the termination letter was received a few days too late—after the negotiation window required by the contract had closed. Inconsistent administration of policy and inability to resolve problems had grievances and arbitrations soaring. Surely, next year the union would get the contract termination notice here on time.

## Add Rapid Change Technologies

At the depths of our depression and frustration, I asked the superintendents if they were ready to try something totally different. It would be unlike anything they had ever seen in a corporation, especially at a plant site. I wanted them to meet two special people who could give us some new options for implementing our strategies. Having run out of ideas, they were intrigued with my proposal and agreed to participate.

The two people were Magaly d. Rodriguez, founder and president of Rapid Change Technologies (RCT), and Carol Ann Cappuzzo, a primary consultant of RCT and a major contributor since the company's inception. I had worked with them in my previous assignment when our department went through the turmoil of downsizing and restructuring.

I recalled my experience of those difficult times. The same forward-thinking boss I mentioned earlier had suggested I contact these two women to help the department get back on track. Magaly and Carol Ann, both experts at bringing to light the outside-of-conscious motivations of learning and behavior, applied brain-based tools and technologies to build community among the department's lead team members and bond them into a real team. Within a couple months, the team plan for restructuring the department was underway which included a process for working together to bond and build back the trust between the Lead Team and the organization.

In my current assignment, I had only talked with Magaly briefly to describe the situation. The company had denied my funding requests to involve RCT and said I had better just find a way to engage them by myself, and furthermore, keep it quiet since it didn't fit consulting guidelines. In other words, we were on our own.

The superintendents were on board, and they were agreeable to juggling the budget and appropriating funds to begin the consulting work. We agreed to keep it very hush-hush. Finally, I asked Magaly and Carol Ann if they were willing to help us, knowing that it would be the ride of their lives. They wholeheartedly agreed, and to this day will tell you it presented the challenge of a lifetime. They had never seen so much anger and hostility in an organization. Even though they used to work with violent gangs, this site was the most resistant to change. The key would be to trust in the process and the human spirit.

## Looking Beneath The Surface

One of the most helpful and beautiful aspects of working with Magaly and Carol Ann is that no matter how bad the individual's behavior, they can always look beneath the surface to see the inner spirit with its magical possibilities. The key is in the positive energy locked up with the spirit, and the challenge is to create an environment where a person can speak their truth without getting killed...or the emotional equivalent, shamed.

When we looked beneath the surface of our visions, goals, systems, and technologies, we found that we were building our glorious improvement structure on an unstable foundation that could not support it. Our base was like quicksand with hostility, negativity, hopelessness, and victim behaviors. Sure, we knew that the albeit familiar environment was not pleasant, but we had never slowed down long enough to address this fundamental need for change.

We needed to make the shift to a dynamic and nurturing environment of trust, honesty, openness, and compassion that was safe for joining teams, taking risks, and learning. Although we didn't know it at the time, this was the key to engaging the whole organization in order to implement the new business systems and technologies we had worked so hard to design. As it turns out, these were critical. We were just missing one important element—people's energy.

## Tapping Into The Organization's Energy

New intra- and interpersonal skills were needed. RCT designed a customized course for us—The Fundamentals of Rapid Change. Not surprisingly, the managers loved the training because it touched some old values that had been lost in the corporate struggles. Although they were hesitant about how it would be received by the operators and clerks, they decided it was worth a try. In the RCT experience, each layer of the organization sees a huge risk for the next, when in actuality, the further away from the senior management layer one goes, the more readily the RCT tools are embraced and used.

Training the managers and supervisors first was critical. They learned how to build their authenticity and engaged in a process for gaining trust. Additionally, they found the courage to listen to bad news along with the good and a process to speak their truth to power. Now it was their responsibility to create this environment for the rest of the organization by applying these processes to calm fears and add emotional safety to the workplace structure.

Next we invited a group of outspoken, contrary operators to

participate in and evaluate the training. Afterwards, three union stewards told me that the training should be offered to each employee on a voluntary basis. They were excited and saw great potential for people. Because of the lack of trust between the management and union, at first managers were not allowed to attend the operator training sessions. Anyone wishing to leave could return to work anytime without retribution. The training was offered as a gift for use with families, community organizations, and in their places of worship. Again, faith in the process told us that it would flow into all areas of their lives, including their jobs.

Adhering to the confidentiality agreements, I did not know exactly what was going on in those courses. When people returned they were energized to join teams and take on new responsibilities. Operators, supervisors, and managers found creative solutions to age-old problems. Leadership skills began to take root and conflict was resolved in the workplace, reducing the need for legal structures. I'm sure Magaly and Carol Ann have many stories to tell about the challenges they faced, but that is for another chapter. In the end, the process and the human spirit won out.

Back at the site we had the business systems ready to engage their energy and ideas in improvement activities. We had learned that the intangibles drive the tangibles:

- emotional safety supports physical safety,
- commitment and caring softens the perceived risk of new empowered behaviors,
- learning and improving can be easier, faster, and more fun,
- inspirational, heroic visions drive breakthrough goals, and
- recognizing a personal stake in the goal clears the way for action and results.

## When Magic Happens

Six months from starting the training, we were facing the major sales promotion of the year along with the deadline for opening the labor contract. In the plant lead team meetings, I was told that we should eliminate all activities other than production.

However, I held to a seemingly radical position that we could do it all: production, along with the leadership and functional training, two quality audits, customer visits and continuous improvement team meetings. Faith and courage prevailed.

At the end of the unusually smooth month, we realized to our surprise that we had accomplished all those activities along with record production and exceeding all the customer service goals. We did not receive a letter from the union to modify the contract since the level of irritation was reduced by resolving more issues as they arose. The employees recognized that the plant had turned the corner. The plant celebrated. Then, we got back to work.

I can't say that we had created a happy factory, but we had focused our attentions on what was good for the people and good for the business. Some people were destined to stay stuck in the past, but the good news is: It only takes 20 percent to start a revolution. Over the next year people commented about enjoying their jobs more than they ever imagined possible.

The business lead team was shocked! They liked the results, but weren't particularly interested in the process that accomplished the turnaround. Oh well, we were an internally powered organization now. In the next eight months the following improvements signaled that continuous improvement was here to stay:

- Annual recordable injuries dropped from four to one, and people knew that they could work injury free.
- The plant was benchmarked as the second highest rate of improvement among 25 similar global sites.
- Batches per day increased by 70 percent.
- Inventory reduced by 30 percent, freeing millions of dollars.
- Fixed costs dropped by 20 percent.
- Hazardous waste was reduced by 30 percent, reducing costs by millions.
- Customer service was above goal all year, and many customer quality awards were received. Operator teams visited customers and customers visited the plant.
- A new, high growth business was awarded to the site because it could be installed at half the cost of other

bids and because of the impressive employee attitudes and quality assurance systems. This insured the plant's existence well into the 21st Century.

## Creating Conscious Paradox

There are many definitions of the high performance organization. Here's mine: The high performance organization is one that pays attention to:

- creating an enriched environment for people which invites the energy and the creativity of the human spirit, and
- creating disciplined systems to channel that energy and creativity into the most useful, highest value work.

Without spirit there is no energy. Without disciplined systems, energy and creativity alone cannot produce results. It's the paradox of disciplined creativity.

The Rapid Change Technologies strategy invites the spiritual intangibles to drive the profitable tangibles, which in this case were worth tens of millions of dollars annually in new sales, cash flow, and cost reductions, in addition to guaranteeing the livelihoods of 330 people and the economic base for a community.

# Part Six

# LEADERSHIP & CONSCIOUSNESS— "THAT'S THE SPIRIT, TOO!"

**Steve Jacobsen** is active in multiple areas of personal and organizational spiritual development. He holds a Master's degree from Princeton Theological Seminary and a doctorate in Educational Leadership from Seattle University. Professionally, he has taught comparative religion at Heritage College in Washington state and worked as a facilitator and consultant for public and private organizations in the northwest. Currently, he is senior pastor of the Goleta Presbyterian Church in Santa Barbara, California. His community involvements have included serving as president of the Advisory Board for the Santa Barbara New Music Festival. Since the completion of his dissertation, he has been active in the ongoing dialogue about spirituality and organizational life through writing and conference presentations.

# 17

# Spirit Matters: 22 Transformational Leaders Reflect On The Role Of Spirituality In Their Life And Work

*Steve Jacobsen*

> I think that all leadership is indeed spiritual leadership.
>> —prominent management consultant and author Peter Vaill

> When the talk turns to the spiritual side of leadership, I mostly want to run.
>> —prominent management consultant and author Tom Peters

Does spirituality play an important role in transformational leadership? As a doctoral student in organizational development, I recognized this to be an emerging issue for management in the 1990s. Recognizing that most of what was said in these debates was based on opinion rather than data, I designed a research project which attempted to discover if there is, indeed, any connection between spirituality and leadership.

I was not prepared for what happened. I never dreamed that I would soon be in contact with a diverse group of 22 esteemed leaders that included a former governor of New York, a U.S. senator from Connecticut, a nursing administrator from Georgia, a Cadillac dealer in Texas, and an employee development manager from Seattle. I was not prepared for the eloquence of their reflections. I did not expect that they would come to consensus on seven tough and sensitive questions. What they have to say about spirituality and leadership may be important for all in business and public service who strive to serve their organizations with integrity and who wonder if "spirit matters" in the turbulent 1990s.

## The Project

The first step was to identify a diverse group of transformational leaders—peak performers in the practice of leadership. That's not an easy task—there's no such category in the yellow pages! I began by establishing a "panel of experts." These people would have seen many leaders perform in many different kind of organizations across the country. They would be able to identify women and men who are *transformational* leaders—people who can not only "get the job done," but do so in a way that creates trust, creativity, commitment, and ethical behavior. Creating the panel was like asking a group of veteran big league managers to pick an all star team, or a group of established choreographers to name the most influential dancers of our time.

Nine people agreed to serve on the panel which included Clark Kerr, former president of the University of California; Theodore Hesburgh, president emeritus of Notre Dame; former NATO ambassador Harlan Cleveland; and management consultant and author Kathy Ryan. I asked this group to each identify 3-5 transformational leaders currently active in secular organizations. This created a list of nominees for the study. I then contacted each nominee, explained the project to them, and invited them to participate. Twenty-two people responded positively. It was a wonderful list—a former governor, a retired U.S. Senator, a Xerox executive from Texas, a health systems CEO from Missouri, a college president from Florida, a foundation head from North Carolina, a stage agency director from Washington, and a California grandmother active in social change. It included seven women and 15 men and members of four different ethnic groups.

These participants were known by a group of experts to be transformational leaders. The next task was to see if spirituality played any part in their performance. I asked each to respond to a series of seven written question about the role spirituality may or may not play in their own life, in their leadership practices, and in the workplace. When all had given their initial responses, I summarized in paragraph form what they seemed to be saying as a group. I asked each to concur or challenge this summary. Suggested changes led to another draft of each statement. Finally, consensus was achieved.

The material created in this correspondence produced seven statements on the role of spirituality and leadership as well as a fascinating portrait of what inspires, directs, informs, and concerns this group of leaders. While space does not permit sharing all the questions, conclusions and insights, three basic findings can be shared. These have to do with the role of spirituality in the formation of values, the influence of spirituality on leadership practices, and the future of spirituality in the workplace.

## Finding: The Role Of Spirituality In Forming A Leader's Values

One of the questions focused on the role spirituality may or may not have played in the formation of their values and beliefs. As a whole, 72 percent spoke in strong and clear terms of the importance of spiritual traditions, while 23 percent described the importance of spiritual principles in their personal development. Specific comments revealed the diversity of backgrounds and experiences in this regard. One participant described a process in which he received the teachings of his tradition as a child, only to take them as his own as adult:

> I became a Catholic because at a stage in my life when I was too young to understand, my mother and father took me to church, had a priest pour holy water on my head and say words in Latin. Eventually, my religion—and its traditional beliefs—became a matter of conviction. Those traditions, while recognizing that we are too weak to do it perfectly, call on us nevertheless to try to do good things for other people.

One person said this:

> I was brought up in a German Lutheran family. I thought everyone was taught to work hard, to respect others, to give of yourself to those around you, to keep your room clean,and make your bed

before you leave the house.

Another person described parental influence as a medium for absorbing spiritual traditions as follows:

> My parents had strict behavior expectations for my sisters and brothers. This included being aware of and respectful of the traditional cultural and religious teachings, customs and beliefs of my people. This included the need to be aware of one's inner self and to do those things to strengthen one's inner self so that one's life would be in balance. This included time alone, meditation, being quiet, listening, and being respectful of others need to do the same.

Of the six respondents who did not identify particular spiritual traditions, five described the influence of spirituality in more general ways. A typical response from this group was from one respondent who said:

> From an ethical perspective, the statement, "do unto others as you would have them do unto you," has helped me to form a sense of fair play and the desire to take the course of action that results in the greatest benefit for all.

Several religious traditions were specifically noted as being influential, including Judaism, Christianity, Native American beliefs, Zen Buddhism, and yoga.

The statement which received consensus indicates the strength of the group's conviction:

> Spiritual traditions or principles have played a fundamental role in the formation of my values, ethics, and beliefs.

## Finding: The Influence Of Spirituality On Leadership Practices

If these leaders' values were so clearly rooted in spiritual traditions and principles, it was important to know how this background impacts their current work in the demanding, challenging, and stressful task of acting as the leader of a secular organization. One of the questions probed this area by asking "Describe how your spirituality/central values influence your leadership practices." A majority—77 percent—said there is a strong and vital relationship between spirituality and leadership practices. One person said:

> ...they can't be separated. I can't sustain my
> energy about those things I don't care deeply
> about. I do best when I involve myself with things
> that are important to me in a very sincere way.

Other respondents echoed this sense of linkage between spirituality and leadership by using language such as "the two go hand in hand," "the starting point for everything I do," "my leadership is grounded in my spirituality," and "my leadership grows directly out of my spirituality."

Five persons (23 percent) identified principles of leadership arising from their central values without mentioning spirituality specifically. One wrote:

> Articulating and practicing principled leadership to
> management team and all staff (using) concepts of
> interconnectedness, stewardship, (and) inclusive-
> ness. Leading by example. Building trust daily.

While the responses were varied, the group was able to agree on a common statement. The statement which received consensus was:

> Our spirituality has a profound impact on our
> leadership practices. It is the foundation of every-
> thing we do. It is our central frame of reference for
> helping us see our role in our organization in
> particular and our life as a whole. It keeps us
> focused on the needs and value of other people. It
> is expressed better in action than words.

At this point in the study, it was clear that spirituality was of great *personal* importance to this group of leaders. The final question dealt with the debate about spirituality in the more *public* arena of the workplace. Do these people advocate a more conspicuous role of spirituality in the secular organizations they serve?

## Finding: The Prospects Of Integrating Spiritual-
## ity Into The Workplace

This question led to the most interesting mix of responses from the group. A majority—59 percent—commented that integration is essential to organizational health and productivity. One person said, simply, that the integration:

> ...not only makes one more productive, but results in a much more fulfilled, happy and peaceful personal life.

One person saw the need as originating in the lives of employees:

> I agree in the context of employees feeling they can make a contribution, meaningful purposeful work which is aligned with a higher purpose and vision... People spend a large portion of their lives at work and need to be able to relate their "spirit," sense of purpose and meaning in this part of their lives.

Still another believes it is important based on professional convictions:

> I think such integration is absolutely essential to the well-being of the individuals involved and, through each of them, to the quality of life in the community. It is increasingly clear that the most successful corporate operations are those that respect individual rights and dignity.

While the majority, then, voiced a positive reaction to this suggestion, a strong minority—41 percent—expressed caution and concern. One person was decidedly opposed:

> I don't think so. It comes with the values of the people who are hired or who are there. It can't be 'interjected.' Look for and reward the behaviors. Overlaying it artificially would be that—artificial and not only a waste of time, but negatively received!

One concern was the danger of talking about spiritual values without living up to them:

> ...verbalizing such values and beliefs when they are not lived leads to more disenfranchisement and cynicism. I would hope that "greater integration of spirituality into the workplace" means that we attempt to live our lives in every sphere in concert with our values.

The reasons for caution, then, were varied and thoughtful. The consensus statement reflected these views:

> Spirituality is the basis for much of people's ways of understanding and acting in the world. There-fore, many of us believe it would be highly benefi-cial for secular organizations to find ways to recognize, affirm, and integrate it into the work-place and public life. This would allow people to have a sense of meaning and purpose—a connec-tion to a greater good—beyond their individual selves. Others among us are opposed to an overt introduction of spirituality in the workplace, but are in favor of supporting leaders, colleagues, etc., whose behavior are congruent with spiritual concepts. All of us agree that, if an organization attempts integration, great care needs to be taken; respect for diversity and a mutual understanding of differences would be essential.

## Implications

On the one hand, what 22 people have to say about a topic doesn't usually create grounds for broad generalizations. On the other hand, when it is a diverse group of peak performers, the lessons for others might be significant. At least two lessons emerge from this study.

First, the project suggests that there may often be a pro-found link between the ability to be a "transformational" leader and a personal sense of spirituality. Spirituality tends to ground us in a greater good beyond the self, helps us value other people, creates in us an aspiration towards ethical behavior, and teaches us that we cannot know or control everything ourselves. When matched with the right skills, discipline, and dedication, a leader can have much more depth and sensitivity. If someone wants to be the best leader possible, it may be necessary to be on this "inward journey" in a significant way. That may mean going back into the tradition of one's childhood. It may mean searching for something new. It may mean learning from a variety of sources. Whatever the path, the soul needs to be nurtured. That is what spirituality is all about. In this sense, Peter Vaill is right on target.

Secondly, the project suggests that there is a great desire to

## Spirituality and Transformational Leadership in Secular Settings
## A Delphi Study

*The Participants*

| | |
|---|---|
| Donna Anderson | President, National Retiree Volunteer Coalition, Minneapolis, MN |
| Ron Anderson | President and CEO, Dallas County Hospital District, Dallas, TX |
| Sharon Anderson | Director, Reflective Leadership Center, University of Minnesota, Minneapolis, MN |
| Mario Cuomo | Governor, State of New York, Albany, NY |
| Jane Dailey | VP–Nursing, South Fulton Medical Center, East Point, GA |
| William C. Friday | Executive Director, William R. Kenan, Jr., Charitable Trust, Chapel Hill, NC |
| Kathy Friedt | Director, Department of Licensing, Olympia, WA |
| David Gershon | Director, Global Action Plan, Woodstock, NY |
| Don George | Director, La Casa de Maria Retreat Center, Santa Barbara, CA |
| Theodore Hesburgh | President Emeritus, University of Notre Dame, Notre Dame, IN |
| Kerney Laday | VP–Field Operations, Xerox Corporation, Irving, TX |
| Michael Lerner | Executive Director, COMMONWEAL, Bolinas, CA |
| Gene Liddell | Director, Department of Community Development, Olympia, WA |
| Roger Meier | COB Rodger Meier Cadillac, Dallas, TX |
| Jeannie O'Laughlin | President, Barry University, Miami Shores, FL |
| Claiborne Pell | United States Senator, Rhode Island |
| Bill Schoenhard | COO, SSM Health Care Systems, St. Louis, MO |
| Kent Skipper | Executive Director, Salesmanship Club, Youth and Family Centers, Inc., Irving, TX |
| Bill Solomon | Chairman, President, CEO, Austin Industries, Dallas, TX |
| Marian Svinth | Employee Development Manager, Simpson Investment Company, Seattle, WA |
| Barbara Wiedner | Founder/Director, Grandmothers for Peace International, Elk Grove, CA |
| Martha Yallup | Deputy Director, Human Services, Yakima Indian Nation, Toppenish, WA |

integrate spirituality into the workplace but also a keen awareness of the problems involved. If we are to get beyond the sense of
fractured, disconnected life, we need to find a way to put our
deepest experiences and values into our everyday work. But not
everyone speaks the same spiritual language. Not everyone is
nurtured by the same tradition. Failure to live up to proclaimed
spiritual values can lead to skepticism and cynicism. Tom Peter's
concerns aren't his alone. Integrating spirituality into the secular
workplace is not a simple or trouble-free process.

Clearly, Spirit matters to this group of transformational
leaders. Regardless of how that spirituality is described, it appears to be a vital part of who they are. When expressed in
concrete action, it makes a difference in the lives of the persons
they seek to serve. As one person remarked:

> You can't be a leader until you know how to follow
> and whom to follow. You can be a much better
> leader if you're in touch with your spiritual self.
> Whether you are a Christian, a Jew, a Buddhist, or
> whatever, you need to live your values and not
> suppress your spirituality. People need to see your
> values in your work product and in your daily life
> because they can believe more what they see than
> what they hear.

**Kay Gilley** is president of Intentional Leadership Systems, with offices in Durham, North Carolina and Eugene, Oregon. She brings nearly 30 years experience in general and human resource management to leadership and organizational development practice. She participated in a delegation consulting with the Ministry of Labor, the People's Republic of China, and Chinese business people on the motivational, philosophical, and technical considerations of developing that country's first-ever labor and employment law.

Gilley received her MISR (Industrial Relations) with a minor in law from the University of Oregon Graduate School of Management, receiving the Award for Academic Excellence for her program. She has also received her Professional in Human Resources (PHR) practitioner designation from the Human Resource Certification Institute (Society for Human Resource Management).

# Conscious Leadership: Bringing Life To Social Responsibility

## *Kay Gilley*

After several months of "putting out fires" in his company, Sam quietly but eloquently began speaking in the middle of a tense meeting. Sam often gave little speeches in meetings, but this one was different. This one came straight from his heart, and it somewhat painfully reflected that he had finally achieved a level of consciousness we had been working toward in our personal coaching sessions.

"It occurs to me that we have been running this company on 50 percent, and 50 percent just isn't good enough any more. I have done 50 percent of what I should have. I have failed to do the 50 percent that I didn't want to do, and no one has held me accountable. In an unspoken quid pro quo, I have let the rest of the management team get by with failing to do the 50 percent of their jobs that they don't like. I haven't held them accountable, and they haven't held me accountable."

"Then," he continued, "they have done the same thing with people that reported to them. At the end of this lack-of-accountability chain, there has been the person on the front-line trying to do a job. We haven't done our job in training, counseling, or following up on the counseling, and then we wonder why the employee isn't doing the job."

"I've gotten by with doing the 50 percent that I am comfortable with, and so has everybody else. Fifty percent just isn't good enough for this company any more."

Conscious leadership is hard because leaders begin to see how they have created what they have blamed others for and how they have created what they wanted to avoid. Conscious leadership is hard because it requires us to give up our illusions. And it is the only way to develop intentionality. It is the only way to achieve the vision, values, mission, and goals that we have worked so hard at developing in recent years. It is the only way that these things take on life and meaning for people everywhere in our organizations.

## Conscious Leadership Cannot Happen Without Self-Awareness

In early meetings with executives, I am often reminded of an old "good news, bad news" joke. In the joke, an airline pilot reports to the passengers, "I have some good news and some bad news. The good news is that we are making really good time. The bad news is that we don't know where we are."

Even a quarter of a century ago, when professional management was still a relatively new science for most businesses, an early writer shared his observation of the effect it was having on our organizations.

> A critical disability that goes with expanding
> competence is the inability (or unwillingness) to
> examine the assumptions by which one operates.
> In order to achieve great competence, individuals
> (or institutions) must put their heads down, cut
> out the peripheral vision that might keep the
> assumptions always in view and run!
> —Robert K. Greenleaf,
> *Servant Leadership—A Journey of into the Nature of Legitimate Power and Greatness*

This is commerce as we have come to know it: business by the numbers, MBOs, action plans, goals, and projections, all based on unquestioned perceptions of reality.

Self-awareness is essential for both leaders and organizations to know "where we are." Every leader has his or her story of "where we are." Most of the time the story is a work of fiction created in good faith and supported by a set of numbers but framed by unexamined assumptions and beliefs about how they want conditions to be.

Self-awareness breaks individuals away from their "stories," by questioning reality. Awareness is like a mirror which reflects without bias. It shows what is, without comment, judgment, explanation or analysis to color it. It allows us to know "where we are." Except by pure accident, a company will never achieve its vision, values, mission, and goals until it knows where it is now.

The geographical equivalent would be to say, "I want to go to Chicago," and to take off without knowing where my journey begins. If I am at my Oregon home, I need to head east and slightly north, but if I am at my North Carolina home, I need to go sharply north and west. Of necessity, my trip is defined by my starting point. Without the mirror of self-awareness for both individuals and the organization, they are largely clueless about how to get where they want to go.

## The Broccoli Seed School Of Leadership

In early meetings with executives and executive teams, I often bring a head of broccoli with me. This does get raised eyebrows and sometimes vegetable humor as people query what we are going to do with the broccoli. I then proceed to explain that I am about to explain the most important leadership lesson they may ever receive.

I point out the general shape and configuration of the broccoli. Then I pull off the next largest division of the vegetable and note that it has the same shape and configuration. Subsequently, I break off each successively smaller units of broccoli, demonstrating how each reflects the size and shape of the whole. Finally, I tell them that if we were to look at a single cell of broccoli, we would discover that, even on the cellular level, the plant retains the same shape and configuration as the whole.

Companies are a lot like broccoli, I say. The leadership of a company is its "broccoli seed." What occurs at the top will be re-created again and again in successively larger business units until it encompasses the whole enterprise. So it is critical that the executive team understand exactly what it is reflecting into the organization. Self-awareness work is the work of discovering the broccoli seed of the company. It removes the illusions that block the mirror and cleans it so we can discover what we really look like.

For a short time, I worked with the executive team of a corporation which had a history of adversarial relations with their union. The group was only interested in blaming the union's leadership and its lack of trustworthiness. Yet in individual sessions members of the executive team had described such deep distrust among themselves that it was not a surprise that they distrusted union officers.

Just as Sam had unwittingly created broccoli seed for his organization which said that "Fifty percent is OK, as long as I don't have to do the things I don't like," these executives had created broccoli seed of distrust. Self-awareness work reveals to individuals and groups what is being created and what is needed to change it. Groups that have done this work can consciously choose to plant seeds of social responsibility, respect for the environment, respect for the whole person in the company, or excellent customer service.

It takes a lot of courage to erase our illusions and objectively see ourselves individually and collectively, and it is the only way that a company will discover what its broccoli seed is. The group I have just described flunked the courage test, as many do, using the excuse that this isn't appropriate for the workplace. Self-awareness is something to be done on one's own, they said. So, they continue planting seeds of distrust as they profess incredulity about "Why can't we just trust each other like we used to?" Sam is passing the courage test, one day at a time, and he is planting seeds of courage and accountability as he does.

## Knowing What We Do Not Know

Clearing the mirror of self-awareness gives us more information about reality, taking us closer to an objective standard of truth. There are four different ways of knowing the truth. Among the possibilities that we know about, there are things that we know we know, and there are things that we know that we don't

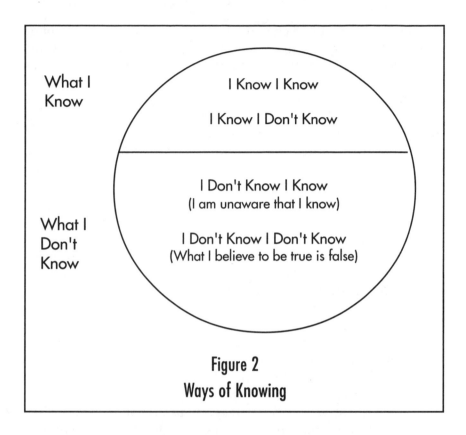

**Figure 2**
**Ways of Knowing**

know. For instance, I know my name, where I was born, and where I live. I am quite certain about these. I am also certain about some things that I don't know about. I know nothing about microbiology, how to speak Chinese, or what it is like to live in war-torn Bosnia.

Among things that we do not know, there are the same two possibilities. There are things that we don't know that we know, and there are things that we don't know we don't know. For instance, there was a time not so long ago that I thought I knew nothing about quantum physics. Then I read a book comparing organizational behavior with quantum physics, and I discovered I really knew quite a bit about the subject. I just hadn't known it was quantum physics. All of us have things that we know about that we aren't aware of knowing.

Inversely, there are many things we believe to be true that are indeed false: we just don't know that we don't know. In the corporation with the union problems, management believed that the union officers didn't care about the company and could not be trusted. After lengthy interviews with those union leaders, I was totally convinced that they cared about the company every bit as much as management did. However, because the management team hadn't done its self-awareness work to discover what they didn't know they didn't know, they had not been able to bring that important part of knowing to consciousness.

Questions invite a higher standard of truth. They help us individually and collectively to discover what we know that we didn't know we knew and what we didn't know that we didn't know. Unless a wake-up call jars our reality, most of us won't choose to doubt that our "stories" are the truth. One of my favorite questions to ask teams of managers who believe they know how things are is: What if the opposite were true? To their astonishment, further exploration often demonstrates that some part of the opposite actually is true. They just didn't know.

Owners of a manufacturing company contacted me because they were having trouble getting more active participation among their line workers. One owner explained, "They have good ideas, and they seem excited. They just don't follow through." The owners had "tried everything," he said, and they couldn't imagine what the problem was.

Upon questioning, the owners admitted that in fact they had started some very important projects which impacted the employees, but the demands of running the company from day to day had prevented them from completing the undertakings. Questions allowed them to come to know that what was occurring in the plant was simply a reflection of what they were doing—the broccoli seed they were planting without knowing it. Questions and awareness delivered a more objective standard of truth.

The conscious mind has the capacity to process seven pieces of information per minute. The unconscious mind can process 300,000 pieces in the same amount of time. The nonlinear, nonverbal right brain has 50 times more brain cells than the overused left brain upon which business has become so totally dependent. Most of this vast library of information is carried around in that part of us that "we don't know." It is the storehouse that, when questioned, can clear the mirrors of awareness and enable a more accurate assessment of "where we are" so that both individually and collectively conscious movement can begin creating the broccoli seed we want in our organizations—the seed that takes us toward the vision, values, mission, and goals of the company.

## Awareness Is The Pass-Key To Leading Consciously

Awareness does not happen overnight but continues to reveal itself over time. However, until individuals and groups begin the journey of discovering "where they are," what their stories are, what they know that they aren't aware of knowing, and what they have believed to be true that is actually false, they cannot begin to either live or lead in a conscious way.

Most of us spend much of our lives on "auto-pilot." Traditional managers auto-pilot their way through interactions and decisions, operating from assumptions that may never have been challenged. When we depend on old assumptions, ignoring all the things "we don't know," we automatically filter out critical information. The American automobile industry in the 1950s and 1960s filtered out critical information about customer dissatisfaction, until foreign competition came along and shocked it from its auto-pilot mode. Swiss watch makers, slide rule and mechanical calculator manufacturers also received belated wake-up calls that shocked them from their perceptions of "reality."

It is foolhardy at best to run any organization from unchallenged assumptions. The more people in a company that continuously challenge what reality is, the more likely it will be to approach a more objective standard of truth about its operational environment. However, if leadership has not done its self-awareness work to discover there are many realities, it will not have planted the broccoli seed which enables a culture of questioning, deliberation, and intentionality throughout.

Until an organization becomes more conscious, more often than not what I refer to as "inverse intelligence" prevails. One would expect that when a group of bright people come together to make a decision, their combined abilities would result in a group intelligence greater than that of any individual.

However, in most groups that I have observed which haven't done self-awareness work, exactly the opposite is true. The resulting group intelligence is significantly *less* than that of any of the individuals that comprise it. In simple terms, if the average intelligence of the individuals in a group is 120, the group intelligence will often be 60, or 70, rather than 150.

For example, one group got together to discuss the process of implementing new technology when installation was nearly complete. A conversion date was selected and a project schedule was developed to meet that deadline. There was apparent enthusiasm, until major problems surfaced. Employees weren't adequately trained. The computer program that drove the new system was incompatible with programs being used in other parts of the operation, and computer codes that should have been rewritten weren't. Suppliers hadn't been notified of projected down time, and distributors had not been informed of possible delays.

When the management group met to assess what went wrong, almost every individual confessed to having had concerns about the schedule, but "since everybody else seemed to think it would work," reservations had not been voiced. Any one of the participants could have improved the quality of the decision but instead, didn't even exercise the judgment that normal individual intelligence would have dictated. Instead of a 120-IQ decision, the group made a decision that reflected a group intelligence much lower than that of individuals who comprised the group. Had this group planted the broccoli seed of consciousness which comes from questioning reality, they would have sought other realities, and both dollar and ill-will costs would likely have been significantly less.

In my leadership development practice, I often do a project which helps groups of executives learn to operate consciously by identifying both the countless realities in their operational and marketplace environments and the dozens of ways in which the company can function well in all or many of them. We then explore many versions of "where we are," often times revealing realities that had been ignored in the past. When we consciously bring them forth, they can no longer be denied and must instead be addressed. Increased awareness allows conscious exploration so more intentional approaches can prevail in the future.

This kind of consciousness is not a "touchy-feely" activity relegated to "when we have the time." It has become business necessity for the company that wants to remain competitive, vital and financially stable. By the time a new competitor or replacement product provides a wake-up call, it is usually too late. At the doorstep of the 21st Century, we can no longer view consciousness as an add-on, frill, or "feel-good" activity. Developing both individual and organizational consciousness is a matter of economic survival.

## Blending Consciousness And Commerce Is The Only Formula For Long-term Success

Many executives view self-awareness and consciousness-building as a luxury, a frill, or something for overstaffed executive teams to do while the "real work" of the organization is being done elsewhere. They dismiss it as taking productive time away from the purpose of the enterprise, or they develop frustration at what they describe as "examining our navels" because they do not understand the long-term importance of the work.

When there is a lack of awareness and consciousness in our organizations, people learn to leave the best parts of themselves behind. New people with creative ideas and questions about how things are done are molded into thinking, saying and doing what is "acceptable here." Most organizations engage in such activity so automatically that they don't even know these are the broccoli seeds being planted in every new hire. Raising consciousness becomes a matter of survival.

Yet, an approach to business which concentrates only on consciousness is just as incomplete and unsustainable as one which overfocuses on the numbers to the exclusion of challenges of reality. It is only by consciously exploring both perspectives and learning to plant broccoli seeds which keep them in balance that we as human beings come to truly understand the important relationships which blending the two can bring to life and to business.

Consciousness without actualization makes little difference to improving the world. This might best be understood by comparing it to a talented painter who sits around dreaming up good ideas for paintings but doesn't have the canvas, paints, brush, or other tools to bring those ideas to life. Unlike Rembrandt and da Vinci who continue to spiritually move people centuries after their deaths, this painter doesn't even influence immediate social circles.

Consciousness brought to life in the world occurs when we use that awareness to discover and experience a strong sense of purpose—a reason that we are on this earth. We come to know what "our work" in the world is, and we begin to consciously live so that we focus upon achieving that purpose. When we are doing "our work," we are creative, internally motivated, energized, peaceful, and joyful—and we leave a legacy. We affect the lives of others in big ways and small ones.

When we blend consciousness with commerce, we achieve the best of all worlds. Commerce provides a vehicle for actualizing our consciousness and our selves, and commerce is more effective and better positioned in a competitive business environment when whole people—their bodies, minds, and spirits—are intentionally and actively engaged with a sense of purpose.

When organizations commit to a collective purpose or mission of improving the world in some way, and when conscious energy is committed to achieving that purpose in big and small ways throughout the enterprise, magic occurs. People who as individuals may feel frustrated at the overwhelming prospect of trying to improve the world, connect in community with others of like mind. What was overwhelming for one person to accomplish not only becomes achievable, but expandable and repeatable.

One of my client organizations is committed to providing an enhanced quality of life for people with Alzheimer's disease and mental illness. Although each is highly committed to improving the quality of life for these people, because of time and energy demands, no one individual could make a significant contribution to even a single life. Brought together with a common sense of purpose and mission, suddenly what was impossible for one person to accomplish begins to happen every day and with dozens of people. They begin to build active communities for what have often been "society's rejects."

From a commercial perspective and largely because of their ability to collectively do what has been perceived as un-do-able, the small company has been nationally recognized as an innovator in their field and has attracted both investors and interest from larger companies.

Perhaps as significantly, the company experiences an annual turnover rate of three percent among employees who complete their trial service period in an industry which averages 70 percent per year. This reflection of both the commitment of people to the collective purpose of the company and to the satisfaction individuals working with purpose experience also pays the real financial dividend of saving the company thousands of dollars each year in turnover costs. This is only possible because leadership consciously and intentionally plants the broccoli seed to allow it to happen every day.

Study after study of companies which are learning to blend consciousness with commerce indicate that this is a winning formula financially, while making the world a better place in which to live and work.

"More than 35 percent of workers surveyed in a 1993 "faxpoll" by *Inc.* magazine reported that a sense of mission and purpose is their single most important long-term motivator. Fewer than half that number were motivated by money," according to *Business Ethics* magazine. When leaders intentionally plant broccoli seed which enables people to experience consciousness brought into the real world, the sense of commitment, motivation, satisfaction and purpose they feel becomes a financial asset.

A 1993 study of firms profiled in the *100 Best Companies to Work for in America* over an eight-year period revealed a 19 1/2 percent annual return for those companies during a period in which the 3,000 largest companies in the United States averaged a 12 percent annual return.

If we are to successfully bring consciousness to the real world, profitability must be an overriding concern. Financial resources can make the difference between talking the talking and walking the talk corporately. I once worked in a daily newspaper which was able to challenge a law which it felt violated the First Amendment only because it had the financial resources to "put its money where its mouth is" and hire the legal expertise to facilitate maneuvers which ended when a special session of the legislature repealed the law. Without the financial clout, the rights of all of us may have been weakened.

It is the clout that has come from commercial success that allows Stonyfield Farm Yogurt to tell farmers that it will not buy milk from cows which have received bovine growth hormone. They have been able to put teeth in their conscious commitment to produce healthy foods because of the loyalty of their customers and their consequent financial leverage. Both of these companies have been very intentional in the seeds they have planted, and their fiscal success has enabled them to act in accord with their consciousness.

# Consciousness Brings Meaning To Social Responsibility

As the Baby Boomers reach mid-life, efforts to make the world a better place have moved from the streets in the 1960s to the boardrooms in the 1990s. Armed with financial results which demonstrate that companies can do well by doing good, the ranks of socially responsible businesses grow exponentially each year.

Some of these businesses have occasionally ended up with egg on their corporate faces because they failed to follow up their commitment by creating the broccoli seed within their enterprises which would ensure that everyone is conscious of how every act of every individual committed in the company's name reflects upon it as a whole.

When a company commits to doing business on the higher road, that should *not* mean that it will always be perfect. It should mean that every mistake or transgression is used to spirit a higher level of consciousness. It should mean that there are a set of questions which every person in the company uses to assess every potential action. Questions like, "Will this action further our company's purpose or mission?", "How do each of our corporate values guide me in *this* decision?", and "Is my course of action in any way motivated by fear or ego?" give people tools to understand and to raise consciousness of their personal roles in perpetuating the broccoli seed of social responsibility. Just saying "We want to be socially responsible" won't do it.

A real commitment requires planting the broccoli seed of social responsibility and raising that commitment to a level of consciousness in every corner of the company. Consciousness is the only tool that will bring actuality to social responsibility. Just as Sam had certain things that he didn't like to do and wasn't held accountable for, leaders in many companies ostensibly committed to social responsibility are not doing the consciousness-raising and aren't been held accountable for that. Those that hope to cash in on the significant commercial benefits of social responsibility must devote themselves just as sincerely and accountably to their role in creating the consciousness throughout the organization to make it happen. Saying the words, developing mission statements, and corporate goals will not create true social responsibility until those things have life and meaning in the daily operational world that every person in the company works in each day.

**Dave Potter** is president and CEO of Concurrent Sciences, Inc. He has been involved in corporate management and training for twenty years. Prior to founding Concurrent Sciences in 1983, he taught instructor-training courses at UC Berkeley and worked as a customer marketing manager for Intel Corporation.

In addition to his responsibilities as CEO, Potter consults with other organizations, most often working with leadership teams and intact work groups. He describes his work with other companies as a "3-D" experience in communication and group alignment—a unique combination of Discovery, Dialogue, and Direction. The 3-D process is the culmination of years of experience with his and other companies that demand a high level of communication and teamwork. He lives in northern Idaho.

# Journey Into The Soul Of An Organization

*Dave Potter*

Almost twenty years ago, my next door neighbor committed suicide. Bruce's violent death shocked and mystified me because he had seemed so well-adjusted He was outgoing and fun to be around. How could this happen? Why? And why Bruce, of all people? He had never even hinted at anything seriously troubling him—he seemed so easy-going. But, as Sherlock Holmes once pointed out to Dr. Watson, the dog not barking is as much a clue as the dog barking. After talking it over with my wife, we realized that the fact that there was no hint of any problems was, perhaps, the major clue to this tragedy. Bruce never, ever, talked about his own personal issues. He could talk nonstop about issues that interested you, and he was a wonderful listener, but his inner life was almost uniformly a mystery to all who knew him. It was only when we read the suicide note that it became clear how distraught he had been about his separation with his wife. He had successfully hidden his inner turmoil from everyone around him.

In these times of accelerating technological and social change, many organizations are also in a state of inner turmoil. This condition is common, and yet tremendous energies are expended to hide the unrest and to bury evidence of discord and inconsistency. But, at what cost to the organization and its people?

What damage is done when...

> ...the division head can't tell his own staff the real reason a key manager is being is "laid off"?
>
> ...the engineering team won't tell management that a project is doomed to failure and, instead, postpone the inevitable by pushing the completion date out further and further, week by week, month by month?
>
> ...a manager has so alienated his staff that they are ready to mutiny, and not one of them has mentioned the problem to his face?
>
> ...a key worker is so sick of working on the same project, month-in and month-out, she goes home every night and complains of her weariness to her husband but, because she wants to be a "team player," has never mentioned it to her team leader?

Every organization has internal conflict, but it is often buried in company or social protocol. This organizational problem of covering up conflict has deep roots. Maybe it begins with parents telling us that "big boys (girls) don't cry" or, "don't tell Aunt Gertrude that you don't like the gift, because she'll be hurt" Our teachers taught us that the penalty for looking like you don't know the answer is to get called on and be embarrassed for not being smart or prepared. Savvy students develop a face and a posture that says, "I'm really here—and I know and understand what you're saying," to hide the fact that they have given up and their minds are many miles away. The people we work with are so skilled at hiding from us what they really think and feel that we may be totally unaware that a key project is about to fall apart. No one wants to look stupid, and no one wants to hint that they don't have it all together. The real problem for the organization is not the conflict, but its unavailability for examination.

## "No Problems Here"

If a casual acquaintance asks how I am, I will probably answer "fine," even if I'm stressed-out about something. Likewise, if someone asks about how my company is doing, I will often say "great" and give a short description of how things

Appearance of Unity

are under control, even when they are not. When I do pre-retreat interviews of individual members of a group I'll be working with, what's really happening in the group may not begin to come out until the interview is nearly over.

Just as we attempt to make our personal lives appear calm and trouble-free, we work very hard to make our organization look like everyone is in sync and pulling in the same direction. For instance:

> ...the marketing director who reports to the president that the ad campaign is in "great shape," even though she knows the two product managers are in the middle of a bitter feud over content and creative control and, without the miracle she is hoping for, it's likely to be over budget and late, or...

> ...the production supervisor who knows there are serious quality problems on one of his lines, but hopes to get it squared away before the upcoming plant inspection.

We may even do such a good job of creating the illusion of unity, harmony, and shared vision that we come to believe it ourselves, and that belief obscures any evidence to the contrary. For instance:

> ...the CEO who proudly points to the corporate mission statement hung on the wall, but none of the employees outside the executive suite would recognize it as being their own if the company logo weren't on it.

Jerry Harvey coined the term "Abilene Paradox" to describe the situation where a group goes, collectively, someplace no one individual wants to go, not because of peer pressure or "group tyranny," but because no one is willing to risk telling their personal truth. It is like the idea presented at a strategy meeting that no one believes is feasible, but there isn't anyone who will risk saying so out loud. Because each member of the strategy team is so skilled at hiding what they really think and feel, when they look around the table, it looks as though all the rest think it's a good idea. So each of them thinks "maybe they know something I don't know" and, out of fear of looking stupid, or being challenged no one says anything and a bad idea goes forward. It is well documented that this is how we got ourselves into the Bay of Pigs fiasco during the Kennedy era and how the Watergate break-in got authorized during the Nixon administration. In both

these cases, the majority of the presi-
dential advisors each thought, privately and independently, that the
proposals were bad, perhaps
even insane, but they said
nothing.

When asked
about the major
problems in his
organization, a
vice-president
once told me that the
biggest problem was the president's tendency to compulsively
micromanage. It seemed to him that every important document
leaving the company was reviewed and red-lined, sometimes
going through five or six cycles before the president approved it.
He said, "It's driving us all nuts! Why doesn't he just do it
himself?!?" He then said, almost in a whisper, that "Everyone in
the company knows his micromanagement is a problem." When
asked, "*Everyone*?!?," he paused for just an instant and then
exclaimed with the shock of realization, "Well, you can't tell the
*President!*"

Admittedly, it takes great personal courage to address
issues directly to those we are in conflict with. It takes even
greater skill to do it in a way that doesn't end with negative and
unresolved feelings. It's uncomfortable and scary. We fear that
our co-workers, our managers, or our employees will ask us
questions we can't or don't want to answer and that it might turn
into an ugly scene, with strong and differing points of view. So,
when we talk about the troubling issues we have with our co-
workers or the company, we normally only do it in safety, with
like-minded colleagues and friends, and not with the people who
most need to hear it.

This unspoken and unconscious collusion not to express
what's really going on is a fundamental problem in organizations.
How many times have you been to a long, lifeless meeting, and the
moment it ends, people gather into subgroups and only then
begin to say, with great animation, what they really think and
feel? Without somehow getting beyond the facade of "we've got it all
together," there is no hope of the organization to discover its essence,
its soul, and to tap the power and creativity of its membership.

# The Gift Of Crisis:
# Discovery

In spite of all our efforts to keep up appearances, inevitably a crisis presents itself which cannot be ignored. The Chinese word for crisis is "wei-ji", and is represented by pairing, side by side, the symbols for danger (wei) and opportunity (ji). The danger of ignoring the crisis or applying a quick-fix, without understanding the underlying dynamics, is that an even larger crisis will result later—and we might not even recognize it as being related to the first! The opportunity the crisis presents is one of discovery, and the rejuvenation and transformation that results if the call to awakening is truly heeded.

## A Personal Anecdote

In 1995, early on a Monday morning, one of my key employees called me into the conference room and, with explosive emotion, told me that he couldn't stand the way he was treated by me and my staff. After a tense and emotional discussion, there seemed to be no possibility of reconciliation. In a final flourish, Matt walked out the door saying, "I've had it—I quit!" Not once in my twenty years of management, had I ever had anyone quit in anger. This was more than a little upsetting and it caused me to question my ability as a manager and my effectiveness in my work with other organizations. If you had asked me five minutes before if there were any serious interpersonal problems on my staff, I would have said "no." Although Matt had experienced some difficulties with some of his co-workers in the past, I had no idea how bad things really were. As a consequence, Matt's outburst had punched a serious hole right in the middle of my illusion of a smoothly-operating corporate machine.

Initially, my staff viewed the incident as "Matt's problem" and his temperamental inability to deal with the inevitable periods of stress in our fast-paced environment. Since it looked to them like an isolated incident, upsetting the calm and efficiency of the rest of the office, it was easy to blame Matt for the ensuing chaos in our office. My business colleagues advised me to get Matt out of there as fast as I possibly could, preferably that same day, before he did any more damage. The logical thing to do was to quickly patch the hole, begin looking for a replacement, and get back to business.

## Into The Abyss:
## Chaos And Dialogue

But we didn't do the logical thing. Instead of simply closing up the hole, we dug deeper and entered a stage of group development M. Scott Peck calls "chaos" in his community-building model. Here, individual differences surface, opposing perceptions and viewpoints are presented and defended, and emotions run high. This is tricky and dangerous territory, and most groups have difficulty here, because they see only two ways out of the chaos. They either:

- avoid appearance of differences, soften opinions, or retreat altogether, or...

- advance into the chaos, with egos blaring, and those with the greatest powers of personal and social persuasion sway the course.

In the first case, the truth is not told, and critical information is lost, regressing the group back to the level of appearances and denial, with no possibility of learning. In the second case, struggle, power plays, and cacophony prevail, and one or more subgroups become alienated—a less than optimal resolution.

There is a third way, however—powerful, but not easy. It requires moving into the area of disagreement and conflict, but with an attitude of curiosity, rather than determining who is right. It's like the Zen method of dealing with pain by bringing awareness into the pain, instead of away from it: Is it constant or throbbing, sharp or dull, hot or cold? Exactly where is it located? What shape does it have, does the position or extent change? It's a technique designed to substitute curiosity in place of the impulse to run away from the pain, and to expand awareness to include and understand the source of the pain.

This third way involves "dialogue," a way of exploring and communicating not commonly practiced in our culture. Popularized by the late physicist David Bohm, dialogue, in this context, has a meaning distinct from the usual meaning of a discussion where different viewpoints are debated and defended. Through dialogue, the collective intelligence and experience of the group are manifested in creative and unexpected ways, in contrast to the more common outcomes of negotiated compromise or majority rule. Although it's beyond the scope of this essay to enumerate the principles of dialogue, they are described in Peter Senge's *Fifth Discipline Fieldbook* and in David Bohm's *On Dialogue*. In his essay, "Dialogue: The Power of Collective Thinking," contained in *Reflections on Creating Learning Organizations*, William Isaacs, of DIA•logos, Inc. and the MIT Organizational Learning Center, says:

> Physicist David Bohm has compared dialogue to superconductivity. In superconductivity, electrons cooled to very low temperatures act more like a coherent whole than as separate parts. They flow around obstacles without colliding with one another, creating no resistance and very high energy. At higher temperatures, however, they begin to act like separate parts, scattering into a random movement and losing momentum.
>
> Particularly when discussing tough issues, people act more like separate, high-temperature electrons. Dialogue seeks to help people attain high energy and low friction without ruling out differences between them. Negotiation tactics, in contrast, often try to cool down interactions by bypassing the most difficult issues and narrowing the field of exchange to something manageable. They achieve "cooler" interactions, but lose energy and intelligence in the process. In dialogue, the aim is to create a special environment in which a different kind of relationship among the parts can come into play—one that reveals both high energy and high intelligence.

To address Matt's departure and to begin the dialogue process, we called an impromptu staff meeting. Although it would have been desirable to have Matt participate, he was not available and some of his co-workers felt strongly that they wanted to meet without him. Using principles drawn from David Bohm's work and the modern practitioners of dialogue, we explored unexamined perceptions, unstated assumptions, and unvoiced convictions. We probed the dynamics underlying Matt's blow up:

- What assumptions had we made about Matt and the cause of his resignation?

- Was it truly and isolated instance, or was it indicative of deeper problems in our group?

- What did it mean about us, individually and collectively, that an important set of work relationships were nearing the point of collapse, and we weren't aware of it?

- What were the lessons embedded in this event?

This was an uncomfortable examination. It was difficult for me personally, because I had always taken special pride in how well our group worked together. People had often commented on the cheerful and cooperative, yet productive, environment that permeated the office. What had happened?

Through this dialogue meeting and other conversations, many of which did involve Matt, we began to realize that Matt's eruption was not his problem alone, but symptomatic of something deeper. The members of the group started to look to themselves to see what part they each might have played. To our dismay, things began to get worse rather than better, and we started to treat each other with even less respect than normal. In truth, the situation wasn't really any worse now than just before Matt announced he was quitting—we simply hadn't noticed before, and now we couldn't hide it. Underneath our illusory "appearance of unity," a whole layer of distrust and conflict had jumped into our awareness.

We began to recall the events of the previous nine months. We could identify many instances of undercutting and undermining, but we hadn't really been conscious of them until now. Yes, now that we thought about it, sometimes we did roll our eyes nearly to the back of our heads when Matt talked. And, we occasionally did it with each other, too. A clique had formed that went to lunch together after the weekly tech meetings, and certain members of the technical staff were never invited. Many examples of reduced efficiency and lack of coordination suddenly came to mind. An air of distrust, second-guessing, and rivalry had crept

into the office, and we hadn't paid attention to the signs because it didn't fit our image of who we were as a group. Now, with Matt's blow up and our probing deeper, things looked worse than ever before. It seemed as though we'd never recover.

## We Give Up:
## Emptiness And Surrender

How well we treated each other was a key part of our corporate identity and our organization seemed to be falling apart with the new awareness that we often didn't treat each other with respect. We were often working at cross purposes. We didn't know what to do. Everything had been said, and there still didn't seem to be any sign of resolution. There was no escaping it—we weren't the organization we thought we were. And creating a corporate resolve that we simply begin to treat each other better and cooperate more willingly seemed pointless and futile, like forcing a five year-old to say "I'm sorry" to his brother, when he doesn't really feel it. We had no answer. Maybe we really were just too different to work effectively together.

At the previous level of chaos and instability, there had been a search for "the answer" that would deliver us from the discomfort of fully experiencing the roots of the problem. As long as we feverishly held on to the hope that there would be delivery from the chaos with a simple answer or by selecting one of the many contradictory points of view as the "right" one, there was no hope of moving beyond this stage. In fact, to the degree that we tried to force our way out was the degree that we were ineffective at moving further. One by one, individuals in the group realized that, indeed, no one had the answer and, paradoxically, each point of view was valid within the experience of the individual. There seemed to be "No Exit"—

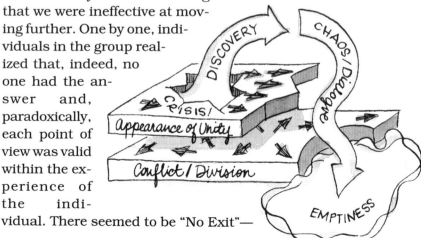

we were stuck and going nowhere. There was nothing to do but to give up. We were deep in the stage M. Scott Peck calls "emptiness" in his community-building model.

If chaos is uncomfortable, this stage of truly not knowing, is by far the most difficult—the organizational equivalent of the "dark night of the soul." Paradoxically, it is in this state of emptiness that we are closest to the soul of the organization. By working through the level of chaos and individual differences using the tools of inquiry and dialogue, a deep knowledge of the group develops, even though no one individual knows what to do with this new awareness.

## Out of the Emptiness: Creative Emergence

> There ain't no answer. There ain't ever going to be an answer. There never was an answer. That's the answer.
>
> —Gertrude Stein

Out of the blue, and without us being prepared for any positive fallout from Matt's quitting, signs of renewed connection began appearing, like crocuses popping through in the spring: Jeff announced that he would no longer attend these exclusive "tech" lunches. Nonexclusive lunches after the tech meetings were OK, but they'd be open to anyone who wanted to come. Some of the insensitive looks that occasionally went across the conference table at tense moments disappeared. Even Matt, who had

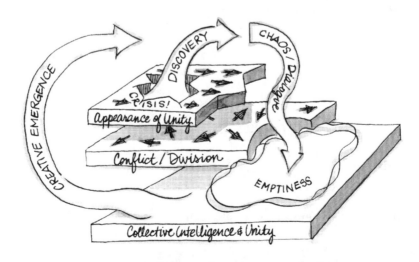

seemed on the verge of doing something vengeful and destructive on his exit, extended his two-week notice to three, and worked evenings and weekends to complete the projects he'd been working on. He did this even though it meant no extra pay, and even though he would still be out of a job at the end of the three weeks.

Something magical had happened, and it had come unexpectedly. Like a leaderless flock of birds turning as one in the sky, we had spontaneously re-formed ourselves and moved to a higher level of organizational effectiveness and well-being.

What happened? After giving up all hope and without mandating a change in our behavior, we had changed. Why? David Bohm once said, "the act of observing thought changes it." Instead of immediately instituting damage control, we had explored the meaning of the disruption and ensuing chaos. We honestly and openly observed ourselves, using the principles advocated by dialogue practitioners such as Bill Isaacs and David Bohm. As difficult and uncomfortable as it was to stay with the process, the resolution presented itself spontaneously and unexpectedly, in its own way and time.

We found that below the layer of apparent unity and that of conflicting energies, was one of collective wisdom, unity, and deep interconnectedness. At this level, after moving through emptiness, the group begins to think as one. Ideas and observations that emerge come as expressions of the group's collective wisdom, informed by the group's previous experience of self-discovery during the earlier stages of chaos and emptiness. *The very differences that were divisive during the stage of chaos and conflict provide harmony, energy, and power at this deepest level.* This level of underlying unity was, and is, always there, but it is typically obscured by the cloak of apparent unity and the noise of unacknowledged conflict.

We had moved through the four phases of discovery-chaos-emptiness-emergence, each with their own dangers and possibilities, and into the fifth stage of integration, where the fruits of the emergence are incorporated into the learning of the organization:

1. **Discovery.** New awareness, precipitated by crisis (or inquiry).
2. **Chaos/Dialogue.** Conflict and differences exposed, exploration through dialogue.

3. **Emptiness.** Group and individual "giving up," surrender to collective intelligence.

4. **Creative Emergence.** Spontaneous, creative, and transformative direction.

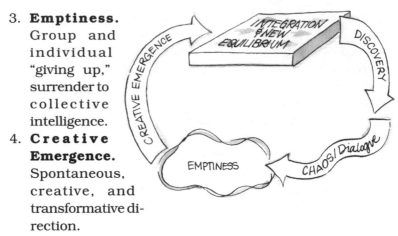

5. **Integration.** New equilibrium at a higher level.

## Continuing the Journey: Cycles of Discovery

Were this a fairy tale, we could end this story with "and the organization lived happily ever after." We had, indeed, reached a new level of cooperation and productivity but, in life and business, nothing is permanent. Our new equilibrium was shattered by events in the marketplace that forced us to realize that our products were lacking in some serious ways. This crisis initiated a new cycle of chaos, followed by dialogue and the painful emptiness of not knowing what to do. Again, after giving up the idea that there might be an easy solution, creative and productive ideas and events emerged out of nowhere, making the company, people, and products stronger than they ever were before. Of course, even this was not the last chapter, with new events later disrupting our new equilibrium, and subsequent renewal and growth.

### Continuing Attentiveness

There's no guarantee of making it even once through the discovery-chaos-emptiness-emergence-integration cycle, much less multiple times, since there are powerful counter-forces at each stage. The paralyzing effect of unexpected crisis, the pain and confusion of looking deeper into the underlying dynamics, the discomfort of being in emptiness and "not knowing", the inability to incorporate transformational insights, all mitigate against the organization completing the cycle of growth and renewal.

If the growth is allowed continue, the cycle winds around and around, in an expanding spiral. Each time, the organization emerges from emptiness, integrates all that it has learned about itself and finds greater unity and expanded effectiveness. Of course, in time, this new knowledge will become calcified, and new events will give the organization the opportunity to grow and adapt.

In a skilled and experienced group, able to withstand the confusion of chaos and frustration of emptiness, the full cycle can appear even in individual meetings, where particularly important and difficult issues are being addressed. For instance, look for chaos, emptiness, and emergence in this description by Tom Portante, a futurist for Andersen Consulting:

> I was reminded of times in our meetings where lots of people are calling out ideas, where it seems that there can be little (if any) common ground in a room full of bright, opinionated and ego-strong participants. At first, it looks like the usual verbal warfare where one person makes an argument, the others listen for weak spots and sites for flanking maneuvers. What invariably happens, after false starts, after a general rapport has developed in the room, after rises and falls in levels of frustration and anxiety, and with a lot of skillful verbal navigational aides by the group's facilitator—is something remarkable. It's as if some of the people are saying 'the answer is 2,' others are saying 'no, the answer is 6,' still others, 'no, it's 5,' and everyone is looking for guidance as to which one is The Right Answer. After a while, there comes the uncomfortable acceptance of the inevitability of an impasse. We may hear a wearisome comment like, 'well, I guess we can all live with 2,' but, somehow, the group neither accepts the compromise nor disbands. Then, unexpectedly, the conversation develops a different cadence, a different rhythm. What tends to happen is that people stop focusing their attention on the most recent speaker's comments and begin addressing some of the underlying assumptions that exist to frame a number of

specific conversational threads. What brings a
smile to my face is when the conversation moves
away from the obvious compromises, to a spirited
exchange that allows us to leave the table with a
near-unanimous decision that, indeed, the answer
is neither 2, nor 6, nor 5, but rather, 16$\frac{1}{2}$. The
creativity that came up with this new answer is
hard to isolate—we often don't even remember who
in the group suggested the thread that led to a
transformation in thinking.

## Summary

The journey into the soul of an organization, into its collective intelligence and underlying unity, is not a trip for the faint-hearted or those looking for quick fixes. It is sometimes painful, sometimes glorious and mysterious, has no final destination and, at each stage, there are strong forces acting against progression to the next phase. In fact, most organizations only rarely move through and beyond chaos and, instead, collapse back into the illusion of unity and solidarity.

When a group is in chaos and is beginning to explore its differences, there is a deep fear—a fear that if the group goes any deeper, it will descend into a bottomless tangle of conflicting egos and unresolvable forces. It's an area of the unknown, with personal beliefs, convictions, and world views that are normally only indirectly expressed. The result of fully and openly exploring this level is paradoxical and is best expressed by M. Scott Peck: "*If you let a group experience its differences, it will actually come together rather than fall apart.*"

Even when there is progression through chaos and emptiness, to creative emergence and integration, it is often by accident, with little learning about how to negotiate these territories the next time. In this era of "permanent whitewater," as Peter Vaill likes to call the continual and constant sea of change around us, can we afford to leave our responses to the inevitable crises to chance? Further, do we need to wait for a crisis to discover the magic that happens when a group becomes more than had previously seemed possible, and its collective mind and soul emerge?

The practitioners of dialogue and community building provide powerful tools for tapping into the ever-present collective, intentionally and consciously, without waiting for the next crisis. Still, it requires courage to move through conflict and chaos, and faith to step into emptiness and the unknown. Although it is a sometimes scary and difficult journey, it is rewarded by those times when the organization transcends the abilities of its individual members, and becomes something far more than the sum of its parts.

**Laura Hauser** is founder of Leadership Strategies International, a consulting and training firm that specializes in the diagnosis and resolution of workplace problems. She is an expert in interpersonal communication and in engaging the creativity of individuals, teams, and organizations to proactively create their future, so they can achieve greater effectiveness and performance. This involves her in strategic planning, business process reengineering, and team and leadership development.

Hauser is a published author and speaker in the areas of team-building, workplace diversity, and the role of executive leadership in affecting customer satisfaction.

Her expertise in leadership and complex systems developed from working with major organizations since 1976 in both specialist and management positions, as well as her academic degrees in communication and organization development.

# 20

# The Intangible Dimension: Can You Afford To Neglect It?

## Laura Hauser

American businesses are in a frantic race to grow and expand in fear of being gobbled up by their competitors. As a management consultant, I work with numerous companies across industries. The leaders of these companies have a lot in common—they feel intensely pressured to increase market share and revenues, reduce expenses, increase customer satisfaction, and ultimately to increase profits.

In response to the pressures of a highly competitive marketplace, companies develop logical, well-planned change strategies to position themselves as advantageously as possible in order to compete successfully in today's and tomorrow's globally competitive marketplace. Communication is carefully planned to describe the compelling reasons for the changes, including the many benefits. Memos from senior managers are generated, newsletters, and other internal communication vehicles are distributed. Managers are coached how, when, and what to say to employees. Systems and facilities are reconfigured, and so on.

But who actually implements the changes? Who puts the plans into action, or not? Employees, of course. To succeed in achieving their business objectives, companies need committed, energized, creative employees to put the change plans into place and achieve success.

Unfortunately, there is increasing evidence that many organization change efforts, such as business process reengineering, downsizing, and corporate mergers, are falling critically short of their objectives. There are numerous examples in business and academic journals of how strategic change efforts have resulted in mixed bottom-line results and have unintentionally demoralized and deflated the spirits of people in the organization. Hence, employees and other key stakeholders view subsequent change efforts as "more of the same" or "the fad of the year." We have seen this with many total quality management initiatives.

So why aren't organizations working as well as they want and need to? Why do projects take so long yet fail to achieve any truly significant results? Why have our expectations for success diminished to the point that often the best we, as employees and managers alike, hope for is "staying power" and patience to endure the disruptive forces that appear unpredictably in the organizations where we work?

## A Spiritual Crisis

I believe there is a spiritual crisis happening in our society and it is directly reflected in American businesses. Many people are working increasingly long hours and expect to have a sense of accomplishment and fulfillment at the end of the day. Rather, at the end of the day, people often feel that they have not accomplished any meaningful work whatsoever. Instead, they feel exhausted and dissatisfied.

We live in a capitalistic society based on the delivery of goods and services and a belief in the external and tangible world. At work we strive to earn more money so we can have a bigger house, a more expensive car, more cash in the bank. Yet, even when we are successful in acquiring these external, tangible possessions, we still feel empty, still feel something is missing. Why? Because possessions alone cannot answer what we as human beings all inherently require—that the needs of the spirit be met. We can buy possessions and even think we can buy people, but we cannot buy energy, joy, love, commitment, or inspiration.

Our history began with the concept of separation of church and state. Yet somewhere along the line, our society forgot that spirituality is not something that started through organized religion. Spirit has been with us since the beginning of time. It is the essence of who we all are as human beings, and travels with us wherever we go, whether it be to work, to church or temple, or to the grocery store. It follows that it must be acknowledged in every context which human beings are found, including business.

The question is—how much do we as individuals and companies allow our spirits to be accessed? Companies who implicitly or explicitly demand that their employees check their spirits at the door, much like checking a coat at a restaurant, cannot tap into the full potential of their employees nor the full potential of their business. They will simply see higher activity and lower productivity, decreased morale, and disappointing business results.

## What Is Spirit?

An individual's "spirit" is the source of positive, creative energy—the intangible, unseen, center of one's being. Spirit in the workplace is the extent to which people feel their work is meaningful, the extent to which people feel connected to each other and the extent of their belief that they are doing meaningful work. Matthew Fox, author of *The Reinvention of Work,* eloquently describes spirit in the context of the workplace in the following way:

> Good living and good working go together. Life and livelihood ought not be to separated but to flow from the same source, which is Spirit, for both life and livelihood are about Spirit. Spirit means life, and both life and livelihood are about living in depth, living with meaning, purpose, joy, and a sense of contributing to the greater community. A spirituality of work is about bringing life and livelihood back together again. And Spirit with them.

Spirit is an intangible but powerful aspect of individual and organizational success. People often refer to it as "heart"— such as "speak from the heart," and "act from the heart." When people's spirit is evoked, they feel energetic, attuned to their work, and committed to achieving successful business results—and results means profit as every CEO knows!

## What Is The Connection Between Spirit And The Bottom Line?

Reengineering, downsizing, and mergers—the cost-cutting profit-making strategies of the 1980s and 1990s—are taking fierce tolls on organizations. More and more, employee morale is depleted. Low morale, in turn, diminishes productivity, which causes the very monetary losses that management was trying to avoid by adapting these strategies in the first place. The spiritual crisis begins for the formerly effective employees who now feel less competent, less appreciated, and less connected to meaningful work and relationships.

As a result of widespread changes that often include staff reductions, the remaining employees often feel overwhelmed by their increased workloads and have had to lengthen their work-day to as many as ten to sixteen hours. Both managerial and nonmanagerial employees feel devalued and understandably dis-couraged; they no longer find their work satisfying and meaning-ful. People feel a loss of energy; they feel psychologically empty and distanced from their work and the organization.

When people are asked to implement change but their spirits are not engaged, they go through the motions, but they do not offer their loyalty, support, concern, and special efforts. Consequently, the change itself often fizzles and gives way to anxiety and frustration. If the organization's own employees do not adapt to the new situation, how can the organization survive and thrive in a rapidly changing world?

What is expected of employees in the frantic race toward the enigmatic finish line is equally difficult for leaders. Leaders are so preoccupied with survival and being in a reactive mode that they focus only on the tangible dimensions of business, such as profits, and ignore the equally critical intangible dimension of business success—the human spirit. To survive and thrive in today's competitive marketplace, leaders must not only focus on the external, tangible dimension of business, but they must also access and nurture their internal, intangible parts of themselves and their organizations. I am reminded of a quote by Warren Bennis, renowned leadership consultant and expert from USC, who says that the process of becoming a leader is much the same as becoming an integrated human being.

The fast pace of change is only going to accelerate in the future and organizations still have to be able to respond with changes of their own. Companies who appreciate the fact that a successful employee is a spirited employee will take the opportunity to reassure and retain valued workers when changes are designed and implemented.

Organizations do have a vested interest in awakening and nurturing the human spirit in the workplace, of leaders and mangers alike, because the presence of spirit has a direct impact on the quality and quantity of work. The extent to which companies care about the quality of the inner lives of the people who serve their customers will inevitably coincide with their ability to transform the workplace and our society. The huge challenges facing our society and our workplaces cannot be overcome by simply implementing new change strategies, even the radical organizational surgeries of reengineering, downsizing, and corporate mergers. The challenges in our society and our businesses are so profound, so fundamental, so universal, that they must also be resolved at the level of the human spirit.

So how can management effect change without disengaging and overextending employees in the process? Companies must spark individual, team, and organizational energy before, during, and after the implementation of strategic-change initiatives. This means that leaders of companies must first reignite their own spirits and then those of employees in the workplace.

There are examples of leaders who integrate both the tangible and intangible dimensions into their personal and organizational lives. One such example is Ryuzaburo Kaku, chairman of Canon (revenues in excess of $16 billion annually). As a renowned philosopher in the international business community, he takes capitalism to a new level of maturity. He believes that business, more than government, is in a position to improve social and environmental conditions. He goes even further by trying to educate the corporate world that not only is it possible to improve social and environmental conditions, but that there is also a direct correlation between doing so and having a more profitable business.

So a leadership that integrates both the tangible and intangible dimensions into their personal and organizational lives can guide the organization toward dynamic business results. This type of authentic and ethical leader provides an environment for people, both employees and customers, to access and manifest their own spirit, which therefore creates an abundance of business success.

## Focus On The Tangible Dimension

Historically, organizations have conscientiously applied principles of expert business strategy and management only to stop short when confronted by the troubling and more amorphous area of communicating from one's heart. We are taught from kindergarten through business school how to make objective and rational decisions, and how to communicate from the head. But we are not taught to listen to and value our inner wisdom, even though decisions made by including this wisdom may in the long run have more integrity than those made solely on the basis of rationality. Hence, we are taught that we cannot—and dare not—communicate and make decisions from the heart.

Because of our academic and work experience, it is only natural that organizational leaders are proficient at dealing with the tangible dimension of success that is based in reality. The tangible dimension focuses on the concerns of one's external world. The business and science literature over the past 40 years commonly refers to these concerns as "task and people (or processes)." Examples of task concerns include profits, market share, expenses, systems, structures, technologies—and using the body analogy: the "head." Examples of people concerns include behaviors, rewards and incentives, decision-making processes, motivation, "taking action," and roles and responsibilities.

## Focus On The Intangible Dimension

Conversely, leaders who, because of their experiences in our society, are less proficient at dealing with the intangible dimension of business tend to dismiss those elements which comprise the human spirit. The intangible dimension focuses on the concerns of one's inner world. Examples of the intangible dimension include vision and higher purpose, meaning, creativity, love, compassion, intuition and wisdom, being in relationship with oneself and others, courage and will, inclusion and belonging, body analogy—and the body analogy: the "heart."

Interestingly, when operating on the basic and authentic level of human interaction, we all become more transparent which is not a problem if we are coming from a position of congruence and integrity. However, when some leaders have attempted to use "spirit" simply as a business strategy to increase results, these leaders are seen immediately by their employees as manipulative, and they quickly loose their credibility. Why?

Because these leaders have not walked-the-talk; they have only talked-the-talk: They have not accessed much less integrated spirit into their own daily lives. They operate only from the tangible dimension.

Our society is acknowledging the importance of this long-denied intangible dimension in our personal and public lives. The acknowledgment of spirit has manifested in many ways, such as the plethora of new books on the topic by authors such as Lee Bolman and Terrence Deal, Matthew Fox, Jack Hawley, Jay Conger, Stanley Herman, Rushworth Kidder, Thomas Moore, Keshavan Nair, John Scherer, and David Whyte, just to mention a few. Even many television, radio and newsprint advertisements now use the "s-word" (spirit) in their commercials.

Every person needs to experience meaning in their job in order to be effective; the importance of purpose, values and ethics in work cannot be overstated. Consequently, a CEO who is able to speak openly and sincerely, not only to heads but also to hearts, is in a position to access powerful energy and creativity. In addition, the organization's leaders must "walk-the-walk" by tapping into their own spirits first, which allows them to align structures and systems in a way that will value and promote human potential. Such a leadership will inevitably achieve a positive bottom line.

## Speaking Of Spirit...

The following model is one of the diagnostic tools I use to help clients assess their organizations and to safely talk about the intangible dimension of business. (See Figure 1.) The use of this simple, yet powerful, tool is a way to engage us in a rich discussion about the organization's real issues, and about the implications of their level of focus on tangibles and intangibles. The rich discussion provides both depth and breadth of knowledge and insight needed to ultimately make decisions about what change strategies, if any, should be implemented to help the organization move toward high performance.

The model works in this manner: I first engage clients in a conversation about what is happening in their organization. Then I draw a vertical line on a piece of paper (any paper will do: even a paper napkin will work) labeled "tangible" and ask them to describe their organization's focus on the level of tangibles in their organization. For example, I ask how much the people in their

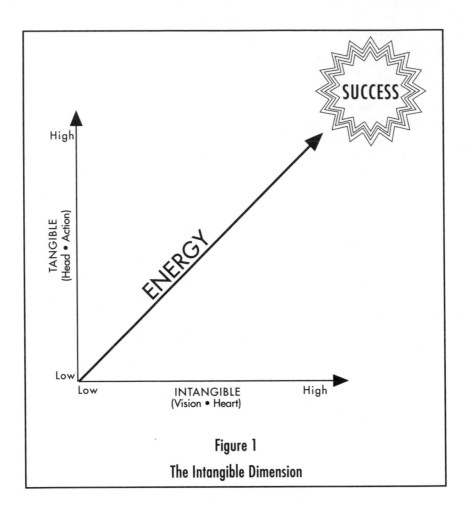

**Figure 1**
**The Intangible Dimension**

organization focus on profits, reducing expenses, and so forth. Most clients plot the (vertical) axis as high; some have even asked if there is a higher rating than "high"! Then I place a dot on the vertical axis to indicate their assessment.

Next, I lead them in a discussion about the intangible dimension (horizontal). It is important to note here that it is not necessary to use the "s-word" if it seems that the word "spirit" would take them aback. I use language that the client is most comfortable with. For example, I may ask some clients, "to what extent do people in your organization feel 'turned off' or 'turned on' about working here? To what extent do they feel valued, inspired to be creative, etc." The response to this question is usually moderately low. I draw the "intangible" line and place a dot on the horizontal axis to indicate visually their assessment. Then I connect the vertical and horizontal dots. Invariably, my clients eyes light up when they discover for themselves that the organization is using only half its potential because of a lack of focus on the *intangible* dimension.

## Case Study In Reigniting Spirit

The following case study illustrates how the spirit of an organization was reignited by integrating the tangible and intangible dimensions of success.

### The Situation

During the summer of 1993, the new president of the mortgage division of a major U.S. bank was under significant pressure from the corporate office to improve significantly financial results, increase market share, and enhance customer satisfaction by year end. When he first joined the company, the division was running behind its financial plan, the processing of residential loans was backlogged, and there was a high level of employee and customer dissatisfaction. Most processes were manual. In addition, employees did not trust one another to do things right the first time, so they were regularly double-checking each other's work. Knowing that the new president was about to embark on a business process reengineering initiative, employees and managers alike had held the unrealistic expectation that a "reengineering switch" could be flipped and conditions would magically change overnight.

The president hired an external consulting company to design a new work-flow process that would decrease the number of days it would takes to process and fund a home loan: decreasing the time from 60 days to 27 days. The new work-flow design significantly changed the structure of the enterprise. When the design was completed, the president realized that the reengineering design was technically sound, but it did not include a plan for ensuring that his managers and employees would support and implement successfully the organizational changes caused by the reengineering. Therefore, the president was concerned that people's level of anxiety, insecurity, and resistance would only increase as the change effort was implemented. He realized that to turn the reengineering effort into a success, he would have to not only plan for the implementation of the technical part of the effort, but also he would have to plan for what he called "the human relations/dynamics" part in order to produce positive bottom-line results.

I had been conducting leadership training for the division's managers and was intimately aware of the issues facing the president's organization and his people. So he asked me to consult with him to help insure the successful outcome of these changes, which was critical to the success of not only the organization but to his own success as well.

### The Intervention

I met with the president and his human resources manager concerning his situation. The overall diagnosis was that the organization had a high focus on tangibles, but it had a low level of effectiveness in relation to intangibles. Therefore, a key intervention needed to be designed and implemented to address the primary needs identified in the diagnosis. That key intervention was the creation of two cross-functional teams. The first, the *project team*, would be responsible for coordinating and overseeing the technical aspects of the new work-flow design. The second team, the *transition team*, would serve as a mirror and pulse-check of people's spirits as the changes were implemented.

The transition team's primary goal was to monitor the impact that all the changes had on the organization and its people and to provide top management as well as the project team with honest feedback as the organizational changes were implemented, much as an anesthesiologist keeps a surgeon informed of a patient's condition as an operation progresses. The members of the transition team followed this pattern of action:

- They identified whatever critical tangible and intangible issues might be impeding the reengineering effort;
- They made recommendations to the president and key executives about how to address these issues;
- They monitored the implementation of approved recommendations; and
- They scheduled similar meetings to follow up on the implementation of recommendations and to address any new issues.

### "Just-In-Time" Problem Solving

The transition team's meetings offer an excellent example of integrating the tangible nuts-and-bolts business issues with the intangible concerns of the business—engaging the spirits of the employees, and communicating with employees at a heart level as well as a head level.

In each case, I facilitated periodic meetings in which the team members met for half a day without top managers, identifying the successes and problems associated with reengineering thus far and creating solutions to recommend to top management. Then, in the afternoon, the president and key vice presidents joined the transition team.

A dialogue ensued. The members of the transition team and the executives openly and honestly talked about positive responses as well as the pain and problems associated with the organizational changes. The executives listened to the team's recommendations and engaged in "just-in-time" problem solving.

Since all of the organization's key decisionmakers were present, therefore decisions could be made on the spot.

Although approval of the team's recommendations was not always automatic, the executives were careful to communicate their belief that the team members were presenting realistic solutions based upon an understanding of the organization's operational concerns. The team members felt truly empowered in that they were able to have an impact on human issues; top management was able to convey its concern about human issues as well as ensure the stability of the reengineering effort. With each subsequent meeting, the transition team followed up with the executives, asking for an update on the agreements made during the previous meeting before proceeding to new issues.

An example of the transition team in action took place one week before the end of the year. The division was still behind on meeting its financial goals, in spite of the fact that it had successfully increased the volume of loans in the system. The problem occurred because the funding department was inundated with the huge volume of loans that needed to be funded. The funding staff, was getting burned out from working long hours and weekends.

At a transition team meeting, the group red-flagged this critical business issue. Rather than becoming engaged in an old pattern of territoriality and blaming, the team members operated from a place of higher service and purpose; they sought out new possibilities; they honored and valued each others' ideas and co-created a resourceful solution—that a "SWAT team" be assembled and implemented immediately in the funding department. The SWAT team members would be people from other departments such as loan officers and processors who had previous funding expertise and whose work load was light, because the majority of the loans had already been processed in their departments and ultimately ended up in the funding department. At the end of the day, the team made their recommendation to the president and his senior operating executive.

The transition team's solution came "just-in-time;" the executives were also aware and concerned about the problem, and were planning a course of action to solve it. The executives welcomed the transition team's recommendation. The SWAT team was implemented immediately. Miraculously, the division ended the year *ahead* of its financial goals, but not without pain and disappointment.

While the SWAT team concept was successful, it didn't work as well as they had initially hoped. They discovered during the implementation of the SWAT team that some team members did not have the skill level required to fund the loans. This resulted in some people feeling incompetent and frustrated; and although the majority of the loans targeted for funding were completed, some of the loans did not get funded in time to meet the year-end deadline.

At the next transition team meeting, members (including the funding department supervisor) spoke about the pain and disappointment of the implementation of the SWAT team concept. Yet, when they also reflected on the accomplishment of the SWAT team, they discovered that the organization and employees learned and benefited significantly from the situation. Team members spoke from their hearts when they expressed one of their key learnings:

> The year-end funding SWAT team created a team-
> building exercise for the organization and a frame-
> work for working together in the future. People
> transcended from "it's their responsibility, it's
> their fault" to "how can I help?" It created great
> energy and a spirit of cooperation.

In addition to operating from a common purpose and accessing the inherent wisdom of the group, the transition team meetings reignited people's spirits in other ways. For example, the meeting structure created a forum for interaction among people who ordinarily would not have interacted. For the first time in the division's history, the "process owners" consistently sat together to understand how their departments interacted and how they could better help one another.

Also the team members were able to see the big picture which, in turn, initiated a process of effective, cross-functional communication. People's language changed from divisive and blaming terminology ("We are not the problem, they are the problem") to inclusive and problem-solving terminology ("We're all in this together; let's figure out how to make things better"). Team members left the meetings with a sense of satisfaction, feeling that they had made an impact on managerial thinking, decision making, and the quality of work life for everyone. And they had.

### Results

Before the intervention, the division was expecting a 75 percent success rate in implementing the new work-flow design. However, due to increased employee commitment, job satisfaction, and quick resolutions of problems, the division achieved an amazing 95 percent success rate!

Other organizational benefits also were realized, as expressed in the president's words:

> Without the team interventions, I think we would have only been at 80 percent of our financial goal. But more important is the positive change in the satisfaction rating of our major customer base and our increase in market share. I am very, very satisfied with the turn. I think what we really learned is the power of the human spirit in the equation. The first half year, I was talking to people's heads by emphasizing the numerical targets, but my message just wasn't sinking in. I said to myself, " I have to switch—I have to talk to their hearts."

At a follow-up meeting I conducted with the president and his senior managers about the intervention, the president conveyed his perspective about how incorporating both the tangible and intangible dimensions of business success also benefited himself and his senior management team:

- Because the process was employee driven, people bought into senior management's ideas.
- Agreements were made and acted upon "just-in-time."

- People really believed that senior management cares.
- Employees were now advocates for senior management and the change initiatives.
- Senior management gained credibility in the eyes of its employees.
- The confidence of employees grew, people gained new skills, they became more comfortable raising issues to senior management, and they felt truly empowered.

## Conclusion

The integration of the tangible and intangible dimensions of organizational success during times of strategic change is not only the key to positive results, it is the element, if absent, which will doom the company in question to loss of morale, loss of profits, and possibly loss of corporate viability.

In these times of Rush-to-Implement-Change, it is precisely the time when successful business leaders must look, paradoxically, back to the tried-and-true basis of corporate success: They must engage the spirits of their employees. Executives, line managers, human resource professionals, and other change agents are in a unique position of creating success for their organization or casting the shadow of failure over the company. If they become the architects of the integration of tangible and intangible, they will be able to build bridges between management and their employees, which will engender success not only for the human spirit but for the revered bottom line. Their first question should be, "How can we tap into individual and team spirit to unleash the energy necessary to fuel not only individual, but team and organizational success?" They will quickly see that the answer lies in valuing the resources that still lie in the true lifeblood of any organization: its people.

## Part Seven

# THE NEW BOTTOM LINE

Chapter 21
### The Self-Healing Spirit Of Commerce
Bill DeFoore

Chapter 22
### A European Perspective
### On Commerce And Consciousness
Gerard O'Neill

Chapter 23
### Humanity Works!
Margery Miller

Chapter 24
### Finding Spirit Through Service
Anita Roddick

**Bill DeFoore**, PhD is an author, consultant, executive coach and president of the Institute for Personal & Professional Development. With his associates, he offers an executive development and corporate training program entitled *Re:Source Development Systems*. He organized and convened the September 1993 Dallas conference entitled "Searching for the Soul in Business" sponsored by the Renaissance Business Associates. He speaks and conducts workshops internationally on emotional intelligence and emotional health in personal and professional relationships.

While teaching psychology and sociology at the college level, DeFoore designed and provided educational programs for Native Americans, Montessori students in Mexico, and inmates of federal prisons. He is author of the book *Anger: Deal With It, Heal With It, Stop It From Killing You*, and co-editor of the anthology entitled, *Rediscovering The Soul Of Business: A Renaissance Of Values*.

# 21

# The Self-Healing Spirit Of Commerce

## Bill DeFoore

In my personal and professional life, I am experiencing several major transitions simultaneously. I am in the process of restructuring my business to adjust to the departure of two long-time associates, and adapting to the introduction of new, challenging work which opens doors to many exciting opportunities. I am transitioning from the role of fiancé to friend in a relationship with someone whom I care for very deeply. I am starting this chapter on my way to Arizona where I will join friends and begin a seven day hike through the Grand Canyon.

I am on the edge of a precipice, with the known behind me and the unknown ahead. I want to leave the past behind, though I still feel a strong attachment to it, and fear the sense of loss as I move forward. I want to leap into the future, though I am apprehensive about the uncharted territory. It seems fitting that I am about to hike into a magnificent canyon, an excursion unlike any I have ever undertaken.

I know that there is a healing for me in these multiple layers of change. As is the case with all healing experiences, this is a time of death and rebirth in my life. So it should come as no surprise that I find my mind turning to that perspective in writing this chapter.

Most of us are well aware of the tremendous influx of psychological and spiritual thought into the business world. Collectively, we have a wide variety of feelings and opinions about the value of this development. Regardless of our position on this issue, no one can doubt the trend, which indicates accelerated growth of these "soft science" concerns in such arenas as management method- ologies, leadership training, and even the more unlikely domain of stock market trading strategies. Commerce and consciousness has been blended, is blending, and apparently will become more blended over time.

As a result of this trend, business leaders, consultants, and social scientists are becoming more astute in observing the behavior of individual human beings, of corporate "bodies," and of the human species in general. It is often unclear from these observations of individuals and collectives whether we are speeding rapidly along a self-destruct course, or whether we are learning how to create healthier, more productive lifestyles and businesses. There are many who would passionately debate either perspective.

From a more detached view, it becomes apparent that neither perspective is completely true nor completely false, and that both contain significant truth. The key to working with paradox is to expand our consciousness and embrace the whole, inclusive truth. *Suddenly, right before our eyes, the glass is both— half full and half empty.*

## Opposing Forces In Commerce And Consciousness

There do appear to be two diametrically opposing forces at work within each of us as individuals and within our businesses. One is positive and promotes increase and growth, while the other is negative and precipitates decrease and deterioration. The energy that fuels these processes appears to be ultimately connected with our human will to live and our naturally occurring death instinct. Reducing this even further to the level of physical science, the will to live can be seen as analogous to an electric, expansive force, just as the death instinct is analogous to magnetic, contracting processes.

Quite naturally, we have chosen to focus our energy on increase and growth, and we do all we can to avoid decrease and deterioration. Growth-promoting consciousness manifests itself in many tangible forms of business success and personal ad- vancement. It is for this reason that we have leaned toward this very electric, masculine aspect in our values, and shied away from the more retractile, feminine, magnetic processes, even calling them "bad" and "counter-productive." We are discovering an interesting phenomenon, however. *Excessive emphasis on growth seems to lead to excessive decline.* This could be seen as a way to understand the current economic chaos we are experiencing. Evidence of these excesses is all around us, where rapid growth followed by a compensatory rapid decline is the norm, and sustained growth over time is the exception. This scenario seems to reflect our current stage of development in commerce and consciousness.

Whatever aspect of reality we deny, reject, or neglect shows up all around us in myriad forms, attempting to regain our acceptance. This appears to be a little-known universal law. Perhaps our overemphasis on positive, masculine, growth-promoting processes has caused negative, magnetic feminine processes to accelerate, as a sort of recoil effect. As a matter of fact, it often appears that collectively, we may be self-destructing with greater gusto than we are self-perpetuating. Fortunately, we also seem to be waking up to this pattern, as evidenced for example by the current popular interest in the phenomenon of "soul," a traditionally magnetic and feminine aspect of our existence. Perhaps this is occurring as a sort of counterbalancing effect against the excessive value we have historically placed on masculine over feminine, increase over decrease, active over passive, spiritual over soulful. One of our biggest mistakes has been to judge significant and valuable aspects of human nature as bad or wrong. If the simple strategy of promoting growth and fighting decline worked, most of us would be healthy and wealthy by now. Since this is not the case, we have to assume that new choices are indicated.

## The Value Of Decline

There is something in the process of decline that we cannot afford to ignore. There is beauty in our endings, a lesson in our losses, a gift within our problems, a healing within our illnesses, and joy in the depths of our sorrow. Our habitual, compulsive movement away from pain toward pleasure, and away from wrong towards right, has taken us further into struggle and confusion. Moralistic judgment, black and white decision making, and compulsive attachment to extreme views are exactly the processes that have helped us to create the messes we are in. Life is too complex to allow polarized, dichotomous thinking and problem solving. We must choose a third view, one based on the value of diversity, contradiction, and paradox.

Perhaps there is something dying within and around us,

and something being born simultaneously. This is quite apparent when we examine the cellular structure of the human organism, which is in a constant process of degeneration and regeneration, death and rebirth. It is also visible in the life process of individuals, and in the transformations we have all observed in the business world. It may be worthwhile for each of us to ask ourselves, "Am I, or is my business, dying or being reborn?" The answer, once again, must ultimately be "both."

The questions now emerge, "Is one better than the other? Is it better to be reborn than to die? Is electric better than magnetic?" Even more important may be the questions, "Is rebirth possible without death? Can electric exist without magnetic? Would we know masculine without feminine?" Anyone who has gone through personal transformation (brought on by heart attack, cancer, near-death experience, spiritual crisis, psychological trauma, loss of loved ones, loss of job, financial failure, war) or corporate transformation (restructuring, reengineering, downsizing, merging) knows that endings are always followed by new beginnings of some sort. The rebirth may be a long time coming, and in some cases does not ever seem to compensate for the pain and tragedy associated with the form of loss that occurred. For many of us, however, the rebirth explains the death, and even gives it meaning to the point of removing the negative value judgment we traditionally place on the tragedies in our lives.

To further explore this idea of blending commerce and consciousness, let's consider the possibility that there indeed are self-promoting and self-destructing aspects living within each of us and working outwardly in our business systems and in our species as a whole. If we were to consider that these are conscious beings who can speak to us, we might imagine hearing messages such as those that follow:

### Self-destructing Consciousness

I am in charge of deterioration, degeneration, and decay. I create the aging experience, however it may be viewed. At my essence, I am completely natural and without me life as you know it would not exist. I am a part of the digestive process in your bodies which breaks down your food to provide nutrition for your sustenance. I turn the leaves brown in the winter and make sure they decay to provide nutrients for the fertile soil from which your food grows.

I create declines in your profit and productivity, which are as natural as nightfall and rain. I mean you no harm, and yet many of you judge me as "bad." You fear the deterioration and decline that I bring, much as you fear your own natural death. This fear transforms me and makes me dangerous.

When you fear, ignore, and reject me, I become a beast in the night who haunts you and threatens to destroy your health, your wealth, and everything you love. When you deny me and fight me, I become a ravenous, power-hungry fiend who ravages families, businesses, and natural resources. Out of balance, I show up in the form of your own destructive behavior, and in the violence, sickness, and despair you see all around you.

All I want is to be accepted and embraced as part of you, part of life. This removes my threat. Fearing, ignoring, or fighting me allows me to take over and rule your behavior, creating what you call "evil" and malady in the world.

Disassociated from your consciousness, I am everything you fear. I am the half-empty glass, the "dark" side, the "shadow." I am the villain, the guilty one. Your fear of me makes me far worse than I really am. Move through your fear, face my true identity and embrace me as a natural part of life, and you will have nothing to fear. When I am accepted as a valid part of you and of life itself, I am an ally and a messenger, no longer a threat to your happiness, success, and fulfillment.

In business, I am the deficit in your budget, the losses of your revenue, the shift in the marketplace, and the nay-sayer in your workforce. The longer you deny my validity as a natural part of your business processes, the larger and more noxious I will become. In balance, I am as natural and harmless as shade under an oak tree on a sunny afternoon, or a predictable decline in a well-seasoned cash flow. Out of balance, I am bankruptcy, a tyrant, a "black hole" in your inner and outer reserves absorbing your gains and draining your energy.

I am desperately trying to get you to accept me back
into your consciousness. I speak to you through your
myths, your stories, your "news," your bottom line
and the saga of your daily lives. I also live in your
deeply-held memories, marked by your emotions of
love and joy, shame and fear, pain and anger.

Having rejected me, you inevitably project me onto
others, thus creating the "bad" people in your life.
When I am allowed to take over human minds and
bodies in my disassociated form, I create the mur-
derers, molesters, rip-off artists, and the perpetrators
of business practices which are based on profit-over-
people motivation. When I am suppressed and
overcontrolled within your psyche, I create depression, bitterness, cynicism and physical malady.

At my worst, I am the aspect of your humanness
which threatens to destroy all life on planet earth.
At my best, when integrated with your total self, I
am an aspect of your healthy personal power, your
creativity, your ability to face problems, your deep
courage and connection with soul.

**Self-promoting Consciousness**
I want only good. I want happiness and health,
peace and harmony. I love the bright and the
beautiful, and I avoid the ugly and the mundane. I
am the half-full glass, the "brighter" side, the
optimism and good intentions you know so well. I
am innocent of any wrong-doing.

Many of you think of yourselves as being like me,
and defend yourselves as "good" people. You
identify with me, that part of yourself that is
indeed good, and you mistakenly create your self-
image as if you were me. I don't have any problems, the problems are outside of me. I choose the
good path, the moral direction. I do the right thing.

The big mistake is to think that I am all that you
are. I am by my nature more appealing than my

counterpart, the "shadow" or "dark side," but there are many things I cannot do for you. In my narrow thinking, I will tell you that all you need to do is to be positive, to decide on the "right thing" and do it. I will try to talk you out of feeling sad, angry or afraid, and convince you that everything is okay. When you have anxiety and depression and cannot sleep at night, however, I can be of no help to you. I am limited. I am at my best only when I am aligned with my counterpart, the shadow.

*You can use my bright, spirited nature to explore your shadow. I am so positive that I can be positive about the negative things in your life.* I can help you to move past your shame and find the benefits of your negative emotions of pain, fear and anger. Then, and only then, I can introduce you to the deep wonders of joy and love. You must learn to use the energy and enthusiasm that I offer you to explore the darker aspects of life. Use me as the leader, and I will guide you on your journey into the soul. Without my soulful counterpart in the uncharted regions of your being, I am but a fragile, delusional emperor playing my fiddle while my empire is burning around me.

At my worst, I am a bliss-ninny, an air-head, a braggart or a naive optimist with multiple blind spots who unconsciously contributes to the very problems I am trying to solve. At my best, when I am integrated with your total being, I am a power-ful spirit who is capable of shedding light on the shadows and bringing vision to your blind spots. When I am in balance with the darker aspects of life, when my joy and enthusiasm are tempered by an acknowledgment of sadness, anger, and fear, I am whole and complete, and I can guide you to realize your most noble of visions, your most worthy of goals. I live in the brilliance of your mind, and in the soaring of your spirit. When combined with my sister soul, I can make your brightest dreams come true.

The challenge that is facing us requires that we open our hearts and minds to the paradoxical dynamics of life as reflected in these two very different views. We must expand in our emotional and intellectual perspective to embrace and include the whole of what is going on in our personal and professional lives.

## Balance And Blending

So what happens when we blend this consciousness with commerce? Could it be that those business leaders who have had the courage to celebrate and encourage mistakes have been on this track? It appears that this blending is already under way. Successful futures trader Ed Seykota studies psychology and is convinced that every trader gets exactly what he or she truly wants, good, bad, or in between. John O'Neill's writing about the shadow in business and Thomas Moore's recent contributions to business philosophy prompt us to examine the darker, more soulful realms of commerce. Perhaps Tom Peters did us all a favor by taking an adversarial role in debate on spirituality and business (see John Renesch's chapter in this book). Maybe he is right...and perhaps everyone who argues with him is also right.

What exactly is in the process of dying, or self-destructing in our business world? Is it the profit motive? Obviously not. We could no more run our businesses without a profit motive than we could sell automobiles which do not move. There are some who believe that the soul of business is dead, or has been neglected to the point that it no longer exists. As long as we have human beings with souls running our businesses, however, this cannot be. So if we are correct in assuming that it is neither the profit motive nor the soul of business that is dying, then what might it be?

It appears that greed, blind depletion of natural resources, and ignorance to human sensitivities may be dying a slow death. This is not because this style of business practice has not proved temporarily profitable, for indeed it has. These processes simply do not produce *sustainable* patterns of continued growth. The growth produced by ravenous consumption of all available resources with no far-sighted plan simply does not sustain itself. Industries which have grown by these means are now struggling to "change horses in mid-stream," in order to survive in a world that insists that its vulnerabilities be acknowledged.

So what is being born? This is the exciting part. Although the evidence of deterioration and self-destruction is more glaring, for those willing to look and listen for it, there is a quiet revolution occurring in business that is becoming more powerful and gaining momentum. *In many a large corporation, its people are being valued as its greatest resource, which is setting many healthy transformations into motion.* The emergence of balance and wisdom is not newsworthy, because it is subtle and does not always create immediate financial gain...thus the *quiet* revolution. A shift in emphasis to sustainable, long-term growth and sensitivity to human needs does not make a big splash, and will never be a news flash. It is happening, however, and each of us can be a part of it if we choose.

## Time To Grow Up

The interest in immediate gratification without regard for long-term consequences is one of the earmarks of immature behavior, whereas emotional maturity is indicated by consistent action toward long-term (often intangible) gains. This is consistent with the perspective that we as a culture and as a species are still trying to grow up and become healthy, mature adults. There is a Myan myth in which Earth is referred to as "the planet of the children." It appears that, in a global sense, we are indeed somewhere between late childhood and early adolescence. William Golding's classic novel *The Lord of the Flies* depicts a group of adolescent boys stranded on an island who end up behaving in a predominately reptilian and barbaric manner, much as the population of the world has behaved since it found itself on planet earth. Perhaps that is what the author was saying...that on a global basis, we are behaving much like adolescents without adult guidance.

Just as "necessity is the mother of invention," we may find that the increasingly urgent need for harmony and balance within human and nonhuman nature will facilitate our maturation as a culture and a species. We seem to have grown out of our need for world war...perhaps we will soon stop making war on ourselves and our planetary home. If we do not grow up and take care of what we have, we will be like the child crying after it has broken its own toy. In our case, however, what we are destroying is the habitability of planet earth, and there is no parent to help us out of the mess we have made.

## New Life Emerging

Although I admitted it to no one, including myself, I was afraid that at forty-six years of age my body (especially my knees) would not hold up to the rigors of the Grand Canyon hike. After two days on the trail I discovered that the path we were taking was known as one of the most dangerous and demanding of all of the routes into the canyon. To my relief and great satisfaction, I got stronger every day. My body loved the exertion and my spirit soared in the beauty of that ancient and magnificent terrain. My fear died, and in its place was born a new sense of exhilaration and appreciation for my body and the earth it walks on.

The aspect of my business that is ending needed to die. It had been in its death throes for some time, creating a long and painful period of transition, as the old systems gradually broke down. The drama and trauma of this ending is being counterbalanced by the birth of a new business that is lively and stimulating. The mixture of joy and sorrow in this professional transition has a rich and spicy flavor, and I find myself inclined to absorb the entire experience as a whole and complete process of change.

The friendship that has emerged from the remains of my romantic relationship is one of great value and radiant health. The romance that has died was in poor health since its beginning. Where there was tension, antagonism, and conflict, I now experience caring, love, and compassion. It's as if the relationship has shed an old skin which had become hard and rough, and the new skin emerging is soft, tender, and vibrant with energy and life. I have to ask myself, would we have what we have now if we had not had what we had then?

Understandably, I have been in a kind of grieving process for a while now, related to these multiple transitions in my personal and professional life. The scabs have fallen off the wounds, and as the healing progresses I am trying to make room for what is being born. I'm still a little tender in spots, but I feel a renewed enthusiasm as I experiment with this novel sense of my identity in commerce and consciousness.

One way of understanding our current human scenario is in terms of our ability or inability to grieve, and our capacity for experiencing true joy. As a general rule, most human beings and many cultures do not know how to grieve. We do everything we can to avoid pain and death, to the point of denying it, medicating against it and distracting ourselves from it in any way we can. If we are to allow the death of that which has outlived its usefulness, and facilitate the birth of that which we must develop in order to thrive, we must learn how to grieve. This means simply that we must value our tears as well as our laughter, our failures as essential to our success, and our weakness as the other side of our strength. There are some who say that human beings are courageous spirits who came to Earth to become co-creators with God. I like that idea...perhaps it's true.

**Gerard O'Neill** is a futurist based in Dublin, Ireland. He has a Masters Degree in Economics from the London School of Economics. He works with the European Commission, some of Europe's largest corporations and local community groups on issues relating to regional, national, and European futures. He currently runs the Henley Centre in Ireland, a commercial consulting firm specializing in futures research and is also European secretary of the World Business Academy and coordinator of the Irish chapter. O'Neill is a global partner in Relationship Marketing International (RMI).

He has lectured on European futures themes in Germany, France, the UK, and Ireland. He has published a number of books and studies, including *Beyond 2000—European Corporations and their Visions of the Future* and *TeleFutures—Prospects for Tele-Working*. O'Neill's most recent book is *The Intimate Future*, with RMI co-founder Chris Davies.

## 22

# A European Perspective On Commerce And Consciousness

## *Gerard J. O'Neill*

> The European Union is based on a large set of
> values, with roots in antiquity and in Christianity,
> which over 2,000 years evolved into what we
> recognize today as the foundations of modern
> democracy, the rule of law, and civil society. This
> set of values has its own clear moral foundation
> and its obvious metaphysical roots, regardless of
> whether modern man admits it or not.
>
> —Vaclav Havel,
> *The Caterpillar and the Bottom Line*

Looking at Europe in the closing years of the 20th Century,
I sense that we are looking at the progress of a caterpillar along a
line: a bottom line if you wish. The caterpillar of European
philosophy and science is coming to the end of one glorious stage
in its life, a life whose future remains unclear. The glory has
manifested itself in the extraordinary achievements of the Industrial Age which had its origins in Europe. But the journey along
that bottom line has come to an end and a new path must be
discovered—before the line ends in a full stop.

Europe's role in discovering that new path could be as
significant as its role in the events of the 19th and 20th Centuries.
Europe is, after all, the ancestral home of the Western concepts of
commerce and consciousness. Indeed, it is the home of the now
predominant techno-economic paradigm shaping and reshaping
our world. A paradigm originating in Aristotle's philosophy of the
analytic method; Plato's insights into how we perceive the world;

Francis Bacon's development of the role of knowledge; Descartes' separation of mind and body; Auguste Compte's model of the positivist method; and Adam Smith's concept of the invisible hand. Home of the industrial revolution and of "rational man," Europe has bequeathed to North America and the rest of humanity a truly planet-changing legacy of wisdom and practice.

Like a boomerang, that legacy is now changing Europe as it finds itself subject to the cultural and technological momentum of the United States and the competitive challenges of Asia. As a result, Europe is at a turning point in its history, not just politically and economically (significant as these are), but also at the fundamental level of values. Where might this turning point lead? European's are, as Havel suggested above, reticent about admitting or revealing their "metaphysical" beliefs. Perhaps we need to quickly lose our reticence—to connect again with our metaphysical roots. The changes under way may help us to do so. As the century draws to a close, Europe has entered a chrysalis much like the caterpillar. We must all wait to see what will emerge.

In this essay I will examine some of the signs of change evident in the European "chrysalis"—change at the level of European society, of European businesses, and European citizens. I will then go on to look at signs of hope which suggest that something very positive is unfolding in Europe with implications for the wider world. Finally, I will explore two scenarios for Europe's future and their implications for the intellectual and spiritual role that Europe might play in the new century that lies ahead.

## Signs Of Change

### The Anxious Society

With some 20 million Europeans unemployed in 1995, Europe is a continent that is fearful about the future. Part of that fear arises from the awareness that many of those employed at present may become unemployed in the future. A 1994-1995 survey found that nearly 60 percent of all full-time workers in the main European economies were afraid that they might lose their job. Of course, these attitudes may simply reflect the type of cyclical changes in consumer confidence that we have witnessed in the United States and Europe during the course of the past ten years of economic boom, bust, and recovery.

On the other hand, they may reflect something deeper and

more structural in nature. Europe, at a national and suprana-
tional level, is reorienting itself in response to current and future
global economic trends. Perhaps the most important of these
trends is competition:

> Many things, undoubtedly, have changed. But one
> thing which has probably changed more than any
> other is the intensity of competition. The latter is
> now omnipresent and immediate. Ask any head of
> business, big or small, and he will tell you that
> that has been the main change in recent years. As
> far as competition is concerned, Seoul or Bangkok
> is now closer to Strasbourg than were Luxem-
> bourg thirty years ago and Manchester fifteen
> years ago.
> —Jean-Claude Paye, OECD Secretary General

Increasing competition, coupled with the privatization of
large parts of the state sector in Europe, is creating a climate of
fear and uncertainty that is not only affecting economic growth
via reduced consumer expenditure, but is also contributing to a
growing uncertainty about the future course of the European
"project," i.e., the creation of an economically and politically
United Europe.

It is now argued in some quarters that we are witnessing the
"Americanization" of European society. This refers to the creation
of a more flexible workforce coupled with reduced job security.
The benefits of this approach is that potentially more jobs could
be created in Europe than at present. The cost is that the
resulting fear and widening income gaps will polarize European
society, giving rise to a scenario of "private affluence and public
squalor." The potential for work to contribute to individuals'
psychological and spiritual development is simply not realized.

## The Ethical Company

How are Europe's businesses responding to the changes
taking place around them? Typically, the response of a company
to increased competition, either from within their own national
market or from abroad, is to cut costs and to become more
customer-focused. Such a response is necessary but not suffi-
cient. What is missing in many European companies is an
awareness of the third leg of successful strategy, namely employee motivation. Instead, the senior managers of too many

companies blunder ahead with cost cutting measures that simply translate into a reduced head count, and then find themselves wondering why those remaining staff are suffering from low morale and a lack of motivation.

Not all companies are making this mistake. Some are responding imaginatively and humanely to the challenges that they face. There is evidence of a growing experimentation with new measures of a company's performance—not just financially but also ethically and socially. In Scandinavian countries there has been a growth in the number of commercial and noncommercial organizations publishing Ethical Accounting Statements which provide an annual quantitative assessment of the organization's performance against a comprehensive range of indicators relating to its relationships with all of its stakeholders—including staff, shareholders, customers, and communities. In the UK, an even more comprehensive Social Audit process has been carried out in organizations such as The Body Shop and Traidcraft plc. The Social Audit incorporates all the features of the Ethical Accounting Statement from Scandinavia, but also includes external benchmark measures of a company's performance.

Such audits get right to the heart of a business' values and purpose. By obliging a company to publicly state what its goals are for all its stakeholders—and not just its shareholders—then a space is created in which values can be explored and developed in relation to how a company treats its own people, the communities in which it is located, and the communities that it serves. Many European companies are now waking up to the obligations and responsibilities that they have beyond the narrow confines of their shareholders. Royal Dutch/Shell, Europe's largest company, learned this the hard way in June 1995 when it had to abort its plans to dump a redundant oil platform in the Atlantic.

Commenting on Shell's "climbdown," an editorial in *The Economist* magazine observed that:

> Companies that choose to defy their consumers'
> political demands are placing their businesses in
> jeopardy. But there is a better reason to hope that
> companies will pay heed to some of these de-
> mands. Just possibly, consumer activism really
> can play a part in making the world a better
> place....No company can possibly satisfy every
> pressure group...Nonetheless, tomorrow's suc-

cessful company can no longer afford to be a faceless institution that does nothing more than sell the right product at the right price. It will have to present itself more as if it were a person—as an intelligent actor, of upright character, that brings explicit moral judgements to bear on its dealings with its own employees and with the wider world.

—*The Economist*, June 24th 1995

The Social Audit and the Ethical Accounting Statement go well beyond the type of Social Statement published in the United States by Ben & Jerry's. Similarly, they are much more significant than the Ethical Codes of Conduct now operated by 45 percent of European companies, and which tend to be once-off qualitative statements, referring to some of the same issues as those addressed in Social Audits. Like Sustainable Development Indicators, Social Audits are a tool for communicating a wider set of values beyond the narrow ones of economic growth and financial performance to a nonspecialist audience. With the European Commission now looking at the feasibility of such measures on a pan-European scale, there is every hope that Europe can lead the way in connecting businesses and other organizations to their wider responsibilities for the whole.

## A Moral Renaissance

What role might Europe's citizens play in exploring and creating a new European model of engaged business activity that is financially and socially sustainable? One that connects the head, heart, and soul of business? Will our sense of fear and foreboding about the future in the face of rising unemployment simply lead to social and moral breakdown? Or will the strong social orientation of European citizens, political parties, and cultural structures provide a platform for innovative actions designed to breakthrough to a new, convivial future for Europe? One that puts the development of people—their minds, bodies and spirits—at the center of economic purpose rather than the maximization of production and wealth?

Part of the answer may lie in comparisons of social values between Europe and the United States. Work carried out by Christine and Ralph McNulty of Applied Futures, mapping different countries' populations onto Abraham Maslow's Needs Hierarchy, gives us some clues. Maslow postulated that a person's needs evolved as certain primary categories of needs were met. Thus the very basic need that everybody has is for Sustenance. Once met we have a need for Security. Above that we have a need for Social Belonging. This gives way to a higher need for Self Esteem, thereafter to Self Development and, finally, to Self Actualization.

Applied Futures has identified three broad groups of people, differentiated by their place on their needs hierarchy. Those near the bottom are called Sustenance Driven, i.e., their main need is for security—financial, physical and emotional. Next there are the Outer Directed, i.e., their main needs are for esteem and status; in other words, a set of values and priorities that puts greatest emphasis on the opinions of others, and on material possessions. Finally there are the Inner Directed, i.e., those who reflect upon their own needs and priorities and who tend to be more focused on nonmaterial goals and values.

Using quantitative surveys, Applied Futures estimated in the late 1980s that ten percent of Japanese adults were in the Inner Directed group, with 55 percent in the Outer Directed group (the remainder falling into the Sustenance Driven category). In the case of American adults, 19 percent were Inner Directed and 51 percent were Outer Directed. Among European adults, 28 percent were Inner Directed and 42 percent were Outer Directed.

Such findings would suggest that Europeans are more aware of and open to nonmaterial values relating to ethics, morals, and personal development than their American counterparts. However, this does not mean that European's are more religious or spiritual than Americans (or Japanese for that matter). Quite the opposite in fact. Belief in God and membership of religious groups seems to be strengthening in the United States, while both are declining in Europe. Some 82 percent of Americans consider themselves to be religious compared with just 59 percent of Europeans according to the European Commission. Also, 44 percent of Americans attend religious services once a week or more often, compared with 26 percent of Europeans. In the case of Europe, there is clear evidence of a continuing process of secularization. Back in 1985, nearly half of all Europeans agreed with the statement "God is very important in my life." By 1995 that proportion had fallen to just over a third.

Perhaps a people living in a continent that produced the Inquisition, the Concentration Camp, and the Gulag may be understandably uncomfortable about "wearing their spiritual values on their shirt sleeves" so to speak. Or it may simply be that Europeans are coming to terms in a more honest and open-minded way with the difficulties of reconciling the intellectual legacy of science and reason that they gave to the world with the heartfelt need for faith and hope in a better, more humane future. But there are, in these changing times, signs of hope.

# Signs Of Hope

## The Sublime Economy

Let us take this idea a little further—that Europeans are more "ready" for the future than their counterparts in North America or in Asia. Outside of Europe there is a perception that the future does not belong to Europe. Rather it belongs to a revitalized, technologically triumphant America or to the economic tigers of China and South East Asia. But Europe—wise old cynical Europe—knows better. America and Asia are reaching the top of the ladder, only to find that it is leaning against the wrong wall. Their moment of triumph in "The Stuff Economy" is made redundant by our shift towards "The Sublime Economy."

Let me explain. The Stuff Economy describes what we have been doing and making over the past 200 years of the Industrial Era. Goods, services, and products—things or stuff that we can buy and consume. It can't go on: already the Earth's atmosphere, seas, and biosphere are showing the signs of an economic system rapidly approaching its limits. Fortunately, we are witnessing the emergence of a new bioeconomic system that will enable us to tread more lightly on the Earth. I have called it The Sublime Economy, after James Ogilvey's scenario for "the sublimation of the economy." In other words, an economy in which the cultivation of human potential becomes the primary driver of economic activity: one enabled by the emerging information revolution. Such an economy would emphasize the role of high quality education through life, and the utilization of information and communications technologies to lighten our load on the planet. It would be a world in which the only stuff that would be made would be stuff that individuals had actually said they wanted. A world at ease with itself and its residents:

> I know of no law of the constant conservation of
> laughter, or any limitation on joy. I see no reason
> to limit our sense of what is possible for the

distribution of delight. These human goods need
not be subject to a law of constant conservation. If
I have more, you needn't have less. Quite to the
contrary, there might be a virtuous circle of
mutual reinforcement in the spread of the sublime
delight, like a ripple of laughter that gains momentum in a crowd. According to the economics of
the sublime, there can be enough for all...We have
struggled up through the realm of necessity and
now stand, more and more of us, on the brink of
the realm of freedom... There will not be one best
way of being human, but a rich ecology of species
in the gardens of the sublime.

—James Ogilvey,
*Visions of the 21st Century*

Creating the Sublime Economy will be a revolutionary act.
And Europe has had some experience in revolutions. We are
already subject to a technological revolution—hence harnessing
that force and directing it towards social and economic goals
congruent with people's needs and beliefs is the challenge now
being addressed by those responsible for European policy on the
Information Society.

Europeans tend to believe that their destiny is shaped by
sociology. While Americans equate destiny with biography.
Europe's greatest strength, therefore, remains its ability as a
society—or union of societies—to galvanize itself towards the
achievement of a social vision that all can benefit from. Just such
a process may be under way in Europe at the cusp of the 21st
Century.

## A Female Future

Who will lead the revolution? I suspect that Europe's women
will play the key role because I suspect that the future is female
anyway. A growing number of Europe's presidents, prime minis-
ters, and party leaders are female. That, and changing attitudes
on the part of men, has meant that there is greater consensus
about social policy, parental leave, child care, and education than
appears to be the case in the United States. This is not to say that
there are no differences of opinions about welfare provisions and
policies: But there is nothing like the ideological hostility to the
Welfare State as is evident in some quarters in America.

Europeans also tend to think about the debate on parenting

and work in terms of "how can my circumstances at work be changed to help me be a better parent?" Americans, again from a distance, seem to consider the key issue to be "how can my circumstances as a parent be changed to help me be a better worker?" We are climbing different ladders, leaning against different walls.

A recent survey by Bates Advertising found that over half of all Europeans would "be willing to give up some material possessions if it means I would have a happier life." Fewer than four in ten adults agreed that "it is important to make a lot of money" (and an even smaller proportion of women). These attitudes and the continuing support for policies that fit work around the family (and not the family around work) reinforce the idea that Europeans are, perhaps, further up the Needs Hierarchy than North Americans—though it is a predominantly secular approach to self development and to inner-directedness.

## Europe's Future

None of the above should be construed as implying that Europeans have collectively embarked upon a strategy of social transformation with human development at its heart. The debate still rages about whether Europe can afford to be "European" any more, both in terms of its welfare provisions and its disastrous record on job creation. But there is a danger that Europe will fail to grasp the opportunity implied in the emerging Sublime Economy and settle instead for a squalid place in an increasingly squalid Stuff Economy.

Below, I have set out two scenarios for the future of Europe, telling two contrasting stories about the next quarter of a century. One story, Risk Society, is about failure. The other story, Mosaic Society, is about opportunities recognized and realized, and about a New Europe finding a place for itself in a New World. I suspect that we are at a bifurcation in time, in other words it really is an "either/or" situation with regard to the future, and not a fudge down the middle. Basically because there isn't time or space for a fudge.

### Risk Society

German sociologist Ulrich Beck coined the phrase "Risk Society." He used it to describe his perceptions of Europe's direction in the late 1980s and early 1990s. It is a society without security. No job security, no security of tenure, and no property security. Europe could become a Risk Society over the next 25 years, especially if some of the trends now evident are allowed to reach their full fruition:

- rapid growth in the number of temporary and part-time workers.
- continuing rises in crime levels, especially against property.
- the reduction and eventual removal of welfare safety nets for growing proportions of the population.
- genetic screening by insurers and employers to exclude high risk individuals and families.
- income polarization giving rise to a greater incidence of poverty.

In effect, the above trends will give rise to what Beck calls "the redistribution of risk:" from employers to employees; from the state to individuals; from the information rich to the information poor. Such a society would not be one conducive to the pursuit of personal development and spiritual growth—other than as human capital investment to enhance "employability."

The European Risk Society could certainly see a religious revival, but it would be the religion of "oblivion," a bolt-hole for those who could not cope any longer with "reality." There might also be a moral resurgence in such a society, but again, it would be a morality of control (especially regarding deviants), against a background of increasing cynicism and anxiety.

## Mosaic Society

On the other hand—perhaps the only "hand" that can be played—Europe might well build upon the Sublime Economy, building a Mosaic Society which viewed human imagination and potential as the most valuable, renewable resources available. It would be a world at ease with experimentation and innovation, at local, national, and continental levels. It would be characterized by choice and diversity: a mosaic of realized potential. Such a society could emerge from some other trends already evident in Europe:

- increasing European entrepreneurship in the information and communications sectors.
- the growth of the Internet and the Information Society.
- growing experimentation with LETS schemes (local exchange and trading systems) and Social Audits—a

genuine commitment by key European countries such as Germany to sustainable economic strategies.

- increasing willingness to experiment with policy innovations such as basic income schemes and energy taxes.

The emergence of the Mosaic Society could herald the birth of an era of social, economic and personal experimentation in Europe without precedent since the 1960s. Such a society would be at ease with new thinking about consciousness and our place in the universe; it would see a revival of rituals drawing on ancient European traditions that celebrated the sacredness of place; and it would witness greater compassion and tolerance towards those with different, even opposing views.

## The Butterfly And The Bottom Cube

What will emerge from the European chrysalis? Will it simply be another caterpillar—only uglier and a sad imitation of more successful caterpillars elsewhere. Or will it be a butterfly—one that embodies the very best of the European story so far, and which carries that story into a new century? Which one?

My heart, and the heart of many Europeans, is on the side of the butterfly. My head says...perhaps. But only if there are more Vaclav Havels. In other words, European political, business and community leaders who are willing to show a little more of their—sleeve: to talk from their heart as well as from their head.

It is especially necessary that we have more business leaders—like Anita Roddick—who are not afraid to challenge the orthodoxy of the caterpillar, the hubris of The Stuff Economy, and leaders who recognize that we all live in a three dimensional world, even business people. There is a "bottom cube" in business, not a bottom line—one with three dimensions, namely: economic performance, social performance, and environmental performance. And if you add time in as a fourth dimension then the same applies to businesses: we are all ancestors to the future. You could even add a "fifth dimension" from which our little reality of "space-time" manifests itself.

Just as Europe shared its scientific, philosophical and commercial wisdom with the world in the 19th and 20th Centuries, so perhaps it can be a teacher (one of several) in the 21st Century, creating and sharing a more appropriate wisdom: one concerned with purpose, priorities and compassion. I, for one, hope so: The butterfly might carry us all on its wings.

**Margery Miller** is owner of Miller & Associates, a manufac-turers' sales agency selling commercial food service equipment to all segments of the food service industry. She was able to structure her company in a way that allows her to follow her true calling, to help businesses develop their people and build empowered workforces that enable both the business and the employees to realize their full potentials. She started People in Business in 1988 and has added Success Unlimited Network coaching to the package she offers small businesses and individuals. She is also author of *Sound Business Bites, a common sense approach to customer service and management.* Miller is working on her second in the *Sound Business Bites* series, subtitled *how to have a life and career at the same time.*

# 23

# Humanity Works!

## Margery Miller

A reporter from *The Dallas Business Journal,* a weekly newspaper, called me a few weeks ago to ask for information on an article she was working on about spirit in the workplace. She had been talking to various people and gathering ideas but she just wasn't clear about what it meant exactly. In fact, when she told her editor what she was working on, he asked her why she thought religion fit into the business environment!

I realized that I don't use the word "spirit" when I talk about this subject—and I suggested a better word might be "humanity." There are many people looking at their lives in a more spiritual way today—but it is hard to define what that really means in day-to-day life—and even harder to explain how to be a spiritual being in the workplace.

When I speak to various groups around town, I tell them I have a mission in life: to bring humanity into business. Where did it go? Why don't we feel it? What can we do about it? Did we have it before? Can we get it back?

I don't think humanity is really lost in the business world, we just don't get to see the best parts of it in most companies. And it shows. People feel the same kind of disenfranchisement in their work lives that we talked about in the 1960s—powerlessness, inability to make a difference, frustration, as if the world is operating around them but they have no voice, no recourse. What they experience is continual fear of losing their jobs, a feeling they have to adhere to policies they have no stake in, and a sense of hopelessness about their ability to change the situation.

What would it look like if business owners and managers considered their employees to be their most valuable assets? How would you feel about work if:

- You could see yourself and your job in a new light?
- You were able to recognize what you're already doing right?
- Co-workers started to notice a more committed atti-tude—commitment to your job and commitment to yourself?
- Customers were not the enemy—and you could start thinking about how to create win-win partnerships with them?
- You felt like you made a difference in your job—without you, the company would not be the same?
- You felt so loyal to your company that you would turn down an offer to work somewhere else for more money because you felt your future was better where you were?

Bringing humanity into business brings all of the above and more! So how do we do it?

The reporter came to my office to interview me so she could understand what all this "organizational transformation" stuff was about. Her conclusion was that it is so simple it seems hard to understand. There are no complicated formulas, no secret methods, no special skills required. All we have to do is create work environments where people are treated kindly, with respect, and given every opportunity to be the best they can be. How difficult is that?

The difficulty is in clearing out the old systems that no longer serve us. The difficulty is in convincing managers that "under the thumb control" doesn't work for employees any more. The difficulty is in opening the minds and hearts of people to look to the positive instead of the negative. The difficulty is in walking our talk once we learn the new words—not just parroting ideas then doing things the same old ways.

I have acquaintances who are members of organizations that profess to be a part of this change process who admit privately that they don't practice "new paradigm" methods in their own businesses because they are concerned that profitability would be diminished. That just tells me they are old paradigm guys with new paradigm ideas. They are not alone. It is one thing to sit around discussing global mind change. It is another thing entirely to put in the painstaking effort of transforming your workplace.

I am happy to announce that I have empirical data which proves that *profitability increases in direct proportion to the amount of effort put forth to humanize—allow soul and spirit to thrive in your business.* My own company continues to grow—we are increasing our growth by eight to ten percent per year during a time when our industry is relatively flat. In the past three years we have been able to institute a retirement plan and spend a significant amount of money upgrading our computer system—without sacrificing bonuses and incentives for our employees. In fact, our employees are the ones who decided what improvements were needed for our network and had the responsibility and authority to implement their plan.

Let's look at the ideas that we practice—and I teach others about in my consulting and coaching work—that are essential to bringing humanity into business.

## It Starts At The Top

When I give talks, I love to speak about leadership and the risk of excellence. I believe the greatest risk we take is the endeavor to be truly great. What is the job of a leader—manager—boss? I see it as twofold:

• To provide vision, focus and guidance.
• To serve the people you are leading.

The vision—where you want to go, the essential elements, the ideal—can be supplemented and enhanced by all the people in the company. But I have never seen a company succeed if the leader didn't have a clear and viable vision first. Very few people want the responsibility for this part. You get to be the leader when your vision is big enough and powerful enough that it engenders so much passion inside you that you *have to act on it!* Vision is what propels us forward—not to a defined outcome, but toward all possibilities.

The leader must be willing—and capable—of taking the most vital parts of the vision and focusing in on what needs to be done at any point. Being able to make the best decisions is a necessity. Focus allows you to blaze a clear path into your future. It also enables others to participate. They know what the plan is and what is expected of them.

Guidance is the most delicate part of this trinity. It requires a willingness to let people learn at their own pace while helping them be mindful of the tasks at hand. It means giving direction without spending all your time directing.

To provide vision, focus, and guidance is to truly serve. You do this by creating a fertile environment with all the necessary tools and elements for each person to become the best that he or she can be. You define the parameters of the job and let them figure out how to do it. You teach them the basics and let them create the rest.

I say "yes" a million more times than I say "no." I listen a lot more than I talk. I ask a lot of questions. My job is to make sure they have what they need, from computers to office supplies to encouragement and praise for good work. And I make doubly sure they know how grateful I am to have them on my team—being and doing their best.

The wonderful part about it is that I take my job so seriously, I don't have to do it 24 hours a day! I have plenty of time to do work outside my office—work that fulfills my passion—which is to help other people do this too. I learned how to hire really good people, create a supportive, nurturing environment and then got out of their way so they could do their work! They spend their work days selling commercial food service equipment. And I make sure we have plenty of money to cover all our needs, and then go out and bring more money into the company doing what I love to do.

The most successful people I know *do not* spend all their time working hard. They spend their time working smart, doing what they love to do and encouraging others to do the same. My employees really love their jobs! And they do them very well. I am sure this accounts for our continued growth and the success of our business overall.

## Power to the People!

When I was part of "the Movement" in the 1960s, we loved this phrase! We said it all the time, probably hoping to someday find out what it really meant. I even tried living in a commune once, and found out that the power belonged to the person who owned the land we were living on, not to those of us struggling to help him build a house on it. So, by the time I was 23 years old, I had figured out that if I wanted to have any power, I needed to have some form of ownership in my situation.

Now in most companies, the employees do not have the opportunity (or even the desire for) financial ownership. Many do not want the liability that goes along with an equity position. So how do we enable these people to become stakeholders in a business without taking an actual financial position?

We give them the opportunity to be powerful in their jobs. We give them permission to voice their ideas, criticisms, viewpoints. We engage them in the activity of growing the business. We act on their suggestions or make it possible for them to do so. We encourage them to offer their opinions by creating a forum for expression. We let them know they matter and that their contributions are valuable.

I think these things have to be systematized to work. Most great ideas are shipwrecked on the rock of laziness. We all get lazy when we don't establish a system for implementation of good ideas.

In 1981 I realized that our company was too spread out for us to have an identity. At the time, my partner and I were working out of the Dallas office and we had another partner in Houston and one in Oklahoma City. Talking on the phone just didn't create the synergy we needed to feel we were building a company. So I decided we would have quarterly meetings. Since that time, we have missed two—and we really felt it. As we added people, these get-togethers allowed us to keep a sense of continuity and flow— even during some very difficult times!

Why quarterly? Because three months is about as long as we can go without losing the momentum we have when we're excited about something. We need reinforcement! We need support! We need encouragement! We need reassessment!

Our meetings are mandatory, and we set them at the beginning of each year. We've been doing this for so long that new employees easily fit into the pattern of attending. Since we are a sales company, we spend all day Friday with our outside sales-people and work on new ideas for marketing, go over problem accounts and share information on how we are doing overall.

Our all-day Saturday session includes both inside and outside sales people (which means all of us because everyone in our company is in sales). We have done everything imaginable in these meetings, from bringing in sales trainers and team builders to an acting teacher for improvisational theater games. We've utilized several different assessment instruments and spent a lot of time learning what makes us tick—as individuals and as a company.

What really happens in those meetings is that we get to be "real" with each other. We get to learn about each other. We get to talk out our differences and confront problems in an open, non judgmental atmosphere. We get to emphasize our strengths and examine our weaknesses—and learn to manage both. We get to experience the process of growth, being able to measure where we are now in relation to where we were.

All of this is empowering. People can respect each other when they understand each other. Petty indulgences lose their importance when people have permission to air their complaints openly. We are all more tolerant when we have been heard.

I invest a lot of money, relative to the size of my company, to bring in outside people to facilitate these meetings. It is very important that I get to participate on equal footing with my employees. In that situation, we are all the same, all there to learn and grow. This kind of leveling is vital to ensure that we don't get stuck in hierarchy. Just because I am the leader doesn't mean I have to exert power over my co-workers. I much prefer that they have a sense of their own power and importance—and value to the company!

Several years ago I came up with a way to do yearly reviews that really helped my people feel they had a voice in the company. I ask them eleven questions and write their answers as they talk. The interesting thing is, I have been using this same review since 1987 and they never seem to remember what the questions are from one year to the next. They are more interested in responding to the questions!

As I write their answers, I rarely comment, but wait until the end and do an overview of what I have heard and bring out any points that I think they—or we—need to work on. I also make an effort to implement all good ideas that come out of these reviews.

I'm going to share these questions with you, because I think they go a long way in helping create an opening for more spirit/soul in business. They are:

1. What do you like best about your job?
2. What are the main problem areas in your job?
3. What could you or someone else do to alleviate problem areas?
4. Which people in the company do you feel most comfortable with and why?
5. What are your short-term goals?
6. What are your long-range goals?
7. How do you feel about company goals?
8. Do we work together well?
9. Do we practice good reassessment?
10. What are our main shortcomings?
11. What could you do in the next four weeks to make yourself feel more successful?

I have observed employees start out with a very foggy, unfocused sense of their own goals and develop into clear strategists over a couple of years. I have seen the power of asking the question lead to awareness and the desire to find good answers. Back in the sixties we called this "consciousness raising." Today, I call it a key to unlocking the potential in an often untapped resource.

I have watched people blossom in an open, accepting environment. I have felt the sadness of seeing people frustrated and held back by managers afraid to let go of their own power positions—never realizing how much more powerful it is to empower others.

## Making Space

How do we cope with the everyday problems of being alive and being in business? Most people put on some sort of mask or persona when they go to work. They become the person they think they are supposed to be in order to get the job done—or even keep the job! What would it be like if you felt free to—had permission to—be the same person 24 hours a day? What if your work environment was conducive to your being your true self? Would you feel differently about your job? Would you be more productive?

I think yes. I decided several years ago that I wanted to be the same person 24 hours a day. I had to create an atmosphere for myself that made that possible *and* I wanted the same for my employees. So I looked at the difficult areas first.

We all do fine when things are going well, but when we are in pain, when we are dealing with life problems, things can fall apart around us. We live in a society in which divorce is common. We can't quit working and lose the one stable thing we have while going through a divorce, but we also can't just function normally. How can the business keep from suffering while we are in agony?

What works for us is to make space. Give people time and space to go through their changes. Give them room to grieve, to cope, to grow into stronger people. We make sure they have time off for counseling. We have a gym set up in the warehouse with a punching bag for getting rid of anger. We encourage mental health days. If it is obvious that they are in more pain than usual one day, we take time to visit a bit, see if some talking would help. Or just let them alone to process without any more irritation added.

Because we spend so much time really learning about ourselves and each other, we can read the signs and use our intuition more easily. We have a healthy respect for privacy and give it readily. I have learned how to ask leading questions that give opportunities without prying. I have learned to mind my own business and not interfere when I see that this person needs to go through an experience without the benefit of my "great wisdom."

The only good help is help which is asked for. I have learned to back off and *not* help—which really was hard for me (a classic caretaker type!). But it paid off in the long run because my employees felt that I respected their ability to handle their lives and, when and if they did look to me for any guidance, it became an interchange of ideas, not me care-taking them.

My father still tells me this old Chinese saying: "Why do you hate me, I never tried to help you?" What a lesson!

We can also be blind to a request for help—by being insensitive or just too caught up in our own stuff to be paying attention. Sometimes it looks like a work problem and it is really a personal issue. If we jump to conclusions too quickly, we might miss it. There is a great deal of subtlety required in dealing with people—hence my reference earlier to "the painstaking effort of transforming your workplace." It takes sensitivity, humility, and patience to be a good sounding board for people—and to really help them work through problems.

Most managers don't want to bother with all that "people stuff"—it takes away from an emphasis on the bottom line! My contention is that it already affects your bottom line, and if you don't pay attention, create space for the soulfulness of peoples' real lives in the workplace, you will feel it in your bank accounts sooner than you think.

## All in the Family

Our work families have become the extended families in our lives. We spend more time at work than any place else! We also tend to re-create our family of origin, unless we have healthy, positive ways to move out of the dysfunctional patterns we were raised with. There is a new emphasis on team building today—and I am a big proponent of this. All the activities we do in our quarterly meetings are designed for this purpose.

And—we need to go deeper. I think each individual needs to have an opportunity to find his or her purpose in life that encompasses more than work, but still includes it. A few very lucky people were born into families that had a driving sense of purpose and direction in society. These few people seem to have an inherent sense of their own destiny. I was more like everyone else, I was just born and tried to figure out how to exist among all these people who didn't seem to understand me!

How can our work families be different from our families of origin? We can create them like we want them! We can be the encouraging, nurturing support group for each other that we yearned for as children! We can look at ourselves honestly and find out what we are really good at and do it—in an environment that nourishes us.

At one of our quarterly meetings a couple of years ago we revisited the "life purpose" question. Our facilitator led us through an exercise that lets us end up with one sentence as a statement of purpose. One of our newest sales people sat there in awe and said, "I'm 46 years old and I never knew what my purpose was! Now I do, and now I know what to do with the rest of my life!" He has been in a steady, productive growth pattern since that time—and I see him being a big asset to our company for many years to come. He has a place. He belongs. And he knows what he wants to do.

What better situation can you create for an employee? Isn't a family a unit that is supposed to have the best interests of its members at heart? Shouldn't a family be a system that allows people their own identity, yet gives them something bigger to be a part of? Don't families that work well together respect the rights and wishes of each other and at the same time pull together for the good of the whole?

Just being aware and conscious of the familial nature of our workplace will take you a long way toward making it a better place to be. Being willing to look at issues from an open, loving-hearted position will take you a long way toward solving problems.

## Humanity Works!

When people feel free to be themselves, express themselves, ask questions and get answers, make a difference and get results from their own initiatives—they want to stay there and keep working! They want to belong to a place like that!

I have often said and heard that money always follows good work. And I believe this to be true. When we put the emphasis where it belongs—on the busy-ness of doing and being good—then we get to reap the vast benefits of our endeavors. We get to feel productive and purposeful. We get to grow as individuals. We get to make a contribution to our communities and to the planet. We get to feel like we are an important part of something bigger than we are. We get to feel empowered, not over powered by forces out of our control.

We get to feel alive, vibrant and useful! We have a future to look forward to and a past we can learn from. We become the people we always wanted to be. What this is really about is basing your business life on core values, expressing those values to your co-workers and all those with whom you do business and letting these values be reflected in all parts of your life.

Does this sound like utopia? Maybe. But why not aim for it? Why not give these ideas a try, a few at a time, little by little, and see where it leads? Not everyone in your company will buy into the new paradigm. When that happens, we call it "graduating." Either they decide to go or we help them leave. We really don't have room for people who have no desire to be a part of the program. But we have no animosity toward them for leaving—it just creates a space for the right person to come along. My rule of thumb: When something doesn't work out, something better's coming.

This to me is real life spirit in the workplace. This is actually spirit and soul working together to create a vital, exciting entity called a company that is a force for good for the whole world. The more good we do in our own home base, the more good we put into circulation. I honestly believe I am serving humankind by being a conscious, soulful, spiritual business leader.

And you can do it too.

**Anita Roddick** is founder and CEO of The Body Shop. Shaped by the social forces of the 1950s and 1960s, she founded the business in 1976 to provide a livelihood for her family. Her inspirations for skin and hair-care products came from the inherent wisdom of the women she met during her travels around the globe. She has always believed that conventional business alienates humanity and set out to make her business the antithesis of the mainstream. From a single shop in Brighton, England, The Body Shop has grown into an international retailer with more than 1,300 outlets in 46 countries. Her company exists to prove that it is possible to fully integrate social, human, and ecological values with successful business practices, for which she has been honored with many awards.

# 24

# Finding Spirit Through Service

## *Anita Roddick*

I don't know what your destiny will be, but one
thing I do know. The ones amongst you who are
really happy are those who have sought and
found how to serve.

—*Albert Schweitzer*

Talking so personally to people whom I may never see, is an
adventure. I ask myself will it be death by disclosure—will raw
vulnerability be apparent—or will I bore the pants off you? I keep
thinking of an old Bessie Smith song: "You keep talking about
love, baby, and you're gonna get screwed."

## Love and Spirituality in a High
## Performance Organization?

You may ask the question: Love and spirituality in a high
performance organization? That is like tossing a hot potato into
a cold bowl of water. The best you can do is warm things up,
right? Not true. The best you can do is better than you ever
imagined!

Work is where the compulsive search for connection, common purpose and a sense of friendship and neighborhood find a

special place. Work is where a continuous sense of spiritual education can take place, and where the word "service" includes both the desire to express ourselves and the desire to contribute selflessly to a greater good.

If this process is managed from the heart, great things in business can and will happen. The only thing that is stopping us is our imagination and as Einstein said: "Imagination is more important than knowledge."

To start at the beginning, I have to journey from my own place, from landscapes and peoples and experiences that have shaped me. All are kept alive in my soul through the stories attached to them. I am the sum total of all these stories and experiences. These stories shaped the geography of my mind, and therefore, shaped my thinking in business.

The places, events, and people that we know make their mark on us like the curves and dots of some inward map which guides us through life. My geography starts with Joan of Arc. She gave me moral imagination. My first heroine stood up for something in a way that caught my imagination: She fought the God of conformism and apathy—always, always examining herself.

Learning about the Holocaust gave me moral outrage and kick-started me at an early age into the belief that everyone must stand up to something and keep their mouth open.

The death of my father offered a profound sense of loss, so a lot of time in my household was spent thinking out loud about life. We talked openly about its meaning its purpose and its significance.

## Challenge Everything!

My mother taught me to challenge everything. She reminds me of the wonderful Walt Whitman quote:

> This is what you should do: love the earth and
> sun and the animals, despise riches, give alms
> to everyone that asks, stand up for the stupid
> and crazy, devote your income and labor to
> others, hate tyrants, argue not concerning God,
> have patience and indulgence toward the people,
> take off your hat to nothing known or unknown
> or to any man or number of men...reexamine all
> you have been told at school or church or in any

book, dismiss what insults your own soul and
your very flesh shall be a great poem.

My mother pushed me to the edge of bravery. She challenged everything and she created a world that allowed my spirit
to flourish. Every time I did anything kind or loving to anyone, she
would delight in it. From day one I was told my genetic pattern
was to have a bold spirit, and to create a world that enabled the
spirit to flourish.

As a child, life was storytelling. Not children's rhymes and
riddles. We were told how we were conceived. We were told stories
of romantic love, deep feelings which defy description. You have to
experience the feeling. The stories guided our relationships to
each other. My mother made things magnificent for us: the stories
of life on the farm in Southern Italy, the anecdotes of the family,
and especially irreverence to the church. There was more majesty
in those stories than in any organized religion. In short, it was all
about love and work.

I came from an Italian immigrant family. At ten years of age,
when my father died, my mother and us four kids worked in a
large cafe. There were no family holidays, there were no family
diversions, except for the weekly cinema—it was work! It was a
livelihood. It was an extension of our home, our kitchen. Court-
ships flourished in that cafe, marriages formed, friendships
connected, the eye was delighted, the music from the jukebox
spoke personally to everyone, and your heart was in the workplace.

## You Can Bring Your Heart To Work With You

It taught me a huge lesson—you can bring your heart to
work with you. It taught me that business is not financial science;
it is about trading, buying and selling. It is about creating a
product or service so good that people will pay a higher price for
it, allowing you the means to fulfill the social projects you had
erstwhile only dreamed of.

It taught me that whatever our society tries to diminish, it is
the family or community that keeps pushing up like flowers in the
cracks of pavements.

My first lesson in community was the Kibbutz. I had arrived
from an academic institution where we believed that academic
people were more valuable than other people because education

is a value-adding industry. Educated people are better than other people because education improves people and makes them good. The purpose of education is to earn more and more money, and the place where education is to be used is your career.

I carried around a set of beliefs that nonacademic work was what filled up the hours before resting, that work was a privilege but for which there was a price to pay. In our modern cultures, I believe that price has come to mean work without joy. However in the Kibbutz in Israel, I learned that work can be noble. Wendell Berry's insights on community are a fitting reflection of what I learned:

> The health of a community depends absolutely
> on trust. One of the essential trusts of commu-
> nity life is that which holds marriages and
> families together. Another trust is that neighbors
> will help one another. Another is that privacy
> will be respected.
>
> —Wendell Berry,
> *Sex, Economy, Freedom & Community*

A community is about a placed people working for a common good. Its people actually know the land and how to care for it. It was a seminal experience for me. I learned that love, labor, community, service, and the land were connective and integrative. It was my first lesson in socially-engaged spirituality. Is it any wonder with experiences like these I walked onto the business stage believing in a better way?

## The Power Of Storytelling

I have always held the belief that what gives me, and ultimately my company, an edge is that I get out of the chair, out of the office, and I move. I move towards people and events that have a clearer vision than I have. These insights are garnished through experiences I share, by storytelling. Every insight I have had, I have shared.

Matthew Fox's observations on the power of storytelling, and the way it forms the basis of the educational systems of tribal peoples, mirror what I have seen by journeying and dialoguing with tribal people, mountain dwellers, desert dwellers, and nomads. In his 1994 book, *The Reinvention of Work*, Fox talks of how the Celtic peoples insisted that only the poets could be teachers and believes that "knowledge that is not passed through the heart is dangerous."

While Fox throws out the challenge for our educational systems to insist that teachers be poets, storytellers, and artists, I see a bleeding need for retailers to be crafted storytellers. Imagine the transformation of the retail environment, in high streets and shopping malls—those monuments to noncommunication, where language is reduced to sound-bite simplification—into a place which functions like a well in a traditional society; where people gather and chat, exchange ideas and information. For me, the notion of gatherings of people, in such a setting, experimenting with products and sharing stories is deliciously seductive.

In their book, *The Path of the Everyday Hero*, Michael Ray and Lorna Catford put the value of storytelling beautifully:

> Myths and stories are the reflection of the human soul. They remind us of our potential, of the divine possibilities of our existence.

Without an awareness of your emotions you are not able to experience reverence. Reverence is not an emotion. It is a way of being. But the path of reverence is through your heart, and only an awareness of your feelings can open your heart. Let me explain by a story.

In 1993 I spent time in what is perhaps the most disadvantaged Native American reservation, Rosebud in South Dakota. I was invited by the tribal colleges to see if I could come up with any creative solution to any one of their huge social problems.

I noticed that in the Badlands sage bush grew wild. Gather the sage bush, extract the essential oil and convert into personal care products. Easy. They had the plants and I had the technology. No. Not easy. They said first we must ask permission from the plant nation. First we must "do a sweat." Then maybe.

What that experience, the ritual—the sweat lodge—told me was simply this: I was not *on top* of nature, I was *part* of nature. It taught me not respect. It taught me reverence.

Living in communities, whether they be indigenous or local, allows me an experiential education. I am able to humanize the issues and share what I have found and what I have been told by grassroots communities in the majority world. Journeying provides insights.

My insight is that the catastrophe is poverty and that if Western governments are to help, they have to put the poor first: as active participants, advisors, and leaders. Any government that mobilizes its grassroots is at least a light at the end of the tunnel because the only true experts on poverty are the poor.

It is poverty that drives the catastrophe when desperate people overexploit their resource base. Nothing incites people to deplete forests, soils, or water supplies more than fear that they will soon lose access to them.

When I visited the Wodaabe Tribe in the Sahel, Africa, they had never heard of the word "desertification" but they knew better than anyone that their soil was exhausted. They too were living out the experience.

## A Poor Man Shames Us All

Forest dwellers in the heart of the Amazon do not need to be told about the mass extinction of species. They know far better than any research biologist what it is to watch their homeland go up in smoke before advancing waves of migrants and developers. What they taught me was that a poor man shames us all.

I am a dogged believer in small-scale economic community initiatives which keep the community together and the culture intact. Increasingly we are developing these initiatives in my company.

Viewed in isolation, these grassroots initiatives are modest. Ten women planting a tree on a roadside, a dozen youths digging a well, an old man teaching neighborhood kids to read—but from a global perspective their scale and impact are monumental. These micro enterprises, these organizations are a ragtag front line in the worldwide struggle to end poverty and environmental destruction.

## Socially-Engaged Spirituality

When you experience their lives, live with their communities, you care. In my job I have a signboard above my office which reads Department of the Future. One of the most important jobs I have to do is develop more opportunities for our staff to spend company time in the service of the weak and frail, to be able to measure their greatness by those experiences and find the heroes in themselves by caring for others.

As Sara Paddison writes in *The Hidden Power of the Heart*: "Care is another one of those four-letter words like love, that cages a powerful frequency band. Care is an oil that lubricates the entire mental, emotional and physical system."

Through service, through compassionate service and caring with passion, people can feel connected and uplifted. I have found it be one of the most important ingredients for both spiritual and physical health and well being. I have found that people become motivated when you guide them to the source of their power. Anything that changes your values, changes your behavior.

The people I work with are mostly under thirty, mostly caring females all in search of present day heroes or heroines. Fox reminds us of Studs Terkel's idea that for work to be authentically human it must be about a search for daily meaning as well as daily bread, for recognition as well as cash, for astonishment rather than torpor. This is what I find in the people with whom I work.

They have a secret ingredient called enthusiasm. Enthusiasm created from the heart guides your whole system, so there is no resistance. Everything flows and seems possible.

## Protecting Your Soul

I have frequently wondered what protected my soul in a business environment that often alienates humanity in every way? I think I know some of the answers. When my husband Gordon and I began, we did not know how to run a conventional business. We had never read a book on economic theories, nor had we heard of Milton Friedman. We valued and respected labor as fuzzy and cuddly, touchy as it sounds.

We had no money. Every "original" idea was based on the experience of that first year's trading. We behaved as people did in the Second World War. We re-used everything. We refilled everything and we recycled all we could.

Then there was our naiveté. We did not know you could tell lies. That grace has stayed with us until this day. We also loved change. We believed everything was subject to change. We shared, and still do, an extraordinary level of optimism about social change.

Let me share another example with you. When a member of our staff, after three exhaustive weeks refurbishing a Romanian orphanage holding babies with AIDS, or campaigning for human rights looks you dead in the eye and says "This is the real me"— take heed, for she is dreaming of noble purposes, not a moisture cream.

In *The Dance of Change*, Michael Lindfield asks us "Is it enough to join a protest march for a few hours to voice our horror at oppression in a particular country and then return home via the local supermarket and pick up a jar of our favorite coffee that just happens to be supplied by the main industry exploiting the people for whom we have recently voiced our support? Global issues are now the politics of place, and local action and initiatives are the means of addressing them." That to me is also service.

## The Politics Of Consciousness

In my company, finding your spirit through service allows us to be conscious participants and practice what Lindfield calls "the politics of consciousness" which he describes as bringing "the power of the inner world into a specific and positive action that can effectively meet human needs."

This has to be the way forward. It does not take a rocket scientist to know a basic truth— that business alienates humanity in every way. Businesses are tough places to nurture tender feelings.

People who do harbor dreams of a more responsible and compassionate world often feel alone and unsupported, except when something occurs to bring their feelings out in the open. Then they find that others have also harbored these same, seemingly subversive, thoughts and feelings.

And so to end: what I have shared with you is not hypotheses or theory. It is service in practice—it is continuous education of the spirit, a defined space, not unlike the community of the Kibbutz. Ethics, spirit and service are part of the moral code that exists only amongst people. So, if the people have no pathway for the compulsive search for connection, neither can the company.

I have found being part of my company's community that I had, and still have, an unprecedented opportunity to create a special place. In that place, service has to be honored and celebrated. The parent has to be served, child development needs to be supported, families welcomed, and values explored and protected.

Community service has to be honored as part of the workplace day. Volunteer programs have to be initiated and supported where people put love and caring into practice, returning to the workplace with stronger values. The workplace also has to inspire creativity and, above all, be fun.

As a company, caring for people includes service to the weak and frail. While traditional business may search for the lowest wages, the lowest environmental regulation, the most passive and desperate workers, we have a duty to the weak and frail to espouse a gentler way of doing business—where core values of community, social justice, openness, and environmental awareness are key.

Let us return to Albert Schweitzer: "I don't know what your destiny will be, but one thing I do know. The ones amongst you who are really happy are those who have sought and found how to serve."

# Conclusion

# **Getting Involved**

If the previous essays have left you wondering, curious, or perplexed, we suggest you read a book we compiled last year entitled *Rediscovering the Soul of Business: A Renaissance of Values.*

In many ways, this book is a sequel to our earlier anthology which contains many fine essays written about "soulful work." Contributing authors to *Rediscovering the Soul of Business* include Thomas Moore, whose *Care of the Soul* book sat on the bestseller list for many months, demonstrating a public interest in the topic. Gary Zukav, award-winning writer and author of *The Seat of the Soul* is also a contributor, offering insights about authentic power from within. And Matthew Fox, the priest who wrote so eloquently about business and organizational life in his book *The Reinvention of Work,* was another contributor. All together, there were twenty-five essays in this earlier book.

As editors of both books, we have been present throughout the conception, collection, development, and manifestation phases of each one—a true thrill encompassing approximately three years all together. During this time we have witnessed the growing popularity of writings, speakers, and programs that address the craving for meaningful work, the increasing demand for doing something that matters, that means something to us.

One of the promises of this book was to provoke our readers to engage in an examination of their own work lives and embark upon a personal inventory of meaning and satisfaction gained from their time in the workplace.

Regardless of where you land, which side of the debate you find the most suitable for your own tastes, at least you will have been engaged in the dialogue offered by our distinguished collection of authors. You will have become involved in the examination of the issues surrounding heart, soul, and work—at least for a short time. Sadly, most people never revisit such basic issues; they merely plod along, day-to-day, desensitized to the gradual "creep" of soullessness in their work and wonder why they feel so listless and bored about their jobs.

Thanks for you attention. On behalf of everyone associated with this project—the contributing authors, our publications staff, editors, production and design people, we thank you for your interest in our book and hope we've contributed some value to your lives.

Each of the authors can be contacted directly if you wish to write them. The contact information for each of us is included just ahead of the Index at the back of this book.

Respectfully,
John Renesch and Bill DeFoore
June 1996

# Recommended Reading

Arrien, Angeles. *The Four-Fold Way: Walking the Paths of the Warrior, Teacher, Healer and Visionary.* San Francisco, CA: Harper Collins, 1993.

Autry, James. *Love and Profit.* New York, NY: Avon, 1991.

Barrentine, Pat, Ed. *When the Canary Stops Singing.* San Francisco, CA: Berrett-Koehler, 1993.

Bartlett, Christopher A. and Sumantra Ghoshal. "Changing the Role of Management," in *Harvard Business Review,* May-June 1995.

Bartlett, Christopher A. and Sumantra Ghoshal, "Changing the Role of Top Management Beyond Strategy to Purpose," in *Harvard Business Review,* November—December 1994.

Beck, Ulrich. *Risk Society—Towards a New Modernity.* London, England: Sage Publications, 1992.

Bellah, Robert, et al. *Habits of the Heart: Individualism and Commitment in American Life.* New York, NY: Harper & Row, 1985.

Benavides, Marta. "My Mother's Garden is a New Creation," in Russell, Letty, Kwok, Pui-Lan, et al., Eds. *Inheriting Our Mother's Garden's: Feminist Theology in Third World Perspective.* Philadelphia, PA: The Westminster Press, 1988.

Bennis, Warren and Joan Goldsmith. *Learning to Lead: A Workbook on Becoming a Leader.* Reading, MA: Addison-Wesley Publishing Company, 1994.

Berry, Wendell. *Sex, Economy, Freedom & Community.* New York, NY: Pantheon Books, 1993.

Bingemer, Maria Clara. "Women in the Future of the Theology of Liberation," in Ellis, Marc H. and Otto Maduro, Eds. *The Future of Liberation Theology: Essays in Honor of Gustavo Gutierrez.* Maryknoll, NY: Orbis Books, 1989.

Blanchard, Ken. *We Are the Beloved.* Grand Rapids, MI: Zondervan Publishing House, 1994.

Blanchard, Kenneth and Spencer Johnson. *The One Minute Manager.* New York: Wm. Morrow & Co., 1982.

Blanchard, Kenneth and Norman Vincent Peal. *The Power of Ethical Management.* New York: Wm. Morrow & Co., 1988.

Block, Peter. *Stewardship: Choosing Service Over Self-Interest.* San Francisco, CA: Berrett-Koehler Publishers, 1993.

Bohm, David. *On Dialogue.* David Bohm Seminars, 1990, Ojai, CA.

Bohm, David. *Thought As a System.* New York: Routledge, 1994.

Bohm, David, and Mark Edwards. *Changing Consciousness.* New York: Harper Collins, 1991.

Bolman, Lee G. and Terrence E. Deal. *Leading with Soul: An Uncommon Journey of Spirit.* San Francisco, CA: Jossey-Bass Publishers, 1994.

Buber, Martin. *The Knowledge of Man.* Highlands, NJ: Humanities Press International, Inc., 1988.

Campbell, Joseph. *The Hero With A Thousand Faces.* Princeton, NJ: Princeton University Press, 1949.

Canfield, Jack and Mark Victor Hansen. *Chicken Soup for the Soul.* Deerfield Beach, FL: Health Communications, Inc., 1993.

Caridas, Evangeline. "Workplace of the Future," in *Sales Consultancy Newsletter,* Fall 1995.

Carmichael, Sheena. *Business Ethics: The New Bottom Line.* London, England: DEMOS, 1995.

Catford, Lorna and Michael Ray. *The Path of the Everyday Hero.* Los Angeles, CA: Jeremy Tarcher, Inc., 1991.

"CEO Follows Founder's Lead With Courage and Vision," *The New Leaders,* Nov./Dec., 1993.

Chappell, Tom. *The Soul of a Business.* New York, NY: Bantam, 1993.

Chittister, Joan, OSB. "Job's Daughter's: Women and Power." *1990 Madeleva Lecture Series in Spirituality.* New York, NY: Paulist Press, 1990.

Cialdini, Robert. Influence—*The Psychology of Persuasion.* New York: William Morrow, 1984.

Conger, Jay A. *Spirit at Work: Discovering the Spirituality in Leadership.* San Francisco, CA: Jossey-Bass Publishers, 1994.

Cousineau, Phil. *Soul: An Anthology.* San Francisco, CA: Harper Collins Publishers, 1994.

Covey, Stephen R. *Principle-Centered Leadership.* New York, NY: Simon & Schuster, 1992.

Csikszentmihalyi, Mihaly. *Flow: The Psychology of Optimal Experience.* New York, NY: Harper & Row, 1990.

D'Aprix, R. *In Search of a Corporate Soul.* New York, NY: Amacom, 1976.

DeFoore, Bill and John Renesch, Eds. *Rediscovering the Soul of Business.* San Francisco, CA: New Leaders Press, 1995.

Dossey, Larry. *Recovering the Soul: A Scientific and Spiritual Search.* New York, NY: Bantam, 1989.

Eck, Diane and Devaki Jain, Eds. "Part VI, Introduction," in *Speaking of Faith: Global Perspectives on Women, Religion and Social Change.* Philadelphia, PA: New Society Publishers, 1987.

Eck, Diane and Devaki Jain, Eds. *Speaking of Faith: Global Perspectives on Women, Religion and Social Change.* Philadelphia, PA: New Society Publishers, 1987.

Eisler, Riane. *The Chalice and the Blade.* New York: Harper & Row, 1988.

Eisler, Riane and David Loye. *The Partnership Way.* New York: Harper-Collins, 1991.

Elgin, Duane. *Awakening Earth: Exploring the Evolution of Human Culture & Consciousness.* New York, NY: William Morrow & Company, 1993.

Ellis, Charles D and James R. Vertin, Eds. *Classics: An Investors Anthology.* Homewood, IL: Business One Irwin, 1989.

Ellis, Marc H. and Otto Maduro, Eds. *The Future of Liberation Theology: Essays in Honor of Gustavo Gutierrez.* Maryknoll, NY: Orbis Books, 1989.

Emery, Merrelyn. *Participative Design for Participative Democracy.* Canberra, Australia: Centre for Continuing Education-Australian National University, 1993.

*Empowerment Statements of SET Ministry,* Milwaukee, WI, 1992.

*Encyclopedia of Religion,* Vol. 1. New York, NY: Macmillan and Free Press, 1987.

"Europe and the Global Information Society," *The Bangemann Report,* March 1994. Brussels, Belgium: European Council, 1994.

Fabella, Virginia and Sun Ai Lee Park, Eds. *We Dare to Dream: Doing Theology as Asian Women.* Maryknoll, NY: Orbis Books, 1989.

Fox, Matthew. *The Reinvention of Work: A New Vision of Livelihood for our Time.* San Francisco, CA: Harper Collins Publishers, 1994.

*Frontiers—Understanding European Consumer Markets.* London, England: The Henley Centre, 1995.

Golding, William. *The Lord of the Flies.* New York, NY: G.P. Putnam and Sons, 1955.

Gozdz, Kazimierz, Ed. *Community Building: Renewing Spirit and Learning in Business.* San Francisco, CA: New Leaders Press, 1995.

Haessly, Jacqueline. *Learning to Live Together.* San Francisco: Resource Publications, 1989.

Haessly, Jacqueline. "Value for the Global Marketplace: A Quest for Quality with a Difference" in Barrentine, Pat, Ed. *When the Canary Stops Singing: Women's Perspectives for Transforming Business* San Francisco: Berrett-Koehler, 1993.

Haessly, Jacqueline. "The Business of Peacemaking" in Ray, Michael and John Renesch, Eds. *The New Entrepreneurs: Business Visionaries for the 21st Century.* San Francisco: New Leaders Press, 1994.

Haessly, Jacqueline. "Soul Work: A Corporate Challenge" in DeFoore, Bill and John Renesech, Eds. *Rediscovering the Soul of Business: A Renaissance of Values.* San Francisco: New Leaders Press, 1994.

Handy, Charles. *The Age of Paradox.* Cambridge, MA: Harvard Business School Press, 1994.

Harman, Willis and John Hormann. *Creative Work.* Indianapolis, IN: Knowledge Systems, 1990.

Harrison, Roger. *Consultant's Journey: A Dance of Work and Spirit.* San Francisco, CA: Berrett-Koehler, 1995.

Harvey, Jerry. *The Abilene Paradox.* New York: Macmillan, Inc., 1988.

Hawley, Jack. *Reawakening the Spirit in Work: The Power of Dharmic Management.* San Francisco, CA: Berrett-Koehler Publishers, 1993.

Heckman, Frank. "Well Being: How to Cut Your Healthcare Bill in Half, Raise Your Productivity and Improve your Quality," self-published article. Mineral Point, WI: September 1992.

Herman, Stanley M. *The Tao at Work: On Leading and Following.* San Francisco, CA: Jossey-Bass Publishers, 1994.

Heyward, Carter. "Doing Theology in a Counterrevolutionary Situation," in Ellis, Marc H. and Otto Maduro, Eds. *The Future of Liberation Theology: Essays in Honor of Gustavo Gutierrez.* Maryknoll, NY: Orbis Books, 1989.

Houston, Jean. *The Hero and the Goddess.* New York, NY: Ballantine Books, 1992.

*International Workplace Values Survey Report.* San Francisco, CA: New Leaders Press, 1994.

Isaacs, William. "Taking Flight: Dialogue, Collective Thinking, and Organizational Learning," in *Organizational Dynamics.* American Management Association, 1993

Isaacs, William. "Dialogue: The Power of Collective Thinking," in *Reflections on Creating Learning Organizations.* Cambridge, MA: Pegasus Communications, 1994.

Isasi-Diaz, Ada Maria. "A Hispanic Garden in a Foreign Land," in Russell, Letty and Kwok Pui Lan, Eds. *Inheriting Our Mother's Gardens: Feminist Theology in Third World Perspectives.* Philadelphia, PA: The Westminster Press, 1988.

Jackson, Phil with Hugh Delehanty. *Sacred Hoops: Spiritual Lessons from a Hardwood Warrior.* New York: Hyperion, 1995.

Jahn, Robert and Brenda Dunne. *Margins of Reality: The Role of Consciousness in the Physical World.* San Diego, CA: HBJ, 1987.

Jin, Yong Tin. "New Ways of Being Church: A Protestant Perspective," in Fabella, Virginia and Sun Ai Lee Park, Eds. "Introduction," *We Dare to Dream: Doing Theology as Asian Women.* Maryknoll, NY: Orbis Books, 1990.

Kadlec, Daniel. "Happy Workers Point to Good Investment," in "Street Talk," in *USA Today,* July 10, 1993.

Karasek, Robert and Tores Theorell. *Healthy Work: Stress, Productivity, and the Reconstruction of Working Life.* New York, NY: Basic Books, Inc., 1990.

Kierkegaard, Soren. *The Sickness Unto Death,* translated by Alastair Hannay. London, England: Penguin Books, 1989.

Korten, David. *When Corporations Rule the World.* San Francisco, CA: Berrett-Koehler Publishers and Kumarian Press, 1995.

Lerner, Michael. *The Politics of Meaning: Restoring Hope and Possibility in an Age of Cynicism.* Reading, MA: Addison-Wesley Publishing, 1996.

Levey, Joel and Michelle Levey. *Quality of Mind: Tools for Self Master & Enhanced Performance.* Boston, MA: Wisdom Publications, 1991.

Levey, Joel and Michelle Levey. *The Focused Mind State.* Chicago: IL: Nightingale Conant, 1993.

Levey, Joel and Michelle Levey. "Wisdom at Work: An Inquiry Into the Dimensions of Higher Order Learning," in Chawla, Sarita and John Renesch, Eds. *Learning Organizations: Developing Culture for Tomorrow's Workplace.* Portland, OR: Productivity Press, 1995.

Levey, Joel. "Creative Intelligence at Work: Toward an Applied Inner Science of Discovery and Innovation," in Frantz, Roger and Alex Pattakos, Eds. *Intuition at Work.* San Francisco, CA: New Leaders Press, forthcoming 1996

Lindfield, Michael. *The Dance of Change: An Eco-Spiritual Approach to Transformation.* London, England: Arkana, 1986.

Machiavelli, Niccolo. *The Prince.* New York, NY: Penguin Books, 1981.

Makower, Joel. *Beyond the Bottom Line.* New York, NY: Simon & Schuster, 1994.

Marschack, Robert. "Lewin Meets Confucious," *Journal of Applied Behavioral Science,* Vol. 29 No 4 December, NTL Institute, 1994.

Marshack, Robert. "The Tao of Change," *OD Practitioner,* Vol 26 No 2 Summer, 1994.

McCarthy, Joseph, "The Spiritual CEO," *Chief Executive,* January/February 1996.

McNulty, Christine and Ralph McNulty. "Effective Strategic Planning — Social Values," in *Journal of Creatia,* Spring 1995. Seoul, Korea: Creatia Management Consulting Co., Ltd, 1995.

"Medtronic CEO Responds to Tom Peters' Column," *The New Leaders,* Jul./Aug. 1993.

Millman, Dan. *Sacred Journey of the Peaceful Warrior.* Tiburon, CA: H.J. Kramer, Inc. 1983.

Mills, Billy with Nicholas Sparks. *Wokini: A Lakota Journey to Happiness and Self-Understanding.* New York, NY: Orion Books, a division of Crown Publishers, Inc., 1990.

Moore, Thomas. *Care of the Soul: A Guide for Cultivating Depth and Sacredness in Everyday Life.* New York, NY: Harper Collins

Publishers, 1992.

Moore, Thomas. "Caring for the Soul in Business," in DeFoore, Bill and John Renesch, Eds. *Rediscovering the Soul of Business.* San Francisco, CA: New Leaders Press, 1995.

Morgan, Marie. "Spiritual Qualities of Leadership in Business," *World Business Academy Perspectives*, 1993, Vol 7, No. 4.

Mottinger, Betty A. *Power, Poverty and the Role/Status of Women.* UMI Dissertation Services, 1991.

Nadler, David A., Marc S. Gerstein, and Robert B. Shaw. *Organizational Architecture: Designs for Changing Organization.* San Francisco, CA: Jossey-Bass Publishers, 1992.

Nair, Keshavan. *A Higher Standard of Leadership: Lessons from the Life of Gandhi.* San Francisco, CA: Berrett-Koehler Publishers, 1994.

Neal, Maria Augusta. "God and Society: A Response to Liberation Theology," in Ellis, Marc H. and Otto Maduro, Eds. *The Future of Liberation Theology: Essays in Honor of Gustavo Gutierrez.* Maryknoll, NY: Orbis Books, 1989.

Needleman, Jacob. *Money and the Meaning of Life.* New York, NY: Doubleday/Currency, 1991.

Neville. *The Power of Awareness.* Marina del Rey, CA: DeVorss & Co., Publishers, 1952.

"Norman Lear Calls for Leap of Faith." *The New Leaders,* May/June, 1993.

Ogilvey, James. "Earth Might Be Fair," in Moorcroft, Sheila, Ed. *Visions of the 21st Century.* London, England: Adamantine Press, 1992.

O'Neil, John. *The Paradox of Success: A Book of Renewal for Leaders.* New York, NY: Jeremy P. Tarcher/Putnam, 1994.

Paddison, Sara. *The Hidden Power of the Heart.* Boulder Creek, CA: Planetary Publications, 1992.

Pascarella, Perry. "Design a Better Future," *Industry Week,* May 6, 1996.

Peck, M. Scott. *The Different Drum: Community-Making and Peace.* New York: Simon & Schuster, 1987.

Peck, M. Scott. *A World Waiting to be Born.* New York: Doubleday, 1993.

Peters, Tom. "America Moving Towards a 'Brain Force Economy'," in *Chicago Tribune,* November 2, 1992.

Peters, Tom. "Top Execs Need to be Spirited Leaders, Not Spiritual Gurus," *San Jose Mercury News,* April 5, 1993.

Rae, Eleanor and Bernice Marie-Daly. *Created in Her Image: Models of the Feminine Divine.* New York, NY: Crossroads Publishing Co., 1990.

Ray, Michael and John Renesch, Eds. *The New Entrepreneurs.* San Francisco, CA: New Leaders Press, 1994.

Rehm, Robert. "Participative Design," self-published article. Boulder, CO.

"Religious Beliefs in Europe," *Standard Eurobarometer No. 42.* Brussels, Belgium: European Commission, 1995.

Renesch, John, Ed. *New Traditions in Business: Spirit and Leadership in the 21st Century.* San Francisco, CA: Berrett-Koehler Publishers, 1992.

Reps, Paul. *Zen Flesh, Zen Bones.* Doubleday Anchor (out of print), 1930.

Roddick, Anita. *Body and Soul.* New York, NY: Crown Publishers, 1991.

Russell, Letty, Kwok Pui-Loan, et al., Eds. *Inheriting Our Mother's Gardens: Feminist Theology in Third World Perspective.* Philadelphia, PA: The Westminster Press, 1988.

Russell, Peter. *The Global Brain Awakens.* Palo Alto, CA: Global Brain, Inc., 1995.

Schneiders, Sandra, IHM. "Spirituality in the Academy," in *Theological Studies*, Vol. 50, No. 4, 1989.

"The Search for the Sacred," in *Newsweek*, November 28, 1994.

Senge, Peter. *The Fifth Discipline*. New York: Doubleday, 1990.

Senge, Peter and Art Kleiner, Charlotte Roberts, Richard Ross, and Bryan Smith. *The Fifth Discipline Fieldbook*. New York: Doubleday, 1994.

Sheldrake, Rupert. *The Rebirth of Nature*. Rochester, VT: Park Street Press, 1991.

Sherer, John. *Work and the Human Spirit*. Spokane, WA: John Sherer & Associates, 1993.

Spears, Larry. *Reflections on Leadership: How Robert K. Greenleaf's Theory of Servant-Leadership Influenced Today's Top Management Thinkers*. New York, NY: John Wiley, 1995.

"Spirit in the Workplace: A Movement on the Verge of Taking Off." *At Work*, Sept./Oct., 1993.

Stevens, Robert Tennyson. *Imagination Activation: Levels I and II*. Asheville, NC: Mastery Systems Corporation, 1994.   TAPE

Stevens, Robert Tennyson. *Outcome Facilitation*. Asheville, NC: Mastery Systems Corporation, 1994.   TAPE

Storr, Anthony. *Solitude: A Return to the Self*. New York, NY: Ballantine Books, 1988.

Terry, Roger. *Economic Insanity*. San Francisco, CA: Berrett-Koehler Publishers, 1995.

"Tom Peters Digs in on Spirituality and Business Issue." *The New Leaders*, Sept./Oct., 1994.

Vaill, Peter. *Managing as a Performing Art*. San Francisco, CA: Jossey-Bass, 1989.

Wang, Lily Kuo. "Ecclesiology and Women: A View from Taiwan," in Fabella, Virginia and Sun Ai Lee Park, Eds. *We Dare to Dream: Doing Theology as Asian Women*. Maryknoll, NY: Orbis Books, 1990.

*Webster's New International Unabridged Dictionary*, 2nd edition, New World Dictionary, New York, NY: Simon and Schuster, 1989.

Weaver, Mary Jo. *New Catholic Women: A Contemporary Challenge to Traditional Religious Authority*. San Francisco, CA: Harper and Row, 1985.

Wheatley, Margaret J. *Leadership and the New Science*. San Francisco, CA: Berrett-Koehler Publishers, 1992.

Whyte, David. *The Heart Aroused: Poetry and the Preservation of the Soul in Corporate America*. New York, NY: Currency Doubleday, 1994.

Williamson, Marianne. *A Return to Love*. New York: Harper Collins, 1993.

"World Values Study Group." Inter-University Consortium for Political and Social Research, *The Economist*, July 8, 1995.

Yong Tin Jin. "New Ways of Being Church: A Protestant Perspective," in Fabella, Virginia and Sun Ai Lee Park, Eds. "Introduction," *We Dare to Dream: Doing Theology as Asian Women*. Maryknoll, NY: Orbis Books, 1990.

Zadek, Simon and Peter Raynard. *Accounting for Change: The Practice of Social Auditing*. London, England: New Economics Foundation, 1995.

Zukav, Gary. *The Seat of the Soul*. New York, NY: Simon and Schuster, 1989.

# Recommended Resources

**Associations and Institutions**

**Business For Social Responsibility**
1683 Folsom St.
San Francisco, CA 94103-3722
Tel. 415.865.2500
Fax 415.865.2505

**European Baha'i Business Forum**
George W. Starcher, Secretary-General
35 Ave. Jean Jaures
Chambery 73000 France
Tel. (33) 7996.2272
Fax (33) 7996.3570

**New Academy of Business**
c/o Anita Roddick
Office 1
3/4 Albion Place
Galena Road
London W6 OLT United Kingdom
Tel. (44) 181.563.8780
Fax (44) 171.208.7697

**Renaissance Business Associates**
P.O. Box 197
Boise, ID 83701
Tel. 208.345.4234
Fax 208.345.3350
email: staff@rbai.com

**Robert K. Greenleaf Center for Servant Leadership**
921 E. 86th Street, #200
Indianapolis, IN 46240
Tel. 317.259.1241

**World Business Academy**
1511 K Street, NW, #1101
Washington, DC 20005
Tel. 202.783.3213
Fax 202.783.3216
email: wba@together.org

## Periodicals

### At Work
*Stories of Tomorrow's Workplace*
(bimonthly newsletter)
Berrett-Koehler Publishers, Inc.
155 Montgomery St.
San Francisco, CA 94104-4109
800.929.2929

### Business Ethics
(bimonthly magazine)
Mavis Publications
52 S. 10th Street, #10
Minneapolis, MN 55403-2001
612.962.4700

### Executive Citizen
(bimonthly newsletter)
10 Rogers Street. #604
Cambridge, MA 02142
617.494.1134

### Leader to Leader
(quarterly journal)
Jossey-Bass, Inc., Publishers
350 Sansome St., 5th Floor
San Francisco, CA 94104
415.433.1740

### The New Leaders
*Bringing Consciousness to Business*
(bimonthly newsletter)
New Leaders Press
1668 Lombard Street
San Francisco, CA 94123
800.928.LEAD (5323)

### World Business Academy Perspectives
(quarterly journal)
Berrett-Koehler Publications, Inc.
155 Montgomery Street
San Francisco, CA 94104-4109
800.929.2929

# How To Contact The Authors And Editors

ANGELES ARRIEN
P. O. Box 2077
Sausalito, CA 94966
415.331.5050

KEN BLANCHARD
Blanchard Training &
Development
125 State Pl.
Escondido, CA 92025
619.489.5005

EVANGELINE CARIDAS
3223 Albans Rd.
Houston, TX 77005
713.662.9926

BILL DE FOORE
Inst. for Personal & Prof. Devel.
4201 Wingren, #201
Irving, TX 75062
214.791.0144

KAY GILLEY
Intentional Leadership Systems
505 Woodwinds Drive
Durham, NC 27713
919.493.5633

JACQUELINE HAESSLY
Peacemaking Associates
2437 N. Grant Blvd.
Milwaukee, WI 53210-2941
414.445.9736
fax 414.444.7319
email: jacpeace@acs.stritch.edu

KYMN HARVIN RUTIGLIANO
Kymn & Co.
165 Edgemont Road
Watchung, NJ 07060
908.754.4437

LAURA HAUSER
Leadership Strategies Int'l
15555 Bronco Dr., #101
Santa Clarita, CA 91351
805.251.0641

BARRY HEERMANN
Expanded Learning Institute
6512 Reigate Road
Dayton, OH 45459
513.438.2175

STEVE JACOBSEN
6067 Shirrell Way
Goleta, CA 93117
805.967.5544

JOEL LEVEY
InnerWork Technologies, Inc.
5536 Woodlawn Ave. N.
Seattle, WA 98103
206.632.3551

KAREN LUNDQUIST
Rapid Change Technologies
6700 France Ave., S., #230
Minneapolis, MN 55435
612.920.3838

MARGERY MILLER
2920 Merrell Road
Dallas, TX 75229-4904
214.353.0498

MARGARET MOLINARI
Organizational Development
Consultant
2730 Avonhurst Dr.
Troy, MI 48084
810.647.6291

SAJEELA MOSKOWITZ RAMSEY
CORE Consulting
(Center for Organizational
Renewal and Effectiveness)
2432 Villanova Drive
Vienna, VA 22180
703.573.7050

GERARD O'NEILL
19 Frascati Park
Blackrock
Count, Dublin
Ireland
353.1.278.2047
Fax 353.1.661.0312

PERRY PASCARELLA
30413 Winsor Dr.
Bay Village, OH 44140
216.871.0276

DAVID POTTER
1191 Tolo Trail
Moscow, ID 83843
208.882.6880

RANDY & BARBARA POWERS
P. O. Box 694
Orinda, CA 94563
510.631.0257

MICHAEL SCOTT RANKIN
4321 Ridglea Circle Dr.
Fort Worth, TX
76126-2225
817.735.9705

JOHN RENESCH
Sterling & Stone, Inc.
1668 Lombard St.
San Francisco, CA 94123
415.928.1473
Fax 415.928.3346
email:staff@newleadersnet.org

ANITA RODDICK
The Body Shop International
Watersmead Littlehampton
West Sussex
England BN17-6LS
44.1903.731.500

DAVID SCHWERIN
900 Valley Rd. # B202
Melrose Park, PA 19027
215.635.5599

RAE THOMPSON
Heartswork
4141 N. Henderson Rd. #825
Arlington, VA 22203
703.522.2179

# Index

# Y

# Z

## OTHER BUSINESS ANTHOLOGIES
### developed by
### New Leaders Press

**Rediscovering the Soul of Business: A Renaissance of Values.**
Authors include Thomas Moore, Matthew Fox, Gary Zukav, Charles
Handy, and twenty-one other contributors; edited by Bill DeFoore
and John Renesch.
*Hardcover; New Leaders Press; $37.75 (U.S.); 379 pp.*

**Community Building: Renewing Spirit & Learning in Business.** Authors include John Gardner, George Land and Beth
Jarman, Jordan Paul, Michael Ray, Marvin Weisbord, and over
twenty others; edited by Kazimierz Gozdz.
*Hardcover; New Leaders Press; $37.75 (U.S.); 441 pp.*

**Leadership in a New Era: Visionary Approaches to the
Biggest Crisis of our Time.** Authors include James Autry,
Carol Sanford, Barbara Hauser, Ann Morrison, Ed Oakley, Kate
Steichen, Barbara Shipka, Tina Rasmussen, Larry Spears,
Elemer Magaziner, Susan Campbell, Robert Rabbin, Margaret
Wheatley, John Adams, Martha Spice, Carol McCall, Max
DePree, Perry Pascarella, and Stewart Emery (interview with
Norman Lear); edited by John Renesch.
*Hardcover; New Leaders Press; $34.50 (U.S.); 315 pp.*

**The New Entrepreneurs: Business Visionaries for the 21st
Century.** Authors include Anita Roddick, Peggy Pepper, Betsy
Burton, Greg Steltenpohl, Ron Kovach, Jeff Sholl, Jacqueline
Haessly, David P. Jasper, Richard B. Brooke, Sharon Gadberry,
John H. Stearns, Cheryl Alexander, Marjorie Kelly, Chris Manning, Paul Hwoschinsky, William B. Sechrest, Nicholas P. LiVolsi,
Bill Veltrop; edited by Michael Ray and John Renesch.
*Hardcover; New Leaders Press; $29.95 (U.S.); 268 pp.*

FROM THE PUBLISHERS OF
## THE NEW BOTTOM LINE

# THE NEW LEADERS

## BRINGING CONSCIOUSNESS
## TO BUSINESS

- Profiles of exemplars in business
- Articles by visionary business
  scholars
- News of transformation at work

---

## SUBSCRIBE TODAY & SAVE!!!

☐  1 year/6 issues, now only $89
☐  2 years/12 issues, now only $159
   (note: foreign subscribers, please add $15/year)

**CALL** 1-800/928-LEADers for credit card orders
            (1-800/928-5323)
**FAX** 1-415/928-3346
**MAIL** your order with payment to:

> *THE NEW LEADERS*
> 1668 Lombard Street
> San Francisco, CA 94123

# THE NEW LEADERS

☐ **P**lease send me a free sample issue of
*The New Leaders* — the business newsletter
that brings consciousness to business.

Name _____
Company _____
Street/POB _____
City _____ St _____ Zip_____ Country_____
Tel: _____ Fax: _____

☐ **P**lease send me a free sample issue of
*The New Leaders* — the business newsletter
that brings consciousness to business.

Name _____
Company _____
Street/POB _____
City _____ St _____ Zip_____ Country_____
Tel: _____ Fax: _____

## BUSINESS REPLY MAIL

FIRST CLASS MAIL    PERMIT NO 26220    SAN FRANCISCO  CA

POSTAGE WILL BE PAID BY ADDRESSEE

# New Leaders Press

1668 LOMBARD STREET
SAN FRANCISCO CA  94123-9706

NO POSTAGE
NECESSARY
IF MAILED
IN THE
UNITED STATES

## BUSINESS REPLY MAIL

FIRST CLASS MAIL    PERMIT NO 26220    SAN FRANCISCO  CA

POSTAGE WILL BE PAID BY ADDRESSEE

# New Leaders Press

1668 LOMBARD STREET
SAN FRANCISCO CA  94123-9706